Scott Walker

A Deep Shade of Blue

*Mike Watkinson and
Pete Anderson*

'Loneliness is a cloak you wear,
A deep shade of blue is always there . . .'

'The Sun Ain't Gonna Shine Anymore'

This edition first published in Great Britain in 1995 by
Virgin Books
an imprint of Virgin Publishing Ltd
332 Ladbroke Grove
London W10 5AH

First published in Great Britain in 1994

ISBN 0 86369 877 8

A catalogue record for this title is available from the British Library

Typeset by TW Typesetting, Plymouth, Devon
Printed and bound in Great Britain by
MacKays of Chatham, Lordswood, Kent

Contents

This one is for Joe Lewis, Catrin Medi,
Davy Michael and Katherine Alexis Anderson

Acknowledgements

The authors would first like to express their love and thanks to Sue Geatches and Lou Cunliffe for their support during the difficult period this book was in preparation. We also want to express our deepest gratitude to the following: Gary Leeds, for his patience during hours of interviews, Lynne Goodall, for discography and photos, Sue Walton, for tapes and videos, Alan Clayson, for his notes on Jacques Brel, and all at Virgin Publishing, in particular Ríona MacNamara and Michelle Ogden, for their encouragement and assistance.

Thanks are also owed in varying degrees to: Graham Alexander, Keith Altham, David Apps, Mary Arnold, Ed Bicknell, Ismene Brown of *The Sunday Telegraph*, Danny Buckland of the *Sunday People*, Martin Callomon, Barry Cawtheray, Al Clark, Dave Clark, B. J. Cole, Chantal Constant, Bill Cotton, Jackie Cunningham, Dave Dee, Simon Dee, Fred Dellar, Simon Draper, Irene Dunford, Robin Edwards, Brian Engel, Mette Engel, Bob Farmer, Paddy Fleming, Moira Franz, Brian Gascoigne, Diana Graham, Muriel Gray, Reg Guest, Bobby Hamilton, Sally Holloway, Mick Houghton, Paul Kinder, Jonathan King, Jeremy Lascelles, Dick Leahy, Frankie Lee, Suzanne Lowry of *The Daily Telegraph*, Nicholas Maffei Jr, Allan McDougall, Barrie Martin, Brandy Maus, Jim Mercer, Marie Moller, Charles Negus-Fancey, Del Newman, James Nice, Jack Nitzsche, Mark Norton of the Performing Rights Society, Maurice Oberstein, Peter Olliff, Drew Ottignon, Tony Peters, Mike Peyton, Arnie Potts, Tim Rice, Helen Richards, Hal Shaper, Dave Shrimpton, Phil Smee, Brian Sommerville, Terry Smith, Dorte Teglbjaerg, John Tobler, Geoff Travis, Ben Turner of *Melody Maker*, Bill Viviers, Michael Walker, Chris Welch, Mike Williams, Freddie Winrose and Simone Wood of Britvic.

Walkerpeople can be obtained from Lynne Goodall c/o 71 Cheyne Court, Glengall Road, Woodford Green, Essex IG8 0DN.

Exorbitant costs limited the amount of Scott Walker lyrics we could use, but the following publications proved invaluable during the course of our research: *Melody Maker, New Musical Express, Disc Weekly, Fab 208, Disc & Music Echo, Sunday People, Sunday Express, The Daily Telegraph, The Sunday Telegraph, Sunday Mirror, News Of The World, Walkerpeople, The Walkers, Music Now, Juke, Rave, The History of Rock, Night Flights, Music Maker, Record Collector, Debut, Q Magazine, Vox, Select, Les Inrockuptibles.*

The following songs are quoted by permission of the publishers: 'My Ship Is Coming In' (Intersong); 'In My Room' (Concorde Partnerships); 'The Amorous Humphrey Plugg' (Miracle Songs Ltd, Carlin Music Corp.); 'After the Lights Go Out' (Derry Music); 'The Electrician' (Marylebone Music); 'Rawhide' (Panache Music); 'Man from Reno' (PolyGram).

Illustrations

The classic image of Scott on stage (*Simon Dee*)

Scott's first bid for solo stardom

Scott playing with The Routers, California, 1963

The two-man Walker Brothers, Scott Engel and John Maus, in 1964 (*Michael Ochs Archive*)

15 March 1966: John, Gary Leeds, Scott and friend celebrate 'The Sun Ain't Gonna Shine Anymore' hitting number 1 (*Syndication International*)

April 1966: The Walkers receiving a silver disc marking the sales of 250,000 copies of 'The Sun Ain't Gonna Shine Anymore' (*Doug McKenzie*)

Johnny Franz and Scott (*Doug McKenzie*)

Scott and Gary backstage with Bobby Hamilton, 1966

Maurice King, with wife Mary Arnold (*Bobby Hamilton*)

Scott and Irene Dunford at the Lotus House restaurant on the Edgware Road, 1966 (*Irene Dunford*)

Scott celebrating the wedding of Bobby Hamilton at Caxton Hall

Brian Sommerville and Maurice King at a Walker Brothers promotion (*Dezo Hoffman*)

Scott on the Simon Dee show *Dee Time* in 1967 (*Dezo Hoffman*)

Backstage at the Bradford Gaumont, October 1968 (*Richard G. Leach*)

1973: Scott, glass in hand, poses moodily for the CBS publicity department

November 1975: Scott just before the release of the Walkers reunion single 'No Regrets'

Scott and John performing on German TV in 1976

Scott in 1984, around the time of the release of 'Climate of Hunter'

Scott, 1984 (*Bob Carlos Clarke/Virgin Records*)

Scott Walker's last British TV appearance to date – in an advertisement for Britvic 55 (*Abbott Mead Vickers/Britvic*)

Scott Walker in 1992: the most recent photograph to be published in Britain (*Syndication International*)

Introduction

'Then someone came along who got the style exactly right – Scott Walker. Scott Walker was a bit of a heart-throb in the sixties. One third of the Walker Brothers at first. He achieved true Arty Neuro status when they broke up and he could sing deep songs by Frenchmen on his own. He also did a lot for shades as a moody device. Shades were the Sony headphones of their day. He wore his shades perpetually and he was very thin. It goes without saying that he was often found in extremely low moods wandering around and worrying about something too big to explain.' ('Neurotic Boy Outsiders' from *Modern Times* by Peter York; Heinemann 1984)

THE FRESH-FACED, PONY-TAILED London record-shop assistant placed the gleaming compact disc on the counter and gazed quizzically at the sleeve of 'Scott 3', a record that was released long before he was born. 'Nice cover,' he said grudgingly. 'But just what is it about this Scott Walker geezer?'

This book is an attempt to answer that question. Why is so little known about one of the most revered figures in the world of rock and pop, and what makes him so special? Older fans, who have shared the singer's ups and downs and stuck with him through thick and thin, will undoubtedly feel that such a book is long overdue, but what explains Scott Walker's appeal to today's young trendies?

Perhaps it is because that seventeen years after his live career ended with a stumbling performance on a Midlands cabaret stage, Walker is perceived as the epitome of cool. Moody images of the mysterious young American, his eyes permanently obscured by shades and brow furrowed beneath a golden helmet of luxuriant hair, make him a pop equivalent of James Dean.

And while Dean died at the age of 24, having completed just three movies, Scott Walker effectively dropped from sight at the age of 26, leaving behind a sizeable cache of buried treasures for future pop generations to seek out and discover. A quarter of a century after the singer's heyday, a steady stream of Walker retrospectives ponder the riddle of the man who had it all, but whose last British public appearance was in a televised orange-juice commercial. A band called Catherine Wheel use his photo on their record sleeve and a Sunday newspaper challenges its readers to find him. Scott Walker, the star who hated the limelight, is as much a sixties icon as shameless self-publicists like Andy Warhol and Nico.

Then there is the mystery surrounding the total eclipse of one of the most photographed faces of the sixties pop scene. In 1969 there seemed no limit to what Scott Walker could achieve. Yet while contemporaries Tom Jones and Engelbert Humperdinck cleaned up at Las Vegas, Walker's vocal talents were confined to places like the Bradford Gaumont.

He turned down an offer for a concert at the Royal Albert Hall in preference to a week's cabaret in a run-down West Yorkshire nightclub. On numerous occasions he trembled on the brink of greatness only to snatch defeat from the jaws of victory. In retrospect, his entire career seems a catalogue of missed opportunities.

As time passed, the lack of confidence which ended Walker's live career infected the area which had always set him apart from his rivals: his songwriting. His once prolific output slowed and, like an ageing boxer struggling to recapture former glories, he made a series of abortive comebacks before finally, to all intents and purposes, throwing in the towel.

'Climate Of Hunter', the last Scott Walker album to date, was released in 1984, since when there has been an ominous silence. As the singer's recorded output slowed, and eventually ceased all together, the legend surrounding him gathered pace until Walker became a leading inhabitant of rock's twilight zone, a remote, flickering filament light years away from the glittering showbusiness path he had seemed destined to follow.

Over the years, countless eulogies have been delivered about the strangest, saddest, most elusive pop star of them all, but no one has delved beyond those piles of yellowing press cuttings to study the character and events which helped transform Scott Walker from No. 1 sex symbol to reclusive cult figure within a startlingly short space of time.

And, make no mistake, Walker was a major star. His fan club membership at one stage exceeded that of the Beatles. By 1969 he had broken new ground with three highly original and immensely successful albums, appeared in his own television series which in turn spawned an album of standards, sung a handful of film themes and established a growing reputation as a record producer. All this following the phenomenal success of the Walker Brothers who, in between unleashing a storm of teen hysteria, issued three classic singles and a trilogy of albums which still reek of class and sophistication.

Above all, there was that golden Walker baritone which could convey sadness, heartbreak, mystery, yearning and joy in equal measures and prompted one critic to exclaim: 'Compared to the sincerity in that voice, the robot vocals of Tony Bennett, the now breathless charm of Sinatra, the studied serenity of Andy Williams and the smug sound of most of our big pop names can get lost.'

Breaking free from the stifling restrictions of teen worship, Walker vowed to shun the latest musical trends and make the records he wanted to make. The series of albums which followed – 'Scott', 'Scott 2' and 'Scott 3' – were hailed as critical masterpieces.

Behind the stark, numeric titles lurked a lavish world of cinematic drama and dark melancholy, the singer's obsession with Belgian songwriter Jacques Brel and his own doom-laden tales of madness, sex and death. The themes were in stark contrast to mainstream British pop and the ignominious failure of the entirely self-penned 'Scott 4' brought Walker's unbroken run of success to a screeching halt.

As the hit albums dried up, chronic stage fright gradually put paid to Scott's live performances. 'When I go on stage I look on it as a battle. Every appearance I make is a fight between me and the stage.' The words actually belong to Walker Brother John Maus, but they could just as easily have come from Scott, who may well have realised that this was a battle he would ultimately lose.

And Walker's entire career can be viewed as a battle. At various times, the opposition ranged from suspicious record company executives, who questioned his increasingly non-commercial output, and nervous television chiefs, who banned his records, to unsympathetic managers who persisted in trying to turn him into a tuxedo-clad supper-club crooner. Lauded by some critics as the 'Sinatra of the streets', Walker discovered that others compared him unfavourably with Tom Jones. He met his opponents head-on and, for an all too brief period, wrested a degree of control over his work that no other pop musician had previously managed.

Yet out on stage Walker could never overcome the enemy within. 'When you see me out there shakin' in front of the camera you know why,' he said. 'It's because I'm frightened – you can't fight that kind of thing if it is inside you.' By the early seventies his career had lost direction and experiments with country and western were largely ignored. A somewhat half-hearted Walker Brothers reunion yielded the unexpected hit single 'No Regrets', but further success proved elusive and Scott pursued his lonely path once more.

A decade on, the Julian Cope compilation 'Fire Escape In The Sky' introduced Walker to a generation weaned on the music of the Sex Pistols and the Clash, although it was to be another three years before 'The God-like Genius' made his eagerly anticipated return. The critically acclaimed 'Climate Of Hunter' created a flurry of interest, but its commercial failure caused the singer to disappear once again. At the time of writing, Scott is reportedly back in the studio, labouring over an album on which so many hopes and expectations are pinned.

In an effort to reach the man behind the myth, our quest for Scott Walker has involved countless interviews with friends, fellow musicians, journalists and family members here in Britain, as well as the United States, Denmark and Australia. Scott himself declined to be interviewed.

While disappointed that he did not feel the time had come to put the record straight, we were not surprised at Scott's decision. He rarely gives interviews unless having an album to promote and has only broken his cover once since 1984's 'Climate Of Hunter'.

But our motivation for writing this book goes deeper than endeavouring to explain what makes Scott Walker tick. Despite the recent release of at least two praiseworthy compilations, we feel that Walker's solo work is still not fully appreciated and that much of today's adulation centres on his moody and reclusive image. Endless 'golden oldie' television and radio shows have ensured that the Walker Brothers hits are endlessly replayed and repackaged while the cream of Scott's solo work has been obscured. Many of the new generation of fans are familiar only with the work of his former group.

It would be nice to think that this book might go some way to redressing the balance, and while we still cannot pretend to understand this complex man, we at least feel able to offer some explanation as to why one of the greatest voices in popular music has been used so sparingly.

Mike Watkinson and Pete Anderson
London, November 1994

Prologue

'First Love Never Dies'

'IF HE HAD WALKED through my front door and asked me to run away with him I would have gone straightaway. All the girls in my class were in love with him. There were about ten of us. We had all been to see the Beatles, the Stones and Manfred Mann but within a few months the Walkers had overshadowed them all as the number one group among teenage girls.

'I could only have been about eleven when I first became aware of him. As soon as I heard "Make It Easy On Yourself" I just had to rush out of the house down to W. H. Smith's in Bradford, which in those days still had those little booths on which you could listen to the latest releases. I listened to it in the shop for hours.

'I was hooked. It was like a drug. I watched them on every episode of *Top Of The Pops* for the next four weeks. I remember I even left school discos early so I wouldn't miss them on the TV. At first it was the drummer, Gary Leeds, who caught my eye, but once I had seen them in the flesh there was only Scott.

'We queued overnight for tickets to the show at the Bradford Gaumont. I was with my friend Susan who later fell out with me because Scott had released a song called "Jackie". I knew he was trying to tell me something.

'We arrived outside the Gaumont at 1.30 a.m. and were right at the front of the queue. By dawn, the line of hundreds of girls, and a few boys, stretched way past Seabrook Fishery more than a quarter of a mile up the hill out of town.

'The doors opened at 10 a.m. and we came out on cloud nine clutching tickets for the third row. We made sure it was not a night the headline act Roy Orbison would remember with any fondness. Everyone at the front had come to see the Walkers. When Roy Orbison walked on we all pelted him with sweets. You could buy liquorice bats by the quarter and they were as hard as rock.

Scott Walker

'To his credit, he braved our liquorice bombardment and finished his set which had opened the show. When the Walkers came on every girl in the house was up on her seat, screaming and waving her arms for just one glance from her particular favourite.

'Lots of girls were fainting but some were faking it as a ploy. They had worked out that if you fainted you were taken through the sidedoors out into the corridor which led directly into the backstage area. I didn't want to miss a single note so I didn't bother. But you can bet your life I tried to nip backstage afterwards.

'There was a ring of bouncers across the whole of the front of the stage and if you got too close they thought nothing of punching you, whether you were a girl or not. We were lucky because we were near enough to hear at least some of the music coming from the stage. They didn't have anything like the sound systems they have nowadays and with this sea of teenagers jumping up and down and screaming at the top of their voices, you'd have needed supersonic ears to hear anything at the back.

'Afterwards, we rushed around to the stage door to catch them leaving. There were hundreds of girls pressing against two lines of police officers who formed a corridor to a limousine waiting with its back door open. The boys ran out and jumped in and it sped off into the night nearly knocking people over as they went.

'We all had tears rolling down our cheeks. Fan worship in those days really was a form of mass hysteria. One person would start and before you knew it you were joining in, even if you didn't know, or even like, the person you were screaming at.

'When they came back the next year to headline themselves it was even more out of control. The police presence had been doubled and the group had taken to wearing crash helmets to prevent their hair being torn from their heads. But it wasn't enough to stop us getting to them.

'I was lucky enough to be pressed up against possibly the shortest police officer in Yorkshire and with the pressure of people pushing behind me, there was no way he could hold us. When the Walkers came out we burst through.

'I was first to reach Scott and grabbed hold of the back of his shirt which was a thick lumberjack type. As other hands pulled at the shirt tail it literally gave way at the seams. By the time everyone had dived on top of that piece of material, I came away with about eight threads which I still have in a tiny sealed plastic bag at the bottom of my jewel box. It all sounds very violent but it wasn't, we just wanted a piece of them for ourselves.

'The show itself was even better than the first time. The curtains went back to reveal Scott lying on the floor in a light-blue two piece suit with a microphone held above his face. He launched into "The Sun Ain't Gonna Shine Anymore" and there was pandemonium.

'The rest of the concert is a blur because every time Scott opened his mouth you couldn't hear yourself think. But I do remember that they were bombarded with teddy bears, and every other stuffed animal you can imagine, all because John had let slip in an interview that he liked teddy bears. He had also revealed that he had recently given up eating eggs because he had only just discovered that they were bird embryos.

'Fortunately I didn't like eggs, so I didn't have to give them up, but lots of girls did. My mum and dad took a bit of a dim view of our infatuation and, without actually banning us from going to that second concert, they refused to help by driving us into town for another all-night vigil queuing for tickets.

'It was about three miles from home into town but we decided to walk it – any hardship was worth it to get one of those tickets. We'd only got about a quarter of the way when we were picked up by a passing police car. They thought we'd run away from home.

'Fortunately they took pity on us when we explained our predicament and they gave us a lift into town and we got front-row tickets. After the show I went home clutching the remains of Scott's shirt, a tear-stained programme and about a dozen different posters bought from the bootleg sellers outside.

'My eyes were half-shut through crying but when I got home to my room I insisted on plastering the walls with each and every one of those posters. During the night my parents crept in and turned them all round so that the faces were to the wall. When I woke up at 4 a.m. I went crazy thinking they'd been stolen.

'The next day we went hunting the band. We knew they were staying at the posh Midland Hotel and a girl from our class had a cousin who was a chef there. He had agreed to leave the kitchen door unlocked at the back of the hotel so we could sneak in. We scoured every floor listening to what was going on behind the doors and hoping to hear Scott's voice behind one of them.

'Eventually, because of the excitement, I had to go to the lavatory so we all crowded into a bathroom. Unfortunately that's all it was, a bathroom with no toilet, and to make matters worse someone had obviously heard our giggles and called the manager. He pounded on the door and the others pushed me forward. Ignoring them for a moment, he decided to make an example of me and frogmarched me down the main stairs of the hotel and through the revolving front door. I don't think I have ever travelled through a revolving door as fast in my life and God knows what I would have done if I had met Scott face to face. I would have probably died on the spot. Looking back now, it's hard to believe we did everything that we did. We must have been insane.

'I even met my husband through Scott. After that second show, I was so overwhelmed all I could say over and over again was "Scott's in blue", because that was the colour of his suit.

'A group of teenage boys overheard me outside and began mimicking me. Years later my husband admitted he was one of them. Poor Raymond, he's had to live with Scott Walker night and day for 22 years. He can't say anything against him because he knows it would be instant divorce.

'But at least there's one convert in the family – my 21-year-old son. He's one of the whole new generation of fans and invariably when I can't find my Walkers CDs, I'll find them in his bedroom.'

Jackie Cunningham, now 41, married with a grown-up son and 'still madly in love with my Scott'.

1 Boy Child

'It'd make a great tragedy, The Walker Brothers story . . . it beats *Hamlet*.'

Scott Walker, 1977

NOEL SCOTT ENGEL was born into a prosperous middle-class family on 9 January 1943, in the small town of Hamilton, Ohio, which must rank as one of rock music's most far-flung outposts. Scott's birth is usually given as a year later, although he did not bother to correct the error and during the youth-oriented sixties frequently maintained that he was a year younger than his actual age.

An only child, he spent the first year of his life in Hamilton, his father's hometown, and does not appear to have ever gone back. His father, who was serving in the US Navy at the time of his son's birth, later became a geologist with an oil company whose work took the family to Texas, the scene of Scott's earliest childhood memories. 'It wasn't a ranch, my dad wasn't a rancher or anything, but it's all a bit barren out there, you know,' he said.

Elizabeth Marie Engel, invariably known as Mimi or Betty to friends and relations, was highly-strung, petite, and blonde. The son she gave birth to at the age of 32 inherited his mother's good looks and strong personality, which in later years led to a tempestuous, but close, relationship. Betty's tall, athletic-looking husband Noel Walter Engel worked for the Superior Oil Company – one of the largest concerns in the States – and by 1967 had risen to the role of vice-president.

Engel's occupation meant the family moved constantly, so any friendships Scott formed were transitory and his early schooling was frequently disrupted. He attended up to seven or eight schools in his early years and took little interest in lessons, knowing that in a few months he would not be seeing his teachers again and would never sit the exams.

Scott, who yearned for a brother or sister, consequently became a solitary child who rarely mixed with others of the same age. One of his kindergarten teachers said she wished he could be more of a child, but Scott was raised around adults and always treated like one. He was an obedient and happy youngster, although his mother later conceded she may have been too strict. 'I wanted everyone to love him, so I went a little overboard on discipline,' she explained. 'However, like any normal child he had his moments and was quite naughty.'

Scott showed musical ability from the age of twenty months, when he discarded his nursery rhymes and started singing ballads and country music. 'Naturally he was asked to sing, usually in front of the family and friends,' said Betty in 1966. 'Never wanted anyone to make a fuss of him afterwards, yet he enjoyed singing. Scott is more at home in front of a big audience than in a living-room.'

On the surface, young Engel had an enviable upbringing. Money was not a concern and he would regularly receive generous amounts of cash from his father right up until leaving high school at seventeen. Yet while Scott was still a toddler, his parents' marriage had run into difficulties and the increasingly tense atmosphere at home was punctuated by screaming matches which were indelibly imprinted on the little boy's memory. Even worse, Scott was badly affected by the acts of violence he witnessed.

'There had been much bad misunderstanding between my parents,' he remembered in a 1966 interview. 'I lived in a nice home – but things were always tense.' Noel and Betty were divorced when Scott was six, and the youngster suffered the added trauma of witnessing his mother's nervous breakdown soon afterwards. This dreadful period ('It was a very bad time for me') caused the boy to side with his mother and hold a deep grudge against his father, with whom he was not reconciled until fifteen years later. 'I held it against Dad – which I shouldn't have,' said Scott. 'He turned out to be a really great guy. But it had been a violent situation between Mum and Dad . . .'

Much later, in the London of the mid-1960s when all and sundry were proudly parading their working-class credentials, whether real or imagined, Scott had no qualms about revealing his privileged background. 'I have a wealthy father,' he told one teen magazine. 'He is an oil magnate, but he never did a lot for me. Once, though, he lent me about two thousand dollars and I blew it on a car. Boy, was he mad!'

Scott was seven when Betty moved to the high-altitude resort of

Denver to convalesce. Her son, who was having to grow up fast, spent much of his spare time at the local cinema where he would weave fantasies of becoming a big screen star. Once the show ended, Scott would race home and attempt to re-enact the hero's part in front of his bedroom mirror. 'He started on a wood-carving spree and almost cut his thumb off,' said Betty. 'One day he was sword-fighting with a friend and Scott almost lost an eye, so that took care of that.

'When we first moved, two little boys came over to play, I went out to check and one was trying to hold Scott down while the other was punching him. I explained to the boys that it wasn't fair, and suggested that if they wanted to fight to let Scott take on one at a time. This was real funny, because Scott's Dad had held the wrestling championship in college and had taught Scott to wrestle, plus box. All Scott had to do was take out the first boy and that ended that. He was respected after that, believe me.' Scott grew to love boxing, the most individual of all sports, and in the sixties attended several top shows in London.

Inspired by his cowboy hero, Roy Rogers, Scott insisted on riding his first horse at the age of seven. To his surprise, the horse promptly threw him and Scott, landing heavily, was knocked unconscious. When he came round, his mother put him straight back in the saddle and within a fortnight he could ride quite well.

Scott was always accident-prone. As a teenager he was involved in several car accidents and suffered a severe injury to his heel while riding pillion on a motorbike. Then, about two months before leaving for England as a 22-year-old, he rode his Yamaha motorbike over a tramline and jammed its front wheel in the rails, causing the machine to flip over three times and 'taking off all his skin on the left side'. Scott's chequered motoring career would continue on the other side of the Atlantic.

'I used to get my way with Mum all the time, so when I decided I wanted to go and live in a big city for a change, we went – to New York City,' recounted Scott, who was ten years old when he arrived in the Big Apple. If he is to be believed, he became 'a bit of a hoodlum', hanging about the city streets with rough characters and experiencing his first taste of racism, which in the 1960s would lead to him becoming one of the first pop musicians to boycott South Africa.

With no fatherly hand to keep him in line, trouble became Scott's constant playmate. 'I was expelled from about three or four schools because I was such a nuisance,' he said. 'I was the guy that got a group around him and looked for trouble. We'd get up to all sorts of things. I was a horrible son and my mother had some real worries with me. I disliked schools and the stupidity of sitting in classes and having a gang was a way of forgetting what a drag everything was. It was a form of rebellion, although I wasn't rebelling about my home, just school.'

Anxious to steer her son clear of further trouble, Betty encouraged him to search for parts in local shows and musicals, but Scott's big break happened completely by accident. One day, a Puerto Rican friend attended an audition for a Rodgers and Hammerstein show called *Pipedream* and Scott went along to provide moral support. 'Except that they heard me sing and I got the part instead,' he related. 'What's more, I was in that show for one and a half years. I didn't enjoy it all that much, but I got paid about $300 a week.'

The money went towards furnishing an apartment for the Engels – Scott had become the family breadwinner before his twelfth birthday. A few months later, he appeared in a televised amateur talent contest at Madison Square Gardens, billed as 'Scotty Engel, baritone from Denver'. In between attending stage school, he also started recording demos for various artists and released a single, 'When Is A Boy A Man' backed by 'Steady As A Rock', on the RKO Unique label in 1957.

When Scott was sixteen, he and his mother moved to California, to be closer to Betty's family. Scott enrolled at Hollywood High where, in order to avoid army training and the hateful prospect of marching around with a gun, he joined the school orchestra, discovered the works of Haydn and Mozart and learnt to play the double-bass. While Scott found rehearsals boring, he stuck with the instrument and progressed to electric bass, so becoming one of the first players in Hollywood and later receiving much session work as a result.

In between school lessons, Scott continued to cut demos and discs for the small Orbit and Ember record companies. A 'Meet Scott Engel' EP consisting of 'The Livin' End' and 'Good For Nothin'' was issued by Orbit, probably in 1959, the year that Scott and his mother arrived in Los Angeles. The cover shows the handsome young Engel rather self-consciously wielding a guitar and looking like a blond Tony Curtis. Sleeve-notes, attributed to 'Teenage Frankenstein', describe him as 'the gonnest gasser of all gassers'. Other singles from this time are 'Charley Bop/All I Do Is Dream' and 'Paper Doll/Bluebell', the latter tracks turning up on an album of early material a decade later.

Scott had developed into a tall, handsome teenager with startlingly blue eyes and a clear complexion, yet despite his blond, angelic appearance music was still taking a back seat to getting into trouble. 'We doused the school into darkness by throwing the master switch,' he remembered, 'but our best thing was blowing up the phone kiosk with a couple of cherry bombs. I did it to test how people would react. It was creative destruction, but I was kicked out for it.' He had barely settled into a private school when he was expelled for using 'profane language' in the street.

Scott was undergoing a distinct change of personality. Previously outgoing and sunny-natured, he became increasingly withdrawn, and displayed a depth of cynicism quite astonishing for one so young. While those abortive attempts to achieve stardom in New York may have soured him, this possible explanation is not wholly adequate. His mother knew the reason, but she was not telling. 'I thought it was because of being let down so much,' she told *Disc and Music Echo*'s Bob Farmer in 1966. 'There is so much (personal problems) that I cannot tell you, that might be the cause.' All Scott would reveal was that he grew 'prematurely cynical and determined to be on my guard against people'.

Caught up among Hollywood types who he dismissed as 'pseudo intellectuals', Scott Engel was the archetypal angry young man. Hollywood was heinous to him. He found its characters boring and dismissed them as 'Hollywood hippies or just plain glory seekers – I wasn't seeing real people.' Bored and directionless, Scott fell in with a teenage gang who used to cruise around in a car at nights seeking trouble. His strong personality must have earned him the respect of his peers. 'We didn't want to hurt people, just the authorities,' claimed Scott.

'Anything that was owned by the authorities – lampposts, seats, anything like that, we damaged. But you had to be quick. Part of being in a gang was having the knack of talking your way out of a tight spot if the police caught you. Not that they caught us much, we were far too quick for them. But all the five guys in my gang could talk, so we were alright.'

One of the gang's favourite pursuits was to head up to Beverly Hills in the dead of night and creep into the gardens of the rich and famous. At that time, beautiful homes were usually built on the edge of a particular cliff overlooking Los Angeles, and Scott and his co-horts took great delight in shoving the outside toilets of these properties over the precipice. 'Some of them were heavy but we'd all get behind and push like mad, and the thrill of seeing it going over was really great,' he recalled. It was just as well some unfortunate insomniac was not sitting answering the call of nature or innocently admiring the city lights during one of these nocturnal raids, other-wise the consequences of such wanton recklessness could have been disastrous.

As it was, Scott was charged with damaging public property on a couple of occasions, but managed to avoid being sent to a detention home or put on probation. 'I must have been the worst son ever and my mother had real worries with me,' he admitted. 'I was horrible. I'd be out late and she wouldn't know where I was and it was always terrible for her when I got into trouble.'

Despite showing promise at English language and literature, Scott did not exactly shine academically (he found mathematics particular-ly incomprehensible), so his later reputation as the great intellectual of pop stemmed from his voracious appetite for books. His restless dreams of escaping the humdrum environs of Los Angeles were fired by the writings of beat culture poets Jack Kerouac, Gary Snyder and Henry Miller, and at sixteen Scott decided on impulse to hitch-hike all the way to New York, encountering his fair share of adventure on the way.

Engel, who took only a small amount of money, would creep into motels just before they locked up at night and leap out of a window early in the morning before the bill arrived. He saw the seamy side of life on that trip and, while these lowlife experiences provided the inspiration for at least one of his later songs, Scott came to view the trip as a mistake. 'I was making myself cynical of everything and everybody,' he said in 1966. 'I've stayed that way and that's half of why many people don't like me today.'

By his late teens, Scott was becoming obsessed by Ingmar Bergman films such as *The Seventh Seal* and *The Virgin Spring* and this, coupled with his love for Mozart, blossomed into a general fascination for European literature and culture. Returning to Los Angeles, Scott strove to get a grip of his life and concentrated on the only subjects which had interested him at school – art and music.

He enrolled at the Walt Disney-owned Chouinard Art Institute in downtown Los Angeles, where he obtained good grades and even worked on some designs for the great man. Scott also learnt to play guitar and started singing again, making demo discs for the likes of teenage idol Paul Anka, as well as playing double-bass for the Los Angeles Youth Orchestra.

'I was interested in West Coast jazz in those days,' said Scott. 'I used to hear Barney Kessel, Bob Cooper and Victor Feldman at Howard Rumsey's Lighthouse Club. I was really familiar with those people and I didn't dig a lot of East Coast jazz. Barney Kessel really started me on jazz and I bought all his albums when I was sixteen and at the time I played guitar myself and was making a serious attempt at the instrument.'

The 'Looking Back With Scott Walker' LP issued by Ember early in 1968, dates from this period and Scott's rendition of 'Sing Boy Sing' apparently prompted Tommy Sands to record the number which became a sizeable hit. Scott's rich baritone is quite remarkable for a sixteen-year-old and his elocution immaculate, yet he still seemed destined to be overshadowed by less talented singers blessed with better connections.

Despite a persistent personality clash, Scott could at least count on the support of a strong-willed mother who was convinced his singing would eventually gain recognition. The mere thought of their offspring pursuing a career in rock-'n'-roll was enough to induce apoplexy in most middle-class Americans, yet Scott at least had no worries on that score. Betty's explanation for his general untidiness ('I was always picking up after him') suggests that, as the only child of affluent parents, he was considerably indulged.

'I miss my mother,' Scott acknowledged soon after moving to England. 'I telephone her very often. I don't actually say I love my mother, I don't know what love is. But I feel more for her than I do for anyone else and I respect her deeply.'

Sometime in 1960, Scott met future Walker Brother John Maus at the audition for a television play. According to legend, Scott accompanied his nervous high-school friend John Stewart to the audition and ended up getting a walk-on part as Maus's brother – a suspiciously similar set of circumstances to those which had led to the *Pipedream* role a few years earlier. After the audition was over, John, who was showing off his guitar, claimed to have mastered at least eight chords. Scott coolly replied that he could play twelve. 'We hated one another right off,' recalled Maus. 'I thought he was a conceited little prig and he thought I was a stuck-up snob.' It was to be three years before they met again.

Despite Scott's flirtation with acting, music remained paramount and stardom seemed assured when Eddie Fisher, the 1950s heart-throb, saw him singing at a Palm Springs lunchtime engagement and offered to become his mentor. For some reason, by the mid-seventies Scott was dismissing this story as 'cock-and-bull', yet his mother distinctly remembered Fisher, then married to Elizabeth Taylor, grandly announcing that he would do for Scott what the legendary Eddie Cantor had done for him. In 1966, Scott himself recalled how Fisher had hailed his promise and booked him on three major television shows.

A 'Scott Engel' EP, exhumed by Liberty in November 1966, comprises four tracks recorded four years earlier which serve as a fascinating insight into Scott's vocal development. On Stewart-McFarland's 'I Broke My Own Heart', *Melody Maker* reckoned Scott sounded 'like a young Dean Martin – sober', and his ballad voice is shown to good effect on 'What Do You Say'.

Unfortunately, Fisher lost interest in his young protégé when Taylor ran off with Richard Burton, whom she met on the set of *Cleopatra* in March 1962. Scott, much to his despair, was allowed to sink back into obscurity and vowed to his mother that he would never sing again. Not for the first time, the harsh world of show-business had kicked him in the stomach.

2 People Get Ready

'Jack Nitzsche did that one record with us, and I took it from there.'
Scott Walker, 1973

STUNG BY FISHER'S REJECTION, Scott vented his frustrations by studiously mastering bass guitar before teaming up with John Stewart, his former Hollywood High schoolmate, to work the clubs in the Sunset Strip area. Scott, who was by now cultivating the long-haired beatnik look and developing an interest in the West Coast jazz scene, quickly became a highly proficient bassist and a highly paid one at that. He and Stewart, alternately known as The Moongooners or The Newporters, backed several well-known artists including The Righteous Brothers and Ike and Tina Turner, and this first taste of success encouraged Scott's initial moderate attempts at songwriting. By the time Engel and Stewart cut a single entitled 'I Only Came To Dance With You' for the tiny Martay Records label, they were calling themselves The Dalton Brothers.

This song, written by P. J. Proby under his Jim Smith alias and backed by Engel and Stewart's 'Without Your Love', was the title track of an LP released by Tower in 1966 and erroneously credited to 'John Stewart and Scott Engel, Original Members of The Walker Brothers'.

Although 'I Only Came To Dance With You', with its precision harmonies and mournful brass backing, has dated quite well, the album itself is a mishmash of only three vocal tracks, studio jams and demos on which the presence of Engel and Stewart is questionable. Scott and his partner also produced a couple of records during this period, most notably Margie Day's 'Have I Lost My Touch/Tell Me In The Sunlight', which carries the production credit of 'Alec Noel' – Stewart's middle name and Scott's first.

'I was nearly killing myself,' recalled Scott. 'Getting up early, going to school, doing homework and going to work at night. We'd start about nine and go through till four. I also had a girlfriend – so

9

I was getting no sleep and was like a zombie. I also used to cut out of school to do session work. In 1963 I played on The Routers' hit "Let's Go!".'

He remained on the periphery of the record business for some time: playing gigs with Stewart in Sunset Strip clubs, working as a van driver for Liberty Records, appearing on Sandy Nelson's 'Let There Be Drums', and undertaking a string of menial tasks at Phil Spector's Gold Star Studios, although never actually playing on any sessions.

Working as a musician for hire proved an extremely tough but invaluable education, and meant that Scott, who backed countless Hollywood celebrities around this time, could play guitar, piano, drums and harmonica by the time he arrived in England in 1965.

One night, Scott was booked to support a singer named Donnie Brooks, who had enlisted John Maus as an eleventh-hour replacement after another guitarist failed to show. After the performance was over, Maus, recognising Scott from the television audition three years previously, enlisted him for a gig at a bowling alley with his older sister Judy. 'So I worked that gig with them, and they were real pleased because we all looked similar and it seemed like a brothers-and-sister act,' said Scott. 'She used to twist – all that stuff.'

John Joseph Maus was born on 12 November 1943 at St Elizabeth Hospital in New York City, the second child of John Maus and his wife Regina. Although entering the world virtually hairless, his famous blond locks soon began to grow and from an early age John liked to wear his hair long. He was humming tunes before he could talk and developed an interest in toy cars, colouring books and clay modelling.

John senior's work as a scientist involved in rocket research took the family to Hermosa Beach, California when the boy was four, and young Maus developed into a proficient and avid surfer as well as a promising Little League baseball player. 'At school I was Mr Athlete,' he recalled in London in 1965. 'I took everything that made you move. I was what they call "end" when we played football. That's the position where you don't get hit. Only one day I did. This guy kicked me straight up into the air and when I came down I had one tooth knocked behind the other, what felt like a broken back and a permanent knee injury that still bugs me in the cold weather over here.'

During several weeks of enforced inactivity, the eleven-year-old

Maus began to develop a serious interest in music, teaching himself acoustic guitar and later progressing to saxophone, clarinet and violin. Deciding to concentrate on guitar, John took a string of part-time jobs to raise money for an electric instrument. By the time he was sixteen he was competent enough to give lessons to a twelve-year-old neighbour called Carl Wilson, a future member of The Beach Boys. John, a lanky six-foot-four with raw-boned Nordic looks, cut a striking figure on the Californian beaches. His main interests were girls, fast cars and sailing and, not surprisingly, this archetypal Californian beatnik later struggled to adapt to London life.

'I just can't get used to England,' John admitted in a 1965 interview. 'I can't get used to the restricted hours your shops and restaurants keep. In the States you can go shopping or get a meal at any time of the day or night. I'm investing a little money in some land in a place called Laguna, just a few miles from San Diego. That's where I'd go back to if we split up. That's where I want to retire to, or work from, as the case may be. Out there it's warm all the year round. The sea is beautiful and the beaches soft and white. I guess I'm just a natural son of the surf.'

By the time he was thirteen, John was developing into a child actor of considerable promise, and attended several auditions for small television roles before landing the part of a 'hick kid' in *Hello Mom*, a 1956 series starring Betty Hutton. 'I was making more money as a child star than I am now as a pop star,' said John, nine years later. 'I was the perfect little gentleman. I had a fringe right down to my nose and I learnt how to deal with the "are you a girl or boy?" routine at a very early age. They always cast me as a country kid with freckles – I was revolting!'

In 1960, the Maus family moved to Los Angeles where John attended El Camino College and considered a career teaching history. However, Regina urged him to utilise his musical talents by forming a group with Judy. Over the next three years, brother and sister played under various names including John and Judy, Judy and The Gents and The John and Judy Four, even recording a clutch of demo records, some written by their mother.

This varied musical apprenticeship meant that, by the birth of The Walker Brothers, John was already a showbusiness veteran. A somewhat tougher character than his adopted relatives, Maus became the natural leader of the group, and his no-nonsense approach enabled him to negotiate deals on their behalf.

By the time Judy, Scott and John joined forces, the latter had blossomed into an accomplished guitarist and vocalist, but one night Scott found himself unexpectedly thrust into the spotlight. 'John got hoarse so I had to do the singing,' he said. 'The club owner groaned at the idea – I was no knockout.' The moody Engel apparently felt the act had no future and did not stay long. He bluntly declared that he could 'make more bread playing cocktail music' (some reports state that he disliked being in a group with a girl) and returned to plunking his double-bass in a trio.

When Scott next ran into John, at another Brooks gig in Pasadena in late 1963, the singer suggested that the pair perform a twenty-minute warm-up prior to his entrance. Scott and John's act was so well received that the management signed them and fired the hapless Brooks.

In those days, all musicians had to be 21 years of age in order to play the Los Angeles clubs. As Scott and John were both under-age, they had to use false IDs simply to gain admission. John's card was in the name of Walker and, because he disliked his constantly mispronounced surname (actually pronounced Moss) and bore an uncannily similar appearance to his partner, it was probably on his suggestion that they became The Walker Brothers.

Together with a huge drummer called Tiny, whose hulking appearance belied considerable technical expertise, Scott and John secured a two-year residency at Gazzari's on Sunset Strip the following spring, working in direct competition with the more established Johnny Rivers at the Whisky-A-Go-Go. Apart from their smooth harmonies, hip image and aesthetic blond looks, Scott and John's hair was outrageously long for the times, provoking disparaging comments and even threats of physical violence from the city's crew-cutted, 'Keep America Virile' fraternity.

Yet Scott's musical tastes were completely at odds with his image. While his contemporaries raved about emerging Los Angeles groups The Byrds and Love, Engel developed a passion for the work of crooner Jack Jones – and did not care who knew it. Jones used to perform in a nearby club and, during intervals at Gazzari's, Scott would slip out of the back door to mingle with Jones's older, tuxedo-clad audience just two doors away.

'I don't count myself in [Jack Jones's] class,' said Scott in 1966. 'But I am working on my own, studying breath control and phrasing so that I can sing in the relaxed manner of artists like Jones. Just to be able to put the kind of styling into a song that Sinatra does in "A Very Good Year", for example. That would mean a lot to me.'

The lines of fans outside Gazzari's grew, as did Scott and John's working hours. They had to play six nights a week from 8 p.m. until 2 a.m., working in twenty-minute slots alternating with the other resident band. Some nights they had to play six hours straight. Scott, left to concentrate on his bass guitar while John handled the vocals, later regarded this period as one of the happiest of his life.

Ben Gazzari, a large jovial Italian, came to 'alove me lika son! He used to get me fat on spaghetti – if it's possible to get me fat on anything. By about 2 a.m. I used to look dreary, my jaws ached from chewing gum and I was a picture of misery. He used to come up to me and cut my tie in half with a pair of scissors. It used to kill me – I'd collapse every time.' Future Walker Brother Gary Leeds, then playing in a Sunset Boulevard club with P. J. Proby, recalls that exciting period:

'The whole connection between all of us was the McKonky Agency which handled groups who played these Twist clubs. When somebody was sick you just switched around because we were all basically playing the same songs. I used to go and watch Scott and John playing across the street in the club opposite. They'd do mostly Top Ten stuff, John playin' the Fender lead and Scott doin' backing vocals. John was a good guitarist and Scott was about the third best bassist in LA.'

Betty Engel worried incessantly about her son. Unaware that Scott was being fed a constant diet of spaghetti and pizza by Gazzari's elderly mother, she feared he was starving himself to death. The long hours he worked at the club meant that home was simply somewhere to crash out. Although he was enjoying modest success on the Los Angeles beat scene, the future was uncertain. Scott had briefly attended business school, but gave it up, saying he needed 'time to think'.

Art, however, remained an abiding passion, so Betty welcomed Scott's decision to major in Commercial Art at Chouinard that fall (he would continue to attend art school at the height of his fame in London). While living at home, Scott ruined every telephone pad with the sketches he drew while talking. Months later, with her son 5,000 miles away in England, Betty would shed many a tear as she gazed down at those telephone pads.

But as Scott became more embroiled in his studies at Chouinard, fate intervened in the shape of Mercury Records' chief, Nik Venet, who had signed The Beach Boys to Capitol a couple of years earlier. Intrigued by reports he had received from Gazzari, Venet ventured along to the club one evening and, after seeing Scott and John elicit an enthusiastic response from the audience, offered them a three-year recording contract. The two Walkers gratefully accepted, and were whisked into the RCA Studios on Sunset Boulevard to record the Eugene Church composition 'Pretty Girls Everywhere' with John on lead. The flipside was 'Doin' The Jerk', Scott's tongue-in-cheek tribute to the latest dance craze sweeping the West Coast.

Both unexceptional numbers, with similar arrangements and brass backing making them sound almost identical, they offer no hint of the famous Walkers sound that was to follow. 'Pretty Girls Everywhere' was at least a moderate hit in Los Angeles and led to the group landing a cameo role in a ghastly surf movie called *Beach Ball*, along with Frankie Valli and the Four Seasons and The Supremes.

This film, which charts the wearisome exploits of a surf group on their way to a talent contest, is worth watching for the sheer awfulness of its cast of suspiciously mature teenage hunks and several dozen bikini-clad blondes with the combined IQ of a kitchen utensil.

Scott and John, wearing grey Beatle jackets, with Tiny's brooding presence on drums behind them, perform 'Doin' The Jerk' in the 'climactic' scene at a sports car parade. John, who roared up to the film set in his beloved Thunderbird, was misdirected into the parade and almost missed the shoot.

The Walkers' career was gathering momentum and when English TV producer Jack Good arrived in town, intent on unearthing new talent, Gazzari's was the first place he went. Good subsequently booked The Walkers on *Hollywood A Go-Go*, where they had a 26-week residency, as well as on his own *Shindig*, where they appeared twice. At around this point, the short-haired somewhat chubby Tiny seems to have accepted that he did not fit The Walkers' image and retired gracefully from the fray.

His departure coincided with the appearance of a wiry, dark-haired fellow who approached Scott and John at Gazzari's one night and regaled them with tales of the exploding pop scene across the Atlantic. Drummer Gary Leeds, who had toured England with P. J. Proby before his work permit ran out, insisted: 'The three of us can go to England and make it bigger than The Beatles!' The absurdity of this statement drew titters from Scott and John. 'I'm serious!'

Gary persisted. 'We've got the hair and the looks and the vocal thing and I just can't see this going wrong.'

'The British pop scene was simply awesome,' Gary says today. 'You saw everyone each week on shows like *Thank Your Lucky Stars*. I specifically had Scott and John in mind when I returned to LA. They were Americans with long hair and I figured it would make the perfect formula. I knew that in England pop groups had this tremendous publicity machine behind them.'

Leeds, the youngest of the three Walkers according to pop reference books, was actually the oldest, born on 9 March 1942. Possibly due to an unwritten law that pop stars of the mid-sixties had to be barely older than the teenagers who bought their records, Gary's year of birth was invariably given as 1944.

'I'm probably the only person in England with two birthdays. When giving their date of birth Americans usually write the month, then the day, then the year. So when I came over to England I wrote 3/9/42 which was naturally read [by the English] as 3 September 1942. I was born in Glendale, a suburb of Los Angeles. It's the kind of suburban town you see in a Steven Spielberg movie; kinda like a movie set in itself, I guess. It's a place that's famous for two things: me and John Wayne. His father was a chemist in the town. Glendale is also where the whole Walt Disney industry took shape because the studios at Burbank are just round the corner.'

Like Scott, Gary was an only child whose father, Don Gibson, ran a doughnut shop and played no part in his son's upbringing after divorcing his wife Violet when the boy was still an infant. Gary, who lived with his mother, aunt and grandmother in various homes around Glendale, was a cheerful and lively boy who created a fantasy world to compensate for the absence of siblings.

He had hundreds of toy soldiers and would spend whole days directing his own war movies, organising battles, developing storylines and even doing voiceovers. His interest in showbusiness was encouraged by a doting mother, who looked forward to the day when her own son's name would be up in lights. In later years, Gary would describe their relationship as 'close, almost too close. She was obsessive . . . kinda like *A Long Day's Journey Into Night*'.

When Gary was ten his mother married Jack Leeds, the general manager of an oils company which produced the flavours for Carnation ice-cream, Dr Pepper and root beer. Leeds's practical, down-to-earth nature proved a stabilising influence on the scatter-brained

Gary, who adopted his name and came to regard him as his real
father. Gary attended Verdugo Hills High where he enjoyed art and
ended up playing drums for the school band on football pitches prior
to games. He developed an interest in drumming from listening to
Jack's cherished collection of jazz records and became a fan of Gene
Krupa.

'There was this kid at school who had a snare drum but he'd
never let me play it, which only made me more obsessed. Drum kits
always cost so much. My grandmother lived in LA and round the
corner was a shop called Drum City. When I stayed with her one
night I sneaked out of the window at 2 a.m. and went down to the
shop. I just stood there starin' through the window at these red
drums wonderin' if I'd ever have a set. That's how obsessed I was.

'The first drums I had were a Gretsch set. I played 'em for three
months and then found out that I'd set 'em up backwards and was
playin' everythin' the wrong way round. Then I got another Gretsch
set, by now I was playin' in a band, and my parents paid $400 for
the red set I'd seen that night in the window at Drum City.'

The Leeds family settled in Sunland Tujunga, a small suburban
town in the hills near Los Angeles, at around the time that Gary
became aware of a record called 'Sh-boom', by a Canadian group
called The Crew Cuts. It was the first rock-'n'-roll record he had
heard, and it was regarded by teenagers as something of a breakthrough after interminable years of Frank Sinatra. Gary, still playing
drums in the school band, would occasionally run through 'Sh-boom'
and some Elvis Presley tunes with like-minded souls at rehearsals.
This led to the formation of a three-piece junior high school group
called The Beltones, whose repertoire consisted almost entirely of
Jerry Lee Lewis material.

Gary's second high school band, The Biscaines, a more serious
outfit which boasted a sax player, recorded 'Blue Skies', an Irving
Berlin instrumental, for an independent label and gained a lengthy
residency at the Riverside club in Los Angeles. There, they frequently
supported crooners Pat Boone and Paul Anka, in between performing
a high-energy act which featured Gary attacking his drums while
standing on a chair.

Leeds left school at eighteen, and undertook a string of menial
jobs before entering Glendale Junior College to study aerospace technology with the aim of becoming an airline pilot. As Hollywood was
engulfed by the Twist craze, he formed a group called The Standells,

who earned a residency at the Peppermint West club just off Holly-wood Boulevard, where they played from nine until two every night. One of their fellow performers was P. J. Proby, who was already developing a reputation for his wild stage act as well as being a songwriter of considerable promise.

The Standells initially concentrated on reproducing Top Ten hits of the day, like Booker T.'s 'Green Onions', although later, at the onset of the British Invasion, their penchant for wigs and collarless jackets led to them being dubbed 'The Peppermint Beatles'.

Gary was a kid with his head in the clouds, but his planned flying career never got off the ground. One day, while giving his mother a particularly vigorous demonstration of the Twist, he fell over, knocked himself out and tore the cartilage in his knee.

Despite his obvious pain and embarrassment, Gary's unseemly tumble almost certainly saved him from army conscription at a time when war in Vietnam was looming. His knee injury caused him to fail the draft board's physical examination and, more disappointing-ly, ended his hopes of becoming a commercial pilot – although he did subsequently gain a private licence. Unbeknown to Gary, it was his rock-'n-'roll career which was set for take-off.

Despite Scott's outward scepticism, he rapidly warmed to Gary's idea of relocating to England. Engel was frequently appalled by the level of violence on the Los Angeles streets and, in contrast, consider-ed Europe romantic and intriguing. While still a schoolboy, Scott had vowed to travel to England, and this ambition had sustained him through those difficult teenage years. 'I knew that [Gary] was talking sense,' he said. 'I'd been aware for some time that my sort of music – ballads and so forth – could sell far better in Britain because, unlike the American public, the British weren't trend-crazy . . . They liked an assortment.'

With the Vietnam war escalating, the fear of the draft helped convince Scott and John that now was an appropriate time to leave, following a final excursion into RCA studios with their new drum-mer. According to Gary, it was he who suggested The Walkers record the Barry Mann/Cynthia Weil song 'Love Her', although Scott has asserted it was the choice of arranger Jack Nitzsche.

Formerly an Everly Brothers B-side, 'Love Her' introduced the distinctive Walker Brothers sound – heavy orchestral backing over which Scott would emote, with John providing high supporting har-monies. In a 1973 interview, Scott said that the disc's Spectoresque feel, achieved by the presence of a 38-piece orchestra, was the brain-child of Nitzsche. 'What he was tryin' to do was achieve something similar to The Righteous Brothers – only a little more refined, because he felt they were gettin' to be a bit of a drag.'

But having worked out the orchestration, Venet and Nitzsche ran into difficulties over the vocal track. Clearly a much fuller, deeper voice than John's ethereal tones was required. Venet and Nitzsche huddled in earnest consultation for a moment before the former broke off to stride over to The Walkers and enquire: 'Which one of you guys sings the lowest?'

John hesitated fractionally before replying, 'Well . . . Engel does.' Much to his mother's disappointment, Scott had rarely sung since the Eddie Fisher debacle two and a half years earlier, and only then when John's throat was hoarse. 'We need someone who can sing bass,' Venet smiled encouragingly. 'Come on, let's do it!'

So, more through luck than judgment, it was Scott who stepped tentatively into the vocal booth while John remained on the sidelines. One of the greatest voices in popular music was discovered that day. 'Scott got stuck with lead because his voice handled it better,' confirms Gary. 'There was no jealousy on John's part, that was just the way it worked.'

Nitzsche, the man who erected the great Wall of Sound which was later rebuilt around all The Walker Brothers hits, is best remembered for his arrangements on Ike and Tina Turner's 'River Deep, Mountain High', and a string of other Phil Spector-produced classics. He went on to write scores for over 40 films, including *An Officer and a Gentleman*, which won him an Academy Award. Speaking from his Los Angeles home, Nitzsche's recollections of the session which spawned 'Love Her' are surprising, especially in view of the record's historic significance. 'It was no big deal,' he says.

' "River Deep, Mountain High"! Now that was a song that mattered to me because it was very special. I cannot compare "Love Her" to that because it was so average. I guess it sold about two copies in the States and you cannot put it in the same category as "River Deep". As we were recording "Love Her", the studio door opened and in walked Mick [Jagger], Keith [Richards] and Charlie [Watts], makin' everyone feel about an inch tall, I guess. When it was over, Venet came out of the control box, jivin'. He was sayin': "That's your greatest-ever arrangement Jack!" – or some crap like that.'

And how does Nitzsche remember Scott? As a fine bassist with latent songwriting talent or a charismatic vocal performer perhaps? 'I remember Scott,' he says thoughtfully, 'as bein' a great hairdresser. That's right! A hairdresser! He was foolin' around in the studio and started rubbin' this gel into my hair. It was called Dep and it wasn't as heavy as lacquer. After he'd rubbed it in, dried it, and backcombed it I ended up looking like I had more hair than when he started! He must have done it three times that day and he was pretty good. I knew nothing of The Walker Brothers before we went into the studio. These small labels used to complete four tracks in each session so it was pretty much another job for me.'

According to Nitzsche, 'Love Her' was originally meant to be recorded by The Righteous Brothers, but the song became available following a disagreement between Spector and Mann. Nitzsche also claims that the actual demo, by a singer called Freddie Scott, was far superior to The Walkers' release. While he remembers Engel as 'a sweet and lovable guy', Nitzsche did not particularly rate his voice and was astounded to learn of Scott Walker's 'god-like' reputation on the other side of the Atlantic almost 30 years later.

'To be truthful, I don't like white music. Scott's white, and he sounds it. Have you heard of a guy called Willie De Ville? Now that's what I call an amazing voice.'

By the time Mercury released 'Love Her' on its Smash label (backed by the unremarkable 'The Seventh Dawn', title track of a United Artists motion picture) The Walkers were feverishly sorting out work permits, saving money and laying plans to launch an American counter-invasion of England. They continued playing at Gazzari's into the New Year, keeping their plans secret from everybody.

When the boys' parents finally found out, their reactions were mixed. Betty wanted Scott to continue his studies at Chouinard, but reasoned that the trip to London would probably only last six weeks and was, after all, the chance of a lifetime. Gary's father Jack generously provided $10,000 to fund the expedition and John's parents wished him the best of luck. Faced with losing his chief attraction, the volatile Gazzari went wild and was only placated when John assured him that the group were merely embarking on a three-month tour to promote 'Love Her'. The Walkers were also fortunate to escape being sued for abruptly terminating their residency on *Shindig*.

On 17 February, the Leeds, Engel and Maus families gathered to see the boys off from Los Angeles International Airport, and by all accounts the farewells became so tearful that the plans were almost shelved. It was a particularly painful moment for John, who a couple of months earlier had become engaged to a beautiful eighteen-year-old pop singer called Kathy Young, who had enjoyed an American No. 1 hit with 'Thousand Stars' in 1960.

Scott, however, was so delighted at finally realising a personal ambition of travelling to Europe that he decided that any pop success which came along would be a bonus. 'I wanted to get out of America anyway and go to Europe, because I'd always been a European film freak and I wanted to see if I could meet Ingmar Bergman and a few other people,' he said later.

As he gazed down out of a porthole at the ugly sprawl of Los Angeles and its surrounding suburbs, Scott could scarcely have realised that two years would elapse before he saw his adopted home town again. In that time he would achieve stardom on an unprecedented scale, but it would come at a heavy artistic and emotional price.

3 My Ship Is Coming In

'I guess we're kinda sellin' Jack Jones through our hair.'

Scott Walker, 1965

TWELVE MONTHS AFTER The Beatles had completed their historic flight into New York's Kennedy Airport amid scenes of mass hysteria, three long-haired Californians made the reverse trip across the Atlantic, arriving at London's snowy Heathrow in vastly different circumstances. The Walkers were completely unprepared for the icy blast of air that greeted them and promptly discussed catching the next flight home. John, who had not thought to bring a coat, emerged from the plane in shirt-sleeves and tore his best trousers during disembarkation.

Apart from attracting some suspicious glances from their fellow passengers, the dishevelled trio aroused little attention, although in the ensuing weeks John would be regularly mistaken for Brian Jones of The Rolling Stones, Gary frequently mobbed by Beatles fans thinking he was George Harrison and Scott, much to his embarrassment, taken for Mick Jagger. 'We took a gamble when we came over,' Scott later told *Disc and Music Echo*. 'We walked out of a twenty-week coast-to-coast TV series – we nearly got sued – and other things were goin' for us too.'

At the time of The Walkers' anonymous arrival, the British music press was reporting that The Beatles, who had 'probably made their last British tour for over a year', were flying out to the Bahamas for two and a half weeks to film scenes from *Help!*; The Kinks were at No. 1 with 'Tired Of Waiting' just above The Righteous Brothers' 'You've Lost That Lovin' Feeling', and Gary's one-time cohort P. J. Proby, whose trouser-splitting antics had led to demands for his deportation, was, according to *Melody Maker*, 'straddling a dazed pop scene like a colossus'. For all Gary's brazen confidence, the next three months would be a period of loneliness and uncertainty for Scott and John, neither of whom took an instant liking to British life or the climate.

The Walkers quickly found a spacious, but sparsely-furnished first-floor bedsit at 1 Onslow Gardens, Kensington, which must have seemed particularly depressing to three middle-class youngsters accustomed to all the creature comforts. In a desperate effort to keep warm, the boys would push their beds perilously close to a tiny electric fire which generated about as much heat as a candle. Despite wearing thick pyjamas and building mountains of blankets, coats and towels on their beds, The Walkers found the cold unbelievable.

This miserable existence, coupled with inevitable homesickness and seemingly indigestible English food which meant a constant diet of cheese and biscuits, slowly began to erode their spirits. The cosmopolitan delights of Harrods' food department provided a welcome source of sustenance – albeit an alarming drain on finances – but, as Scott would later recount, it rapidly became clear that John in particular required more incentive to stay.

'So the three of us came over [to London] and started going broke slowly. Nothin' was happenin' and we were freezin' to death. Straight from Southern California to this in February 1965 – Jesus, it was cold, and we were walkin' around the streets lookin' for a flat. John had one foot on the banana skin and the other on the plane, so to speak, and I decided to head into Europe.'

On Gary's insistence, The Walkers turned down offers to play one-night stands, hoping that bigger offers would shortly come their way. Although the trio were virtual nonentities on the London pop scene, they adopted the attitude of big stars and made sure they were seen and photographed in fashionable clubs like the Cromwellian and the Scotch of St James. It was all part of what Scott termed 'The Big Exercise'.

Although he never would have admitted it to the others, Engel's own homesickness was acute. Early in April he rang his mother to announce he was coming home and wished to be enrolled again in art school. Two days later he called and said they were going to stay. 'Then I thought I would die, but reasoned with myself and knew that this was his life and he had to live it,' Betty recalled.

Philips, who issued all Mercury recordings in Britain, released 'Pretty Girls Everywhere/Doin' The Jerk' and waited in vain for a reaction. The second release, 'Love Her/The Seventh Dawn', seemed similarly bound for the bargain bins and the dispirited Walkers were in two minds about whether to return to the States. Then suddenly, without any plugging from the group, the disc started to move, breaching the *Melody Maker* Top 50 on 8 May, the week in which The Walkers attracted considerable publicity by criticising an apparent backlash towards British artists in their native country.

'Love Her' was voted a hit by the *Juke Box Jury* television panel, but when the group emerged from the wings the heads of the lanky Scott and John were out of camera range. A couple of nights later, Scott and Gary were mobbed in the audience at a Kinks/Yardbirds show in Walthamstow. Gary's initial delight at being mauled by several screaming teenage girls quickly turned to dismay when he realised that one of them had made off with his wristwatch, a cherished gift from his mother.

Nevertheless, Gary was considerably heartened by developments and wasted little time in introducing the group to the music press, reasoning that as they had not approached The Walkers, it was now up to The Walkers to approach them. *Melody Maker* writer Chris Welch was somewhat taken aback when the boys arrived unannounced at the paper's Fleet Street office.

'It was certainly not the usual way you would first get to hear about a new group. I don't think they had a record contract and they certainly didn't have much PR. London was in full swing, very much the epicentre of the music scene, so an American group was quite unusual.

'They did give the impression that they were brothers, and they did make an attempt to look identical with these Beatle hair-dos. I discovered later that John and Gary were wearing wigs; Scott was wearing the real thing. They were all very bright and articulate and good fun to be with, as opposed to some of the British R&B artists who were around at that time. Gary was the cheekiest and most natural; John was a little sullen and suspicious; Scott was very charming and had this sort of amused look about him as if he thought everything was a bit of a joke which he couldn't bring himself to take seriously.'

The mystique that was developing around The Walker Brothers would have been considerably damaged by the claim that two of them wore wigs. At the end of the year Gary would, through the columns of the music press, indulge in a public slanging match with P. J. Proby, who had the temerity to question whether the drummer's hair was indeed his own. Proby was possibly referring to the days when Gary played with The Standells, who did indeed wear Beatle wigs on stage at Peppermint West.

Scott Walker

It may seem a case of splitting hairs but, for the record, Bobby Hamilton, one of The Walker Brothers' road managers, says he always denied fans access to the dressing-room because a member of the group wore a hairpiece over his forehead. Hamilton refuses to name the guilty man but, since he saw both Scott and John blow-dry their hair, the conclusion seems obvious. 'No way did I wear a wig,' insists Gary, whose firm denials are supported by long-time friend Allan McDougall. By March 1966, when Gary was the subject of *Melody Maker*'s Pop Think-In, the subject of wigs had clearly become rather tiresome. 'I knew that one would come up,' said Leeds wearily. 'I wear one under each arm.'

The great wig controversy was still to come, but on 21 May – the day The Walkers' work permits expired – the *NME*'s Keith Altham revealed that the trio were not really brothers at all and had been promoting themselves with $10,000 from 'a mystery backer' – i.e. Gary's father, although the drummer told journalists that the money came from the Mafia. (When John threatened to fly back to the United States, Gary would say: 'But how will the Mafia feel, John? They'll be waitin' for you at the airport.') Altham, who dubbed the group 'the blond Beatles', was particularly impressed by John's hair, which at the time was probably the longest on the London beat scene.

'We adopted the long hair because it was different,' explained John. 'Some of the other groups would like to as well, but they don't have the guts.' Maus, normally the most taciturn member of the group, revealed that The Walkers' best friend in England was called Oz and lived in the flat below them. He said he often chatted to Oz over a cup of English coffee which Scott and Gary apparently found disgusting. No snippet of information was regarded as too banal for pop readers of the mid-sixties.

By now The Walkers had been in Britain for three months and had yet to find a manager, or even perform live. Brian Epstein and Andrew Oldham, respective managers of The Beatles and The Rolling Stones, had both ignored Gary's overtures and, amid backbiting rumours that the group were phonies who could not play at all, The Walkers' first British gig came about through totally unforeseen circumstances. An on-stage dispute at Cardiff between The Kinks' Dave Davies and drummer Mick Avory had been swiftly and bloodily resolved when the latter whacked the guitarist over the head with a cymbal, inflicting a wound requiring several stitches. The Kinks were thrown off the Arthur Howes package tour and The Walkers drafted in to complete the remaining four dates with The Yardbirds.

Scott, John and Gary made their début at the Leeds Odeon, performing a 'slickly presented slot with the emphasis on beat. Green and red spotlights picked out their casual outfits as the bass guitarist Scott announced "There's Pretty Girls Everywhere" [sic] followed by "I'll Be Satisfied". A long introduction led into "Money" which Scott and John sang at separate microphones, drummer Gary simply providing sound backing.'

NME's Gordon Sampson reported that The Walkers' fifteen-minute slot ahead of The Hollies had caused wild audience reaction, while noting the obvious disappointment at the non-inclusion of 'Love Her' and the group's refusal to play an encore or even take a bow at the end of their set. Bolstered by performances on Ready Steady Go, Thank Your Lucky Stars and Top Of The Pops, the disc rose to No. 24 by 4 June, peaking at No. 18 a week later.

Despite snide insinuations about their perceived lack of playing ability, The Walkers were probably at least as proficient as their British counterparts. John's performance on his Fender Telecaster was a highlight of these early shows, while Scott was clearly a talented bassist. Even Gary, who was later confined to the role of spectator in the studio, had developed a rudimentary drumming style after years of playing the Los Angeles clubs. 'He could hold a beat,' recalls one journalist of the day. 'He was certainly as accomplished as Ringo, or Dave Clark.'

Pop writers earnestly reported that The Walkers had met when Scott and John, careering around Los Angeles in the latter's Thunderbird, drove into the rear of Gary's car at a set of traffic-lights. It was said that during the ensuing roadside argument Scott noticed a set of drums in the back of Gary's car and asked him to join the band. In the naïve, fresh-faced world of sixties pop, a little imagination could go a long way.

Years later, Scott would pinpoint the group's Thank Your Lucky Stars television appearance at Birmingham's ABC studios as the start of his personal nightmare. On arriving at the studios, the boys had not taken any notice of a group of girls gathered on the pavement, as they assumed they had no British fans. 'Suddenly,' related Scott, 'they hit us and damn near tore us apart. I got inside and I was bleeding and shocked. I looked at John and John looked at Gary. "Jesus Christ!" was all I could say . . .'

Following a repeat of these scenes back at the hotel, a panting Scott tottered into the bar with torn coat and bloodied shirt. 'They're still out there y'know,' he told the incredulous barman. 'Tried to get through the door lately?'

Around this time, Altham had a full interview with Scott, who was sharing an avant-garde flat in Chelsea with Gary. 'There are fifteen mirrors in one bedroom,' observed Altham, 'a cavalry sword on the wall, a bust of nobody in particular on the mantelpiece, an enormous aspidistra in a pot and a secretary who "kinda came with the flat".'

Scott was moved to elaborate on this mysterious girl: 'She was sittin' in the middle of the dining-room carpet when we arrived. She was cryin' and everythin', sayin' that she was an out-of-work actress and had nowhere to go. So we hired her to answer the phone for us.' Just at that moment, the phone rang. Scott picked up the receiver and, covering the mouthpiece with his hand, sheepishly explained: 'She kinda went out to act or somethin'.'

As Scott dealt with the call, Gary explained how the pair had been forced to find a new flat because of John's late night activities. 'John is very fond of the club scene in London. He kept coming back at ridiculous hours in the morning and the landlady was going out of her mind. He would insist on playing this one guitar run at about 2 a.m., so we decided to compromise and left.'

Gary also talked easily about the boys' new-found popularity and how it had taken their new road manager, Claude Powell, by surprise. 'He's just over from the States and, well, he doesn't know just how wild the fans over here are. We went to *Top Of The Pops* in Manchester yesterday and there were about seventy-five kids outside . . . Claude's famous last words were: "Don't worry. I'll hold them back." He lost his cufflinks, his watch and his jacket and they did the mashed potato all over his face. We just stayed in the car and fell around laughing.'

Altham, who like Chris Welch would interview Scott extensively over the next four years, always looked forward to meeting the most enigmatic Walker, who even at this stage was evidently a different kind of pop star. Interviews would generally take place at Associated Rediffusion's studios in The Strand, from where *Ready Steady Go* was televised, or at the *Top Of The Pops* studios in Manchester. Scott, whose time-keeping was appalling, would saunter into the canteen or dressing-room two hours late, remove his by-now trademark shades, and say: 'Hi, I guess I'm real early for this one, huh?' He always said it with such charm that any irritation Altham felt would instantly vanish.

'He was always looking for another horizon; searching for something more significant than what he was actually doing. He tended to wallow a little in his melancholic streak and all the girls would flock round him. He would sit in front of the dressing-room mirror and claw his face with his hands after making sure that someone was watching. If you were seeing the three of them, Scott would always be the last to put in an appearance, in much the same way as Jagger is always the last Stone to get on the tour bus after a concert.

'At the same time, Scott was sufficiently intelligent to have a sense of proportion about his brooding qualities and he could laugh at himself. John appeared the more balanced of the three and Gary was one of those characters that everyone has in the band; a garrulous comedian who was out to enjoy fame as much as he could while he still had it.'

The modest chart placing of 'Love Her' in no way reflected the group's growing popularity. While Scott's vocal capabilities were still not fully appreciated, the trio possessed an image that most pop managers would later have killed for. Scott himself described The Walkers' appeal as 'neurotic romanticism'. The three mysterious, tragically good-looking Americans were exotic creatures from another dimension in the eyes of British teenagers weaned on the cheeky gap-toothed pop of Gerry and the Pacemakers and Herman's Hermits.

Pop stars like Freddie Garrity thrived on their wholesome boy-next-door image but, somehow, it was difficult to envisage Scott Walker, his eyes permanently obscured by shades, as the boy-next-door. He would discuss existentialism and actually knew what it meant; while most pop stars' reading material did not extend beyond the *NME* and *Melody Maker*, Scott was discovering Jean-Paul Sartre and Albert Camus as well as Hemingway, Dickens and Dylan Thomas; as John downed bourbon at the Cromwellian and Scotch of St James, Scott could be found in a quiet corner of Ronnie Scott's in Frith Street, happily immersed in the unfathomable depths of modern jazz; and while Gary and his friends played Russian roulette with cartons of cream cakes ('First one sick is out!') Scott would slip off to see the latest Ingmar Bergman movie.

The Walkers' star was on the ascent, but this was still not enough to cure John's unhappiness. Of the trio, he was the one who found the move from California's sunny beaches to London's crowded streets the most traumatic, and his general unhappiness was exacerbated by the fact that the girl he was engaged to marry was several thousand miles away. 'I've gotta get back to Kathy,' he kept saying.

John had threatened to pack his bags so often that it had become a standing joke. Then the crunch obviously came, and he booked himself aboard a Los Angeles-bound flight out of Heathrow. The night before John was due to fly, Gary burst into his flat and excitedly announced that he had found the group not just one manager but two. John immediately cancelled his booking.

Maurice King and Barry Clayman ran a small stable of acts which included Van Morrison's Them and Birmingham outfit The Rockin' Berries from their office at 185 Bickenhall Mansions, Baker Street, but The Walkers would become the jewel in their crown. Despite being diametrically opposed characters, King and Clayman teamed up in 1964 to form Capable Management, which Scott, in later years, would sardonically refer to as 'Incapable Mismanagement'. King, a dark, thick-set, pugnacious figure who was born at Westcliff in 1927, grew up in London's East End and broke into showbiz in the early sixties, through his ownership of the Starlite Club in Stratford Place off Oxford Street.

Despite its glittering name, the Starlite was actually a dingy establishment frequented by dubious characters, and King numbered the notorious gangsters Reggie and Ronnie Kray among his personal friends. King was louder and more assertive than Clayman and, when displeased, had been known to threaten some artists with physical violence. 'Maurice was a liar and a con merchant but he had a great personality and artists listened to him,' recalls his widow, Mary Arnold, who today runs her own showbusiness agency in south-west London.

'He handled quite a few artists over the years, but Scott had the potential to become the biggest of the lot. Maurice had so much front that when he shouted everyone jumped. People were afraid of him but he was a teddy bear. Scott loved him almost like a father and they had a very close relationship. Scott liked the fact that Maurice would take the piss out of him.'

Bobby Hamilton, the former Walker Brothers road manager, agrees that King 'couldn't just talk the hind legs off a donkey, he could talk four legs off a bloody stallion'. Clayman was a far quieter and more easy-going individual who, to many people, appeared to be King's underling although they were, in fact, equal partners. Today he is one of the top promoters in Britain – responsible for Michael Jackson's tours – and too busy to discuss Scott Walker. Back in June 1965, Engel was becoming ensnared in fame's spiralling vortex and the prospect of being managed by such a streetwise individual as King was appealing.

'Scott wanted King as his manager after noticing that his eyes curled up at the corners – the definite sign of a villain,' says Allan McDougall, a London-based music journalist and publicist in the mid-sixties. 'Both he and John remarked on those eyes and reasoned that no one would give King any shit.'

Scott received uncomfortable first-hand experience of King's dodgy connections on his first visit to the Starlite. During the course of the evening, the constant playing of Tony Bennett's 'I Left My Heart In San Francisco' ('All gangsters loved that song', recalls McDougall) drove Engel to distraction and prompted him to sabotage the jukebox.

'I'd learnt this trick during a misspent youth in Glasgow,' says McDougall, who later enjoyed success as a record producer in Hollywood. 'You simply pulled the jukebox out from the wall and pressed a button at the back which ejected the record that was playing. Scott suggested the idea that night, so he'd obviously learnt the technique in LA. Anyway, we managed to eject Tony Bennett once and were in the process of repeating the manoeuvre when this sharp-suited, tough-looking thug with slicked-back hair comes up and says, "I don't think Ronnie would like that". Shortly afterwards, one of King's henchmen told us that the guy who came up was Reggie. Scott started quaking and I needed a swift change of underpants.'

King first became aware of The Walker Brothers when Gary, who had been given his home telephone number by McDougall, dragged him out of bed at three o'clock one morning. Angered at being disturbed by some semi-inebriated American kid, King bluntly reminded him of the hour and hung up. Gary's follow-up call received a more menacing response: 'Don't you EVER ring me at this time of night again,' hissed King through gritted teeth. Undeterred, the drummer besieged the Capable Management office to such an extent that King ordered his secretary not to field any more of the calls.

A few days later King was listening appreciatively to 'Love Her' on his car radio when the disc jockey's disclosure of this new American group's identity almost caused him to collide with a double-decker bus. The Walker Brothers! King screeched to a halt as he recalled the drawling Californian who had plagued him the previous week. Swearing venomously, he drove like a madman back to Baker Street and burst into the office. 'Marilyn!' he shouted at his startled secretary. 'We've got to find that Gary Walker bloke!' The following day King and Clayman watched in satisfaction as Scott, John and Gary signed on the dotted line.

The job of publicising the new group fell to Brian Sommerville, a 34-year-old former *Daily Express* journalist from Huddersfield, who had fulfilled a similar role for The Beatles before falling out with Brian Epstein. Sommerville's best publicity stunt was getting Ringo Starr driven through the streets of Paris in the car that won the 1964 Monte Carlo Rally. His worst came when he persuaded Brian Poole of The Tremeloes to leap into the fountains on the Champs Élysées and ended up getting arrested himself.

Balding, bespectacled and permanently attired in suit and tie, Sommerville was clearly someone to be respected following his work with The Beatles. Now a successful barrister living on a farm near York, Sommerville remembers that during his first meeting with The Walkers at Bickenhall Mansions, John – still clearly the group's leader – leaned forward intently and said: 'You've done it once. You've made The Beatles so big. Now you've gotta do the same for us.'

Sommerville: 'Scott I had to treat with a certain amount of reserve because I felt there was something rather strange about him. He was such an introvert in his relationships with people. He hid behind his dark glasses like Greta Garbo and had a phobia about the girls who hung around outside which only encouraged them even more, because it seemed he was playing hard to get.

'But it was no good telling Scott. That would have been fighting human nature. He had certain fixed ideas on some things like honesty and integrity. If anyone he knew breached confidences or showed any ulterior motive for wanting to do something, he just didn't want to know them any more.'

Arthur Howes, the country's top promoter, booked The Walkers for a series of summer packages at popular holiday resorts around Britain. At the same time it was announced that John would be taking a ten-day holiday at the end of month. What Scott and Gary and the group's growing number of female followers did not realise, and were considerably enraged to discover, was that the reason for John's hastily-arranged trip back to California was his marriage to Kathy Young.

'I must admit we were very shocked,' Scott told Rod Harrod of *Disc Weekly*. 'We were mad at first, but now we're over it.' When Harrod asked whether John would be allowed to take his wife on tour he was left in no doubt of Scott's disapproval. 'I'd get very, very annoyed if Kathy started to travel around with us on dates,' he said sternly. 'I used to even get annoyed when he brought her to TV shows before I knew they were married. He should definitely keep his work and home life separate.' Although John and Kathy returned to London together and found a flat in Regent's Park, the recent furore over Tom Jones's marital state persuaded Maus to keep his mouth shut – for a few months at least.

Live appearances the following month caused riotous scenes at Manchester, Stourbridge, Blackpool and Sheffield. Screaming teenage girls stormed the stage and made it increasingly difficult for The Walkers to complete the set, let alone hear their own playing. Shirts were ripped, limbs were bruised and hair wrenched out by the handful. 'You know, on every date so far we've only been able to get ten minutes through our forty-minute set,' Scott told *Disc Weekly*'s Penny Valentine the morning after hitch-hiking back from Birmingham. 'Last night I went all the way down. Right off the stage. The bouncers were hurtin' me almost as much as the kids were.'

Recalling their reception at Manchester's Oasis Club, John said: 'They took us outta there in coffins. The kids went wild. They wanted pieces of face, y'know, our cheeks, noses, things like that.' At Scarborough's Futurist Theatre, the boys watched aghast as one girl climbed on to a parapet high above the stage and, ignoring police threats of arrest, announced she was not coming down until she had met one of The Walkers. She finally got her way when Gary clambered up to give her a kiss.

The kind of fan fever generated by The Walkers had not been seen since the early days of Beatlemania. Gary had his expensive corduroy jacket torn off his back, chewed up and stamped on. John lost his shoes at one all-nighter and returned to the hotel in bare feet. Scott had his favourite blue shirt reduced to ribbons. 'The other day six hundred kids started to rush the stage and the place we were playing in only had two bouncers,' said Gary. 'We just try and run for it. Often it's impossible. They're everywhere. When this happens we just lie down where we are, cover our faces with our hands and hope for the best. We are spending twenty pounds a week each on new clothes.'

The group's Ford Cortina, used to transport The Walkers to these early dates, was virtually wrecked by girls who, not content at smearing lipstick messages all over the paintwork, would also wrench off the wing mirrors as well as parts of the seats where their idols had sat. Scott and Gary's Chelsea flat was quickly located and the appearance of either on the doorstep would be greeted by a burst of screaming from crowds of girls sunbathing in the park opposite.

Privacy, something which Scott had always taken for granted, was now a thing of the past as The Walkers' new-found popularity saw them plunged into an exhilarating, but exhausting stream of one-nighters all over the country. 'I guess we know just about every stone along the M1,' reflected Gary. 'And I've been in that Blue Boar roadhouse so often I feel like I own the joint.'

Maurice King watched the mounting scenes of hysteria with mixed feelings. He and Clayman had one of the hottest outfits in the country, yet their stage act was being reduced to a shambles every night. The Walkers originally augmented their line-up with the keyboards of Jimmy O'Neil, who formerly played with Birmingham band The Uglies. However, as Scott and John were finding it impossible to play their instruments with two or three weeping teenage girls clinging to their backs, King proposed a more radical solution. Scott and John would swap their guitars for hand microphones and, in future, backing would be provided by a soul band called The Quotations, led by a six-foot-one, 18-stone organist who called himself Johnny B. Great.

During rehearsals at the Starlite, however, it became clear that something more than Gary's limited drumming abilities was required to hold the whole thing together. By supplementing Gary's sound with the drums of sessionman Jimmy Butchart, The Walker Brothers/ Quotations became possibly the first British band to boast two drummers. 'It was a good idea and one we wanted to try anyway,' says Gary. 'Everythin' else seemed over-amplified at the expense of the drums. The three of us did play initially, but the sound wasn't powerful enough and didn't make for a good stage show.'

The rest of the support band consisted of a four-piece brass section – trumpet, trombone, tenor and baritone sax – as well as a five-piece rhythm. Before the two merged bands hit the road, however, The Walker Brothers were lined up for their first recording session with producer Johnny Franz at Philips Records. It was to prove a momentous occasion.

4 Make It Easy On Yourself

'We try to make the whole thing, voices and instruments, an entity, and make each record sound like a performance. When you're doin' a painting, you don't concentrate on one eye, you bring in the whole face.'

Scott Walker, 1965

'FREDDIE, WE'VE GOT AN AMERICAN KID over here with a good ballad voice but he hasn't quite got the range. Can I send him over? . . . Tomorrow afternoon sounds fine . . . Oh, by the way, his name is Scott Engel.'

Johnny Franz replaced the telephone receiver, sat back in his chair and surveyed countless music sheets sprawled across the large oak desk. He sipped thoughtfully at a mug of tea and lit his umpteenth cigarette of the day, seemingly oblivious to the blue smog enveloping him. Through an open window came the distant drone of double-decker buses rumbling around Marble Arch. Franz paused for a moment before swivelling in his chair and placing a record made hot and sticky by the midday sun on a nearby turntable. Seconds later, the deep, mature resonance of Scott Engel's voice filled the room for the fourth time that morning.

Franz, a dark, good-looking man with twinkling eyes and a pencil-slim moustache, had developed a legendary reputation during the eleven years he had been Head of Artists and Repertoire at Philips Records. A unique talent-spotting ability matched with an uncanny knack of creating hit records established him as the foremost record producer in the country prior to the emergence of George Martin in the early sixties.

Born in Hampstead in 1922, the man who would exert such an immense influence on Scott Walker's early career began his working life as a fifteen-year-old office boy for Francis, Day and Hunter music publishers in London's Denmark Street. Music was Franz's life and, despite suffering an arthritic condition which left him with a permanent stoop, he developed into a first-rate pianist who accompanied cabaret performers and earned bookings in various West End clubs. During the Blitz, Franz and George Shearing, the famed jazz pianist, regularly performed at the Tottenham Court Road tube station, where Franz introduced the American to his future wife.

After the war, Franz orchestrated for the BBC and worked with singers Frankie Vaughn and David Whitfield, but was perhaps best known as an accompanist for Anne Shelton, whose popularity was such that a children's comic called *Radio Fun* ran a cartoon series entitled 'The Adventures of Anne Shelton and her pianist Johnny Franz'.

Franz became Head of Artists and Repertoire at Philips Records in 1954 and began a remarkable career that spanned 23 years and spawned no fewer than 77 Top Twenty singles. By 1965, the year that he married Moira Creamer, his long-time secretary, the company was situated at Stanhope Place in an imposing building overlooking Hyde Park and Franz had produced a wide range of singers including Susan Maughan, Marty Wilde, Shirley Bassey, Dusty Springfield and Harry Secombe. Although his success ratio had declined by the onset of the 1970s, Franz produced hit records to the end and was working with MOR (Middle of the Road) duo Peters and Lee at the time of his death, from a massive heart attack, in January 1977.

The producer's easy-going nature and immense personal charm was evident to all, from the biggest recording star to the lowliest minion at Philips. More importantly, Franz's own distinguished musical background enabled him to develop a strong rapport with the artists he recorded. The role of an A&R man was to sign artists to the label and select their repertoire. Franz himself was best qualified to explain the job's requirements: 'First, musical knowledge, second, a flair for anticipating what the public's taste will be in three weeks' time, third, complete integrity and fourth, a hundred per cent love of the job.'

Much of Franz's time was spent selecting songs for various artists on the Philips label, hence the fact his desk was always awash with music sheets. He would frequently lunch with publishers at the Lotus House Chinese restaurant in the Edgware Road, which became almost like an unofficial canteen for Philips staff. Franz loved Chinese food and red wine and would occasionally nod off at his desk after a particularly good lunch, although it never affected his command of the studio, where he could sometimes still be found working in the early hours of the morning.

Having selected a particular song, Franz would often routine it on the grand piano in his office, although his lack of singing voice meant he could never give an actual demonstration to the artist.

During recording, he adopted a laidback approach and would rarely venture into the studio, but oversee operations from the control room.

Franz's right-hand man in the studio was Peter Olliff, who engineered on virtually every recording Scott made during his eight-year association with Philips. Olliff, a bearded, dapper little man who discusses recording techniques with the precision of a brain surgeon, is today PolyGram's Director of Media and Technology and based in an office at Berkeley Square. He remembers Franz as 'a one-off' whose perfect pitch – the ability to recognise any given note – proved invaluable.

'Perfect pitch is exceptional even in a musician, and meant that Johnny could listen to the run-through of an orchestration, push the talk-back key to the studio and say: "The second viola was playing an F-sharp instead of an F-natural" – that's how good he was. Scott and Johnny seemed to form the perfect partnership. Johnny was tremendously influential in helping with the orchestrations, picking songs and leading everything from a musical point of view, which enabled Scott to develop within himself.

'Scott, who was very intelligent, probably realised at a very early stage that this man could do a great deal for The Walker Brothers and help him realise his own musical ambitions – something which is difficult for some artists to accept. A lot of them are so egotistically driven that they want to do it totally their way. Later, Scott was able to go on and write his own material because Johnny was totally sympathetic to what he was trying to do.'

Scott, then, was particularly fortunate to meet someone like Franz during this crucial part of his career. At 43, the producer was old enough to be his father, yet the pair found they had much in common. While it would be exaggerating to say that Franz was effectively the father-figure the singer had never had, the older man undoubtedly became a trusted friend and confidant at a time when Scott's deep mistrust of his fellow man was becoming alarmingly apparent.

They regularly dined together at the Lotus House, and Scott was a frequent visitor to the Franz's large house on the edge of Hampstead Heath. The producer was enthralled by the quality of Scott's voice and subsequently came to admire his professionalism in the recording studio, so it is probable that Engel's plans for a solo career were first hatched during one of their earnest conversations at the Lotus House.

Philips released 'Love Her', unaware that The Walkers had de-
camped to London and were now literally on their own doorstep.
After The Walkers made their British TV début, miming to 'Pretty
Girls Everywhere' on the 26 March edition of *Ready Steady Go*, the
record company assumed they had taken the next flight back to the
States. The Walker Brothers did not fit their preconceived image.
Maurice King, on hearing the group's name, apparently assumed that
they were black. Similarly, Johnny Franz received a surprise when
Scott, John, and Gary sauntered into the Philips studio one morning.

Franz, intrigued by the voice on 'Love Her', had thought it belonged to some middle-aged crooner, not some hip, long-haired 22-
year-old American whose permanent wearing of shades suggested
they required surgical removal. He quickly came to view Scott as a
future star with a long and potentially lucrative showbusiness career
ahead of him. The singer would often disappear into the producer's
office ostensibly for a business meeting, only to end up routining
standards like 'Stormy Weather' and 'Summertime' hour after hour
while Franz accompanied him on piano.

Franz frequently dispatched Philips artists to the Denmark Street
studio of vocal tutor Freddie Winrose whose famous breath control
technique – a closely-guarded secret – taught them to increase their
range. By the mid-sixties, Winrose had worked with the likes of
Helen Shapiro and Kenny Lynch, but, speaking from his farmhouse
in the wilds of mid-Wales, he remembers Scott as his most fascinating pupil.

'He was totally untrained and used to laugh whenever I discussed
ways of improving his range. He learned quickly, but if he was away
from me for three months his voice would lose up to an octave,
which makes me wonder what he sounds like now. Johnny Franz
once said to me: "Freddie, we are going to have the finest ballad
singer in the world." I had to agree with him. Scott's potential was
enormous.'

Winrose immediately taught Scott to clock himself for breath
control. When out walking he would take in a breath, hold it, and
release it after seven steps. 'My pitching is fine – it's always been
pretty fair,' said Scott. 'On a good day I've got a two and a half
octave range which is pretty phenomenal. My biggest problem is my
breath control. I guess I'm not healthy enough.'

Scott later acknowledged his debt to Winrose by presenting him
with an inscribed gold chain bearing the words 'To Freddie – the

maestro', and in a 1990 reference he described how the vocal coach had increased his understanding of the singing art in general. 'He greatly increased my range, dexterity and confidence. But most important for me was his way of teaching breath control which I found most valuable.'

If 'Love Her' was The Walkers' launching pad, Franz's task was to produce a record that would blast the group into orbit. The publishers he occasionally met over lunch would invariably be trying to sell songs which had been hits in the United States. The London-based record companies would buy a song, decide upon a release date by gentlemen's agreement, simultaneously put out their rival versions on the same day and then plug them as hard as they could. At a time when few musicians wrote their own material, it was not uncommon to have three or four versions of a song in the charts at the same time. 'Make It Easy On Yourself', the Bacharach–David composition which Franz and Engel chose as The Walkers' first Philips-produced single, obliterated Decca's rival interpretation by Bern Elliot.

Philips was confident that it had the right group, the right image and the right song. What was now needed was the right sound. 'Love Her', a moderate success, had dramatically illustrated Scott's vocal capabilities while its Spector-ish orchestral backing pointed the way forward.

A few months earlier, Spector had produced The Righteous Brothers' 'You've Lost That Lovin' Feeling' which topped the charts on both sides of the Atlantic and was undoubtedly still fresh in Franz's mind. Using 'Love Her' as a blueprint, the challenge facing the Philips team was to create an original and distinctive sound. In 'Make It Easy On Yourself', a song which Jerry Butler took to No. 20 in the American charts in 1962, Franz believed they had found the ideal vehicle.

In 1965, song demos were exceptionally primitive and often bore no relation to the finished article. Scott, however, recognised the song's potential and Franz appointed the classically-trained Ivor Raymonde as arranger. Raymonde, a veteran musical director who co-wrote Dusty Springfield's 'I Only Want To Be With You', would arrange each of The Walkers' three massive hits before defecting to Decca. Recalling the creation of the British 'Wall of Sound', Olliff insists that it was not merely a case of copying Spector.

'The basic idea had formed, but the actual development of the sound was made in the studio. No single individual can take sole responsibility, the sound emerged from the creative genius of several people. Scott never discussed Phil Spector at any time. If you listen to the recordings you'll find that the sound is unique. It's all to do with the orchestration – the way the arranger has written it, the instruments actually played and the acoustics and balance of the sound as it was manufactured during the recording.

'For example, the bass line is quite unusual in that there would quite often be a bass guitar, a string bass and perhaps the left-hand side of the piano all playing the same bass line together. By doing that either in unison or in harmony you achieved a very unusual effect. When mixed in with the whole sound picture the effect was quite surprising – and that was on just one little group of instruments within the whole orchestration.'

While Olliff asserts that the creation of the cavernous sound was a team effort, Scott, who cannot fail to have been influenced by the recording techniques he witnessed at Spector's Gold Star studios, was undoubtedly the prime mover. Reg Guest, who played keyboards on each of the Raymonde hits and later took over as musical director, remembers Scott constantly striving to create what he called a 'cataclysmic' sound effect.

'Scott, coming from LA, was aware of the Spector sound and probably had a good idea of how it was achieved, so it was him who wanted three keyboards, three guitars, three percussionists and so on. There'd also be two bass guitars making a heavy, almost monotonous noise, which all helped to get this big sound going; basic piano organ and harpsichord, presumably to give an edge to it, and then a large orchestra on top.

'The end result – and it always took quite a long time to get it going – was this big swirling noise which became quite famous. It was very attractive to a lot of people, but very boring to actually play. Scott was fond of literally flattening you with noise and yet on top of it would be a tender vocal with a heavy emotional feel. It wasn't a case of listening to Spector and saying: "Let's do that." The actual sound was in Scott's head.'

In 1973, however, Scott revealed that Spector had been a major influence throughout his career. 'Although I knew how to do what Spector was doin', the only way I could get that mammoth sound was to use really large forces and pre-plan everything before goin' into the studio. The reason for this was that there was a union problem [in Britain] and you couldn't overdub anything.

'Now the way Spector gets his sound is by overdubbing. I did it by usin' large forces in a studio that "leaked" – at that time a very inferior studio which nobody was usin'. So all this leakage of sound – plus the fact that I was usin', say, five percussionists, two basses, three pianos – was responsible. It was outrageous. In the studio everyone was on top of each other, but that's how it was done.'

The Philips studio was indeed astonishingly small. For a typical Walker Brothers session, anywhere between 25 and 35 musicians, their equipment and instruments surrounded by a forest of microphones, would squeeze into an oblong-shaped room 60 feet in length, 20 feet wide and 25 feet high. In those days quite a few people smoked, and the building's primitive air conditioning was scarcely adequate. The chain-smoking Franz probably got through about 60 cigarettes a day as well as four pots of tea during each three-hour recording session.

Most orchestrations had a rhythm section with string bass, bass guitar, drums, an electric guitar or two and acoustic guitar. Keyboards would be either piano, organ or harpsichord. The percussion section would consist of timpani, tubular bells and various Latin American toys, while the string section would include violins, viola, cellos and quite often woodwind and brass. The drum booths were situated at the back of the studio enclosed within an acoustic screen like the other sections of the orchestra.

The cost of employing the musicians was so high that three or even four titles would be recorded in each three-hour session, which included a twenty-minute tea-break. It says much for the calibre of these sessionmen that, although they had never even seen Ivor Raymonde's arrangement before walking through the door, after one rehearsal they were generally ready to play it.

'We had a 40-piece orchestra plus John and me,' Scott related afterwards. 'We did weird, weird ballads and way-out Ben E. King numbers. Our new single will take a lot of accepting. It's very Phil Spector-ish.'

Scott's fears were groundless. 'Make It Easy On Yourself' is today regarded as one of the finest records ever made. Its gothic orchestral architecture and gargantuan production, topped off by an extraordinary vocal, paint an evocative image of the scene in that cramped studio as Raymonde's orchestra tackle his arrangement while, up in the control room, Engel, hands on hips, and Franz, cigarette in hand, cast a critical eye over proceedings. The record established a sound identity which set The Walker Brothers apart, although it would ultimately become a millstone around their necks. Peter Olliff says that if 'Love Her' was The Walkers' blueprint, 'Make It Easy On Yourself' was their patent.

'We had the song, the group and the arrangement, but we also needed the magic fairy-dust sparkle to make the thing different and to make it commercial. We experimented by putting some reverberation echo onto the backbeat of the drum and it seemed to achieve the right effect, so the way the sound was achieved was partly through innovation and partly through accident. I thought Scott possessed just about the best commercial voice I had ever heard and I saw the potential for an enormous career. He had a voice and phrasing technique comparable with Sinatra and Tony Bennett.'

By the summer of 1965, the initial wave of excitement created by the coming of The Beatles two years earlier was subsiding and within the music press there was much speculation about 'the next big thing'. With the Fab Four away on a lengthy American tour, the day of The Walker Brothers had arrived.

5 Get Behind Me

'When they throw me out on to a TV set or a stage it's like puttin' a
hermit who has lived all his life in isolation suddenly in the middle of
Times Square.'

Scott Walker, 1968

'**M**AKE IT EASY ON YOURSELF', a soaring ballad sung with
remarkable intensity and emotion over a backdrop of
sweeping arrangements, created an image of Scott
Walker as the great doomed romantic which remains
as potent today as it was in 1965. Resigning himself to the end of an
affair, Scott urges the girl not to prolong their torment but to go to
her new lover, adding dejectedly that no words of consolation will
make him miss her less. Scott's brooding good-looks and projected
air of vulnerability were a killer combination and the song was
scheduled for release on 6 August, backed by Guidry and Gayten's
more upbeat 'But I Do'.

First, however, The Walkers had a few dates to fulfil with their
new backing band. There were outbreaks of Walkermania at Great
Yarmouth's ABC Theatre and Morecambe's Winter Gardens before,
on 31 July, the boys were dragged from the stage by screaming fans
at Nelson's Imperial Ballroom.

Two weeks later, with 'Make It Easy On Yourself' appearing at
No. 41 in the *NME* charts, The Walkers signed for their first ballroom tour of the Midlands and the North. There were dates in Bury,
Stockport, Boston, Nelson, two in Blackpool and one apiece in Reading and Harlow. Barrie Martin, The Quotations' baritone
saxophonist, says the quality of The Walkers' performance would
have been fantastic – if only Scott and John could have been heard
above the screaming.

'It was a pity because the Odeons and Gaumont cinemas we
played were proper theatres once they had lifted up the film screens.
They were small and intimate so nothing could compare to them for
sound, acoustics, and atmosphere. It was different in the gambling
clubs up north, but at least you could hear what you were playing
because the audiences hardly screamed at all in those places.

'We'd open the show by doing a number or two and then the stage would go black. We'd then launch into the James Bond theme as roving spotlights passed over the band. Just as the theme reached its climax the announcer would shout: "Ladies and Gentlemen: John, Scott and Gary – The Walker Brothers!" and the place would just erupt. Gary would walk on first and the kids would go crazy; when John appeared they'd go totally berserk and then when Scott came on there'd be absolute pandemonium.'

Although the Walkers would be forever identified with moody ballads, their stage act was built around up-tempo numbers like 'Land of 1,000 Dances' and 'Dancing In The Street'. Scott and John would shimmy and shake while their twirling, extravagant hand movements raised the level of hysteria. Away to the right, the huge, bearded Johnny B. Great would pound away on his keyboards as the rest of The Quotations swung from side to side in time with the beat. Gary revelled in his individual spotlight, safe in the knowledge that any technical inadequacies were being neutralised by the professional expertise of Jimmy Butchart. Occasionally, Leeds would take centre stage and belt out an exuberant, if rather tuneless, version of 'Dizzy Miss Lizzie' in the style of P. J. Proby, while Scott thrashed about on drums.

While all concerned, including Maurice King, agreed the shows had improved drastically, one particular aspect was the subject of growing unease: Scott, by now increasingly identified as the leader of The Walker Brothers, was quite simply scared to death. Always a highly-strung and nervous individual, who tended to jump at any loud noise, Scott's obvious torment before hitting the stage was deeply disturbing to witness. Virtually every performer experiences stage-fright at some time or other, but this was something else. The singer's face would drain of colour and he would tremble and sweat, clench and unclench his fists and claw frantically at his face.

Scott was six-foot-one of nervous energy and a mass of nerves, particularly during the first five minutes of a performance. When he sang 'Make It Easy On Yourself', he would shut his eyes tightly to blot out the sight of the frenzied teenage horde in front of him and raise his left arm in much the same way as a pedestrian shields his eyes from an oncoming car's headlights at night. Anyone sitting as far as ten rows back could see the singer's hand shaking uncontrollably. Barrie Martin, observing this silent terror from just a few feet away, found it difficult to comprehend.

Scott Walker

'I just couldn't understand it because if I had a voice like he had I would have gone on stage with all the confidence in the world. He obviously had to psyche himself up to go out there every night.'

Scott's fear of performing live was nothing new. When The Walker Brothers had played their first gig as a duo in California, the sight of the audience rushing the stage caused Scott to freeze. His first reaction was to retreat to the sanctuary of the dressing-room, and only some fast talking from his fellow Walker Brother, who agreed to hit the stage first, had persuaded Scott to go on, although, in John's words, he was 'still absolutely physically scared'.

Bearing this in mind, Scott's nightly ordeal during that frantic summer of 1965 becomes a little easier to understand, especially when what had happened to him within the previous four months is taken into account. Having arrived from the United States as an obscure bass guitarist in an unknown American combo who nursed vague ambitions to write songs or produce records in between the odd spot of sightseeing around Europe, he now found himself the focal point of a pop phenomenon which threatened to rival The Beatles.

The rise of The Walker Brothers was remarkable even in an age of overnight sensations. The imminent release of 'Make It Easy On Yourself', a song of obvious quality, which invariably received a tumultuous reception when performed live, must have made Scott realise that The Walkers had a monster hit on their hands and that his professional and personal life would never be quite the same again. 'In those days I had a very screwed up attitude,' he reflected some years later. 'I honestly didn't understand why it was all goin' on.'

Scott's greatest friend and closest confidant during the 1960s was Jonathan King, the Cambridge undergraduate and pop personality who had a huge hit with 'Everyone's Gone To The Moon' in 1965 and 'Una Paloma Blanca' a decade later, as well as countless others under assumed names.

It was an unlikely alliance: the moody, introverted Engel and the brash, outrageously camp King – yet they were kindred spirits. Not only was King of superior intellect to your average pop musician, but he cocked a snook at the business through a series of progressively outlandish publicity stunts and took delight in pricking more than a few egos from his *Disc & Music Echo* soapbox – a maverick role he continues to perform with relish.

He and Scott would laugh at the absurdities of the pop world and the latter appreciated King's forthright and occasionally brutal honesty in an industry where sycophancy was rife. The bespectacled, bearded King won Scott's confidence to such an extent that the singer frequently sought his opinion on recording techniques and song material.

When they went out together, Scott was delighted to discover that his extrovert companion deflected attention away from him. Considering King's extraordinary apparel of the time, which ranged from a Chinese mandarin jacket to a full-length Cossack ensemble, this is not perhaps surprising. Today, sitting at a pavement café just off Baker Street, King warmly describes their association as 'one of the deepest friendships of my life'.

'We were very similar in many ways. We were exactly the same size and used to swap each other's clothes all the time. We both, in a sense, had intellectual pretensions in that we didn't want to be just interested in pop culture. He knew I was at Cambridge where I was studying English Literature, and I knew that he had some brains and was therefore interested in reading books by quite significant people. One of his fascinations was Jean Genet and it was through discussing the character of this rather bizarre man that we found we had a lot in common.

'On the recording side, Scott loved Johnny Franz and valued his experience. He certainly had far more time for him than I had. I actually thought Johnny was a rather boring old buffer who was totally out of touch with the current scene, but Scott never put him down at all and always defended him against my criticisms. He needed people who could provide some foundations for him, some rocks that he knew he could rely on. I sort of became that in friendship and Johnny was Scott's rock in the music industry.'

Scott, who certainly seemed to regard King as his guardian angel, called him 'the Cocteau of the pop business. He could never handle his own situations, but he could certainly handle mine.'

Press reaction to 'Make It Easy On Yourself' was wildly enthusiastic. *NME*'s Derek Johnson commented that the song was much in keeping with The Walkers' style with Ivor Raymonde's score featuring 'lush, sweeping strings, heavenly choir and a steady beat ... A likely top-tenner, convincingly handled by the boys,' he concluded prophetically. Dave Clark's verdict: 'Nice but not commercial', in *Melody Maker*'s Blind Date spot, must have come back to haunt him; his further observation; 'big backing with a full sound' was spot-on, though.

Scott Walker

That same edition carried a rather rambling interview with Scott who, groaning and clutching his cheek, staggered melodramatically into the Philips studio and told a bemused Chris Welch that some stranger had attacked him on his own doorstep the previous night. 'It was about 4 a.m.,' related Scott. 'He came to the door drunk and said he lived there. I called him a **** and he laid me out! When I finally got up the guy had gone. Can you see that bruise?' He pointed to a faint blemish.

Scott admitted to laziness, but revealed he had written a few songs with an effervescent young singer called Lesley Duncan who provided backing harmonies on several Philips records of the time. Their 'You're All Around Me' crops up on The Walkers' début album and was the B-side for 'My Ship Is Coming In', although the collaboration appears to have been short-lived.

Recalling the previous night's activities, the bleary-eyed Engel ('Excuse me, I've got a terrible hangover') confessed to having visited about four nightclubs, but had decided he hated them all and the type of people they attracted.

'You see people in their hip gear and it's really funny . . . They're all such nothing people and the people that have really got something are probably walking about in the street. You find all the new beat singers down there that have no talent and they are throwing their money around and looking cool. When I got back I played this album you have gotta hear . . . it's completely weird, by a Frenchman, Charles Aznavour. He looks like a dustman with a five o'clock shadow but his songs are beautiful . . .'

Both the article and its accompanying headline: 'Someone Walked All Over A Walker Brother' appealed to Scott's perverse sense of humour, and he subsequently appears to have been a little more forthcoming with Welch than he was with other journalists. Welch believes that Scott initially enjoyed being part of the Swinging London scene although the novelty of being the centre of attention quickly wore off as, temperamentally, he was entirely unsuited to the pop world.

Welch found Engel an exceedingly complex character. He sang pop, but preferred classical music and jazz; he could be the most friendly, humorous and intelligent of companions or morose, uncommunicative, bad-tempered, sharp-tongued and generally difficult; one night he would happily discuss music, play records or chat with a few friends, the next he might wind up in a club, drinking himself into a void of boredom and depression. Welch was never quite sure which Scott Walker would turn up for the interview.

Gary, meanwhile, had decided from the outset to make the most of his fifteen minutes of fame. Aware that his contributions both in the studio and on stage were limited, (he was said to be unable to play on the records owing to 'contractual reasons') Leeds appointed himself as the group's unofficial spokesman, a role which he has conscientiously fulfilled right up to the present day, and the press embraced this pop star who would never turn down an interview.

The drummer's love of the rock-'n'-roll lifestyle was indicated by his endless clubbing and relentless pursuit of girls. As far as groupies were concerned, the newly-married John was more selective, but showed a disquieting fondness for drink; it was, perhaps, significant that he christened his two alsatians Scotch and Brandy. John continued to dote on the animals even after Scotch left two large toothmarks in his forehead.

Scott, whose blond hair, blue eyes and improbable good looks made him the object of most girls' lust, virtually shunned the groupie scene in preference to serious relationships. His first girlfriend in London was Irene Dunford, a blonde nineteen-year-old model. In later years, Scott, who once said English girls possessed 'a terrible beauty' demonstrated a predilection for European women. They might have been Dutch, German or Danish, but all of Scott's girl-friends possessed above average looks and intellect, were not the types to be found hanging around stage doors and were also extremely discreet. 'I don't date girls in the business,' he said. 'I'd rather go out with dentists' daughters.'

Pop's newest 'most eligible bachelor' met Dunford at an official reception at Philips to mark the release of 'Make It Easy On Yourself'. Dunford, who says she was quite a shy person herself at the time, believes this encouraged the rather tongue-tied Engel to come over and attempt some small-talk. The young model had already chatted to John and Gary but, having unsuccessfully tried to establish eye-contact with the slightly aloof, self-conscious figure in opaque shades on the other side of the room, had concluded that Scott was not interested and was too scared to approach him. She almost dropped her drink in surprise when he suddenly appeared at her shoulder.

'My first impression was of someone very highly-strung and talented. Gary had the best personality, John was a bit of a loner, although not difficult to make friends with, while Scott seemed to be in it purely for the music. I think he liked the fact that he'd had to approach me instead of the other way round. Afterwards he gave me a call and we met for lunch; after that we'd often get together for a drink and a quiet talk. I had a boyfriend at the time and I think that suited him because he certainly was not looking for a steady relationship.

'We struck up a really close friendship before we began a relationship. He was genuinely lonely and would invite me round to his flat for conversations. He had quite a funny side to him too, but he had to trust you first before this side of his character came out. He could become a bit of a prankster after downing a bottle of bourbon. It did loosen him up.

'One night we staggered home from a club, Scott so drunk he could hardly stand. We arrived at his front door and he couldn't find the key. When I said I'd get in by breaking a window he looked at me as if I was crazy. Anyway, he helped me up on to the top of these railings and I hurled myself at the window ledge about four feet away. There was a fifteen-foot drop below but it's amazing what you can do when you're drunk. I clung to the window ledge, smashed the glass with my fist, yanked up the handle and hauled myself inside. That really sobered him up. When we inspected the damage the next morning neither of us could believe what we'd done. I don't think he touched the bourbon for some time after that.'

Scott's discomfiture at the initial onslaught of fame was becoming more apparent as 'Make It Easy On Yourself' accelerated up the charts. He would drive Maurice King frantic by disappearing from the flat he shared with Gary for days at a time. When Scott eventually reappeared at Capable Management's office, he would casually explain that he had been away 'replenishing my energies' in a way that never failed to infuriate King, who must have occasionally questioned the wisdom of managing a singer whose own mother jokingly referred to him as 'The Madman'.

Engel, despite all his assertions to the contrary, was a workaholic who wasted no time in negotiating with the agency on behalf of the group as well as taking on a major role in the studio. His growing load of responsibilities possibly help to explain these occasional disappearances which earned him the nickname 'Scoot'.

'Make It Easy On Yourself' entered the *NME* chart at No. 25 on 20 August and gathered no moss as it surged upwards over the following weeks. It rose to No. 14 on 27 August, No. 4 for two weeks and then No. 3 for a further two weeks, peaking at No. 2 on 1 October. The previous week, the record had displaced The Rolling Stones' 'Satisfaction' from the top of the *Melody Maker* charts. It eventually reached No. 16 in America after selling over 250,000 copies in Britain and earning The Walkers their first Silver Disc.

'The Big Exercise' had paid off. Seven months after their shambolic arrival at Heathrow, The Walkers had scaled the pop pinnacle. Halfway across the world, the telephone rang in Betty Engel's Hollywood home. 'Mother,' Scott's excited voice crackled down the line, 'you won't believe it, we've done what we wanted to do.' Betty clutched the receiver to her chest and wept.

Back in London, Scott's first impulse was to get roaring drunk, and the group's growing army of young fans would have been horrified to learn that the leader of The Walker Brothers ended up being treated to bed and breakfast in a West End police cell. 'When "Love Her" made the chart I consumed quite a bit of alcohol. But when "Make It Easy On Yourself" made No. 1, I just fell over,' Scott later admitted.

One of the great unreported pop stories of the day began innocently enough when Scott, whose drinking grew in direct proportion to his fame (Scotch and Coke was his favourite tipple), decided to forget the stresses of the past few months by embarking on a lone pub crawl along the King's Road, finishing up in a somewhat rowdy hostelry 'surrounded by a bunch of freeloaders and a couple of beatnik artistic types'.

Alcohol often revealed a surprisingly aggressive and unpleasant side to Scott's character and, a couple of hours and several beers and whisky chasers later, he was tossed unceremoniously out into the street. 'Funny thing, none of those freeloaders came to see if I was all right,' he bitterly remarked to Bob Farmer of *Disc & Music Echo* a year later. 'Instead, the two beatnik painters picked me up – but I was really stoned and started throwin' rocks at cars. The police picked me up and locked me up, saying I should be ashamed of myself . . .'

Scott enjoyed two strokes of fortune when he awoke in a cell the following morning, unshaven and unkempt. Firstly, the police decided not to press drunk and disorderly charges and secondly, waiting pressmen, who were clearly on his scent, inexplicably surrounded a red-haired man when Scott and his fellow cell-mates stumbled down the police station steps, grimacing and blinking in the morning light.

As reporters fired questions at the bewildered man, Scott was able to sidle off in the confusion, thus ensuring that no story ever appeared in the papers, although he appears to make a fleeting reference to this incident in the breathtaking 'Such A Small Love' from his first solo album.

Only a few weeks later, he was arrested following another drunken disturbance in Oxford Street. (An annoyed policeman apparently told Engel to stop shouting and singing – he refused.) This time, the police recognised him and summoned an angry Maurice King, who managed to reach Scott before the press did.

Aware that their luck could not last, and determined to avoid a repetition of these incidents, King (much to Scott's fury) put a 'tail' on the singer for the next six months. The man's brief was literally not to let Scott out of his sight, yet his charge still managed to disappear for a four-day period, causing the cancellation of two gigs and subsequent legal action. Engel, however, was unrepentant. 'OK, I was an idiot, but I was working my arse off,' he said. 'The pressure around me made me do it.' According to Chris Welch, Scott's evident dissatisfaction with his new-found fame was accompanied by myriad self-doubts.

'He started to drink very heavily. I remember having a strange telephone conversation with a girl who worked for Philips. Without any prompting from me, she said they'd had to cancel some shows and Scott was being difficult and he didn't want to work. She said he was admired by everyone and had a wonderful voice yet he was treating himself really badly by getting drunk, falling down and making a fool of himself. People close to him were clearly upset that he was destroying himself for no apparent reason.'

Brian Sommerville, saddled with the unenviable task of trying to publicise a pop star who hated publicity, confirms that drink could affect Scott badly. 'He had the awful vice of drinking on his own. He would sit alone in a darkened room because he claimed his eyes were very sensitive to the light. In fact, the only time Scott asked me not to bother him was when he had a hangover. I can remember many occasions when the phone had been off the hook and he said: "Well, I'm sorry about that, but I had such a hangover".' Both Johnny Franz and Reg Guest frequently had bottles of Mateus Rosé (allegedly Scott's favourite wine) sent to their homes by fans.

One night, Scott and Irene Dunford had a terrible row in his flat after she accused him of drinking too much. 'When he was in a foul mood he would become abusive about other pop singers and say they had no talent,' she remembers. 'He'd say Tom Jones would lose his voice within five years if he carried on singing at that rate. He felt he screamed out his songs without putting any finesse into them.

'On this particular night he was in such a bad mood that I didn't feel like sitting through two bottles of bourbon until he snapped out of it; I said it would be best if I left. He got angry and propped a chair under the door handle to stop me from leaving and then sat there in a typical Clint Eastwood-style pose, chewing a matchstick with his arms folded.

'He just sat there glaring defiantly at me and rocking the chair back on two legs. But whenever he struck a pose it would often go totally wrong and, sure enough, the chair suddenly went from under him, he landed on the floor in a heap and the matchstick got wedged in his gum. We both ended up laughing.'

Then on 1 October, a Walkers' spokesman announced that, due to repeated riots at ballroom concerts all over the country, the group would restrict its appearances to theatres once the current batch of dates was completed. 'The fans' demonstrations are now making it impossible for them to complete their act, wherever they go,' he added.

As if having to perform live every night was not bad enough, escalating fan mania left Scott feeling acutely vulnerable on stage, where the threat of physical injury was now very real.

The presence of an orchestra pit at most theatres was usually enough to halt the advance of all but the most determined 'screamagers' as Scott called them, but at ballrooms, which had no seating, only a thin line of security men separated The Walkers from anything up to 2,000 hysterical girls. Photos of a dazed, semi-naked Scott struggling to stay afloat in a raging sea of female bodies starkly illustrate the inadequate security at some of these venues.

Indeed, The Walkers were forced to miss two performances at Great Yarmouth because their lead singer was suffering from shock and nervous exhaustion after being pulled off the stage at Dunstable's California Ballroom. The group's road manager, Drew Harvey, who tried to rescue Scott, was taken to hospital with spinal injuries. Jonathan King recalls that this sort of incident fuelled Scott's growing hatred of stardom.

'I've never known anyone who hated stardom so much and from about the second day of knowing him, I was well aware that he was not going to keep on putting up with it.

Scott Walker

'The only person in the world who could persuade him to go on stage when he decided he wouldn't, was me. I was quite often sent for by Clayman or King when I was down at my mum's who lives in Surrey. I used to have to drive for about an hour and a half, go into the dressing-room and say: "Stop being silly, go out there on stage," and he would finally concur.

'Firstly, he suffered from horrendous stage-fright and was shit-scared of going out there. Secondly, he had absolutely no confidence in his ability and I had to keep telling him what a great singer he was – although to this day he probably thinks I was only saying that because I was his friend.'

Scott's problems were not confined to the live circuit. Soon after 'Make It Easy On Yourself' prised 'Satisfaction' from *Melody Maker*'s top spot, he and Irene Dunford, sitting in a corner of the Scotch of St James just below and in front of The Rolling Stones and their entourage, had several lighted cigarettes thrown at their table. 'I knew exactly where they were coming from and I also knew that Jagger was very jealous of Scott,' she says. Although Dunford tried to diffuse the obvious tension, Scott was clearly enraged at The Stones' malevolent behaviour, although he steadfastly refused to move to another table.

'[Jagger] uses my cigarettes to throw at Scott,' Gary later complained. 'I can't smoke 'em afterwards because they're full of Scott's hair. He threw cigarettes at Scott and he didn't even offer us a light.' The incident deepened Scott's disenchantment with the London club scene, which he articulated on 'Saturday's Child', (a track co-written with Lesley Duncan that appears on The Walkers' second album) the story of a frivolous and naïve London swinger who falls prey to the shallow characters of clubland.

6 We Came Through

'I think we were probably the drunkest group ever.'

Scott Walker, 1973

B Y AUTUMN, the task of ferrying The Walkers from one venue to another was having to be planned like a military operation. While The Quotations travelled in a van, Scott, John and Gary would be driven to the night's venue by Bobby Hamilton, usually in a Rolls-Royce or Mark 10 Jaguar, cars with sufficient leg-room to accommodate three gangly Americans. Cars were never used twice as they invariably came back with hub-caps missing, wipers broken and paintwork damaged.

The success of 'Make It Easy On Yourself' meant The Walkers were now recognised wherever they went. Even lunch at a motorway café had to be organised in advance. Hamilton, a laconic eastender who had previously toured with The Byrds and Van Morrison's Them, would telephone ahead and make arrangements for Scott, John and Gary to eat in the relative privacy of the kitchen.

Yet even there The Walkers would be subjected to the curious gaze of chefs, waiters and waitresses and a steady stream of autograph requests. They tended to order large meals but eat very little. While an order of half a dozen T-Bone steaks might have seemed reasonable when ordering, by the time the food was served, The Walkers' appetites had often diminished, possibly as a result of the stress caused by their manic lifestyles. The England of the mid-sixties was a difficult place to get decent food anyway, and on tour sandwiches formed the group's staple diet.

Hamilton's main task, however, was getting The Walkers safely into theatres, and during the next two years he would learn a thousand different tricks. On arriving at a town, King, Clayman and Hamilton would seek police assistance to steer The Walkers through the chanting masses congregating around the local theatre. When one Chief Inspector grandly announced that the deployment of every available officer would ensure the group's safe passage, King, clearly not sharing his confidence, retorted: 'That didn't work for bloody Kennedy, did it?'

The Walkers' car, surrounded by a heavy police escort, would pull up in front of the theatre amid mass screaming. In the back, Gary would be glimpsed waving cheerily, John grinning from ear to ear and Scott, frowning and pensive. The journey from the car door to the stage entrance might only have been a few feet, but, depending on the adequacy of police security, it often resulted in torn clothes, scratched faces and pulled hair which led to the group resorting to the ingenious use of crash helmets.

On other occasions, the boys, wearing thick parkas with the hoods up, crash helmets and goggles, would pull up outside the theatre on scooters, dismount, and file unnoticed through the doors past queues of unsuspecting fans whose devotion to The Walkers knew no bounds. Girls would stand outside the group's hotels for days, and in all weathers. Once, The Walkers' car knocked down a fourteen-year-old outside a ballroom in Portsmouth. On regaining consciousness, she immediately asked an ambulanceman whether Scott was OK.

Having reached the sanctuary of their dressing-rooms, The Walkers would often be imprisoned there for up to nine hours before the actual performance. Then, after the show was over, there was the problem of returning to the hotel. Hamilton remembers on one occasion pushing three policemen dressed in long coats and wearing crash helmets out of the stage door while The Walkers made their escape through the foyer. The girls outside the stage door ripped the decoys' clothes to shreds.

'Sometimes, as they were finishing their performance, we'd be waiting in the wings with long coats for them. As soon as they left the stage they'd put them on, slip downstairs and out with the crowd. With their long hair they looked just like girls from behind, and it was such a daring stunt that none of the fans suspected a thing. We got away with that one quite a few times.

'Another time, we pulled up outside the Albany in Birmingham to find around two thousand girls surrounding the place. On police advice we drove right up on to the pavement within inches of these big sliding doors that opened automatically. The boys piled out and we had to follow, leaving the keys in the door. The kids were yelling and the hotel manager was doing his nut because the doors kept opening and shutting like crazy and no one could get into the car to turn off the ignition. This copper ended up having to smash a side window with his truncheon.'

Scott actively disliked the adulation that John and Gary revelled in. On spotting a group of schoolgirls, the latter might instruct Hamilton to pull over, wind down a window and whisper 'Hi' just to observe the hysterical reaction. While being driven through the West End, Gary would persuade Hamilton to stop alongside a foreign tourist at a bus-stop. 'Excuse me,' Gary would say. 'Do you know where Oxford Street is?' The man would reply, in faltering English, that he did not. 'Well, you head down here for half a mile and it's the first on your left.' 'Oh, thank you very much,' the bewildered tourist would stammer.

John and Gary became new lords in London's pop aristocracy, living it up in the trendiest nightclubs and restaurants and spending money as if there was no tomorrow. Gary acquired a red Marcos sports car costing £1,700, and spent a similarly huge sum on a pair of infra-red binoculars which kept him occupied ('Lorry three miles ahead!') on the long trip down the M1 from a northern venue one night. John, to whom cars were still an obsession, treated himself to a new Bentley and then a custom-built Marcos and a Lamborghini. Scott initially drove a silver Mini with smoked-glass windows. Then he bought an old American Army jeep in a dubious state of repair.

By now the weather was turning decidedly chilly, so whenever Scott fancied a drive he had to wear a scarf and several layers of clothes, as the vehicle did not even possess a proper roof. Whenever he called at Irene Dunford's Islington flat, Scott always made sure there was a coat in the back to provide her with extra protection from the cold. Considering Engel's obsession with privacy, his choice of vehicle was bizarre. The jeep afforded little cover to its occupants; indeed, they must have been highly visible. Scott would not have appeared more conspicuous if he had ridden a penny farthing around Piccadilly Circus at the height of rush-hour. Dunford soon came to dread that khaki-coloured jeep.

'Being a passenger in that thing was so scary because there were bits hanging off and flapping in the slipstream. He never got it fixed and I used to hang on to this pole like grim death. Scott's driving mirrored his personality. He was very erratic: always swerving in front of cars and pulling up in the nick of time cursing the other drivers.'

The Walkers' dramatic ascent to the top of the charts coincided with Maurice King's announcement that they would not take part in pop package tours unless receiving top billing. 'We don't want them over-exposed, that's why we're turning down tour offers,' he said. Having stopped playing ballroom dates for security reasons, the group launched their new two-concert-a-week itinerary at Bristol's Colston Hall on 21 November.

There had been near-riots at the Portsmouth Birdcage the previous week when the group failed to appear, with compère Jimmy Saville battling to restore order to the crowd. No reason was given for The Walkers' non-appearance – Scott may have done one of his disappearing acts, or perhaps the group was not contracted to appear, as was the case at Oldham's Princess Ballroom a couple of months later.

The following week saw the release of their eagerly-awaited new single 'My Ship Is Coming In'. Reviewing the disc in *Disc Weekly*, Penny Valentine gushed enthusiastically: 'It's tremendously, tremendously romantic with Scott doing the lead with that gorgeous voice of his. It's a song full of pessimism [*sic*] about the bad times being over.'

'My Ship Is Coming In', penned by American songwriter Joey Brooks and a US hit for soul singer Jimmy Radcliffe, is notable for its optimistic lyrical content which contrasts starkly to anything else The Walkers put down on vinyl. Dark, menacing clouds miraculously part to reveal exploding shafts of sunshine as Scott, uncharacteristically displaying the joyous exuberance of a man who has just won the football pools, assures the girl who has faithfully stuck by his side through the bad times that 'things are gonna be different now'.

NME's Derek Johnson described 'My Ship' as 'a typically modern rockaballad with a shattering crescendo – a beautifully convincing performance, enhanced by a colourful and imaginative Ivor Raymonde backing. Melodically, it didn't hit me quite so hard as 'Make It Easy On Yourself' on first play, but obviously it's a disc that grows on you. Another big one.'

The B-side, 'You're All Around Me', written by Scott and Lesley Duncan, he found rather more intimate and reminiscent of the legendary singing group The Drifters.

More cynical contemporary critics find Brooks's lyrics corny and unconvincing and argue that 'My Ship' floats uneasily alongside its more celebrated cousins 'Make It Easy On Yourself' and 'The Sun

Ain't Gonna Shine Anymore'. While the song is unquestionably a radical departure from style, almost akin to The Stranglers covering Rodgers and Hammerstein's 'Happy Talk', Scott's powerful delivery and Raymonde's dramatic production effortlessly create another classic. 'My Ship' steadily ploughed its way to No. 3 on most charts, paving the way for the début album 'Take It Easy With The Walker Brothers', which was released a fortnight later.

The LP, produced by Johnny Franz with accompaniment directed by Raymonde, carried a cover photograph which, although clearly intended to be moody and evocative, now appears almost laughably contrived and stilted. Gary, flanked by an apprehensive-looking Scott and a sullen John, looks particularly gauche and awkward. The record itself, however, more than makes up for the disappointing sleeve, with most of the dozen tracks standing the test of time extremely well.

'Make It Easy On Yourself', the opening track, is followed by 'There Goes My Baby' with its dynamic intro featuring timpani and trumpets culminating in the arrival of Scott's lead and the string section. Philips' plans to issue it as a single were apparently vetoed by Scott on the grounds that the song had been recorded a couple of months earlier and was no longer 'fresh'. 'First Love Never Dies', which highlights Scott's superb elocution, has a slow beat with strings and trombones providing the intro as the singer laments a first love that failed to work out.

'Dancing in the Street', with its lively brass and girl backing singers, showcases John's bluesy voice and became an integral part of The Walkers' live act. Scott, in a reference to the tight recording deadlines set by Philips, later opined that John had needed more time on this particular track. 'Lonely Winds', part-written by Mort Shuman, a lyricist who would later play a key part in Scott's solo career, is an upbeat number with Scott and John's superb harmonising swelled by a chorus and swinging string passage. Side A closes with David Gates's 'The Girl I Lost In The Rain', the weakest track on the album.

'Land of 1,000 Dances', featuring a particularly brilliant piece of brass orchestration, was the closest The Walkers ever came to capturing their early live sound, although Scott denounced his own performance as 'terrible'. 'You're All Around Me' highlighted the dramatic improvement in Scott's songwriting a mere twelve months after he had implored teenage Californians to 'do the jerk'. Bob Dylan's 'Love Minus Zero', with its characteristically abstract lyrics, was described by Scott as 'the most melodic thing he has written so far' and is followed by the singer's own personal favourites, 'I Don't Want To Hear It Anymore' (penned by Randy Newman) and 'Here Comes The Night' (Pomus/Shuman).

The influence of the former, which finds Scott eavesdropping on gossiping neighbours questioning the fidelity of his girl, is evident in the voyeuristic feel to many of Engel's later compositions. Scott's powerful delivery is also truly exceptional for a 22-year-old, a fact that was not lost on John. 'I was standin' right next to him at the time and, man, I just couldn't figure out where this voice was comin' from,' he said. Maus attributed the famous Engel baritone to the singer's physical shape: Scott had short legs and a long body which enabled his voice to well upwards from deep within.

'I haven't got the same kinda depth to my voice that Scott has,' John admitted. 'But I do have a good voice for the up-tempo discs. More of a rock-'n'-roller's voice, I suppose. Surprisingly, though, it's a higher pitch than Scott's – I sound like a violin compared with a bass when we sing together.' The album closes with the raucous 'Tell The Truth', in which raving trumpet and trombone solos and girl backing group The Breakaways whip up a minor riot behind Scott and John.

Scott, while by no means delirious with the end product, liked to think of the album as a shop window for some of the writers he admired. 'We were tryin' to find songs which are good from people who aren't very well known yet, and give 'em a kind of showcase and start-off,' he told *Disc Weekly*. The record's chart placing of No. 3 confirmed The Walker Brothers as a major force and established Scott as a favourite pin-up in girls' magazines.

Scott's fastidiousness over his appearance and constant preening in front of mirrors could have been the result of insecurity or a slightly narcissistic streak, but he does seem to have had genuine hang-ups over those inherent good looks, no doubt fearing that he would be viewed as just another pretty face destined to be readily exploited and discarded.

'I'm not handsome, I'm skinny,' he protested to a sceptical Penny Valentine while sitting on the floor of his flat, surrounded by little animal mascots and albums by Carmen McRae, Frank Sinatra and Jack Jones. 'The fan mail is perfectly evenly divided between John, Gary and myself. Look, I can walk around the streets and people don't even recognise me,' he said heatedly. 'I hate people thinking

I'm good-looking, it's real bad. Good looks to me mean someone like Alain Delon, the French actor.' Keith Altham was another journalist who witnessed Scott's mounting personal conflict.

'Scott certainly wanted to get away from the fan mania and the screaming. Not only was there a problem of being idolised for something that they weren't, they also couldn't be heard for what they actually were. He felt diminished as an artist. As far as live performing went, it virtually didn't matter whether you were out of tune, out of key or out of sight.

'Scott had one of the great romantic voices of all time, which was a problem again for him because he didn't really want to be a romantic singer. Being in The Walkers was something he did not believe in and had no empathy for. He wanted to be seen as a serious artist and songwriter and a singer of songs that had some substance.'

On the surface, however, all was rosy in The Walkers' garden. Tour offers flooding in from Australasia, Asia, Europe and America spectacularly illustrated the success of Capable Management's gamble in taking on the group. The Walkers had been voted Brightest Hopes for 1966 by *Melody Maker* and Scott was firmly entrenched as the country's No. 1 sex symbol.

After the group had recorded a special festive edition of *Ready Steady Go* and a *Top Of The Pops* Christmas spectacular, King and Clayman presented the boys with a gift-wrapped portable television which became an essential part of their touring luggage. John, Kathy and Gary flew back to California to spend Christmas with friends and family, leaving Scott, no doubt lamenting his lack of roots, behind in Chelsea. Christmas Day was spent in the company of a Greek family he had befriended and, by all accounts, a riotous time was had by all.

The Walkers featured prominently in the *NME* 1966 Annual alongside established favourites like The Beatles, The Rolling Stones, Elvis Presley, Cliff Richard and The Animals. Scott was, somewhat surprisingly, placed only 21st in the world male singer category of the *NME* poll with 221 votes. Elvis was top with 6,002 votes, Cliff second with 4,848 and Scott only just pipped Ken Dodd who scored a remarkable 216. The Walkers, however, were seventh in the world vocal group section. The Beatles walked it with 9,320, a full 3,000 ahead of the second-placed Stones. The Walkers totalled a respectable 1,284, just ahead of compatriots The Beach Boys.

'Make It Easy On Yourself' came a disappointing 10th in a best new disc section dominated by the world's two most popular groups. The Beatles may have won the accolade in the best group section but 'Satisfaction' was the year's most popular single. The Walkers (or more likely King and Clayman) diplomatically commented: 'As Americans we feel honoured being placed so high in your poll with all those great British groups competing. What can we say but thank you.' What indeed?

A thriving fan club run from 185 Bickenhall Mansions confirmed The Walker Brothers' elevation to the pop hierarchy. The club issued a monthly magazine offering readers the chance to win a pair of Gary's drumsticks by composing as many words as possible from 'Walker Brothers'; received 2,000 cards addressed to the boys at Christmas; employed seven area secretaries based all over the country; and attracted a group of 'screamagers', whose permanent presence outside the office doors forced Scott to enter and leave via a toilet window at the rear.

On 9 January, a transistor radio, socks, art books and an enormous spider were among a variety of gifts received on Engel's 23rd birthday, which a fan in Blackpool marked by jumping on to a garage roof at the stroke of midnight, waving a banner and yelling 'Happy Birthday Scott!' while a friend beat out an accompaniment on a dustbin and turned up a record player as loud as possible. The girls then observed two minutes' silence before toasting Scott with Scotch and Coke and wishing him luck in the forthcoming year.

Yet beneath all this euphoria, the centrifugal forces that would rip the group apart were already beginning to stir. When The Walkers had appeared on the Christmas edition of *Ready Steady Go*, Gary, most uncharacteristically, had thrown a temperamental fit over what he considered was the unfair amount of coverage devoted to Scott and John.

'I wasn't in the picture at all,' he complained later. 'When it gets to my turn they show scenery and dancers. I think the only way I'll get seen on that show is if I go as a dancer . . . They don't leave Ringo out.'

A distinct whiff of mutiny hung in the air. Partly as a result of Gary's discontent coupled with his frustration at being unable to play on the group's records, and partly due to the demands of fans angered by the drummer's eclipse, King and Clayman decided to launch him as a solo artist. A song entitled 'You Don't Love Me' was released on the CBS label on 11 February by Derry Music, a publishing company recently formed by Engel, King, Clayman and John Stewart, whom Scott had summoned from Los Angeles and placed on a retainer as a writer.

The song, credited to 'T. Raye', produced by Engel and Stewart and backed by the latter's 'Get It Right', bears more than a passing resemblance to Tommy Tucker's 'Hi-Heel Sneakers', but heavy feedback on the distorted production blends with Gary's rasping vocal quite well and it is surprising it did not reach higher than No. 26. Mick Jagger, who reviewed the disc for *Melody Maker*, remarked of it: 'I've heard that riff before. Could well be a hit. Quite a good sound.'

It was, then, particularly unfortunate that Gary chose that very edition to mount a fierce attack on The Stones' leader. Behind the cheery visage of mid-sixties British pop lurked a cauldron of seething jealousies and rivalries, and a trawl through the papers of the day reveals a quite astonishing amount of bitchiness amid all the superficial mateyness. Gary's gripe centred on the fact that Jagger had jokingly dubbed The Walkers' current hit 'When My Shrimpboat Comes Home' – an obvious reference to his girlfriend Chrissie Shrimpton.

'It's really ridiculous,' fumed Gary. 'You hear everyone knocking each other . . . let's sign a truce.'

'The Sun Ain't Gonna Shine Anymore', which emerged a week later on 25 February, staged a total eclipse of Gary's début disc as well as that week's other releases. This classic record, which remains the song most readily identified with The Walker Brothers, was penned by Bob Gaudio of The Four Seasons and the group's record producer Bob Crewe, who had previously written 'Rag Doll'. The Walkers' towering version bore little resemblance to the weedy original. Maracas, tambourines and trombones establish a mid-tempo pace until the backing builds with strings, timpani and harpsichord to create a faint Latin flavour before Scott begins to sing.

The record was a monster hit which dwarfed the success of 'Make It Easy On Yourself'. It remained at the top of the charts for a whole month, comfortably seeing off all rival contenders, and peaked at No. 13 in America.

'The Sun Ain't Gonna Shine Anymore' was everywhere during that spring of 1966. It reverberated around the London discothèques and cafés and spilled out on to the streets. Milkmen whistled the tune, wistful schoolgirls sang it while gazing dreamily at their Scott

Walker posters and little old ladies at bus-stops hummed its mournful refrain. The record was playing on a juke-box in The Blind Beggar pub in Bethnal Green when Ronnie Kray strolled in, drew a Mauser pistol and shot gangland rival George Cornell between the eyes. 'The sun wasn't gonna shine for him anymore,' said Ronnie, recalling the murder years later.

The Walkers were elated when 'The Sun' soared to No. 1. 'Make It Easy On Yourself' had failed to top all the rival charts but this time there was no mistake. On hearing the news one morning, Scott burst into the flat Gary was now sharing with Graham Nash of The Hollies, shouting: 'We made it, we're number one!' and all three started leaping around the room.

The Walkers' forthcoming British tour, on which they shared joint billing with Roy Orbison, was only a week away, and Scott vowed that his mother would be in the audience for the opening night at the Finsbury Astoria on 25 March. He duly wired two tickets to Hollywood and booked Betty and his aunt Cile into London's Grosvenor House Hotel, where they stayed for three weeks. Scott's attempts to take them to dinner at his favourite restaurants were ruined, however, by persistent autograph requests. They ended up dining in their hotel room, much to the bewilderment of Scott's mother and aunt, who found it difficult coming to terms with the extent of his fame in Britain as he remained a virtual unknown in his own country.

Within a few months, however, Walkermania would be imported to Hollywood in the wake of the group's moderate impact on the American charts. The man who ran Betty's local newsstand in Hollywood unwisely broadcast the fact that she bought her copy of *Disc Weekly* there every Monday and the following morning she was mobbed.

Yet while 'The Sun' deservedly ranks alongside such timeless epics as 'You've Lost That Lovin' Feelin' ' by The Righteous Brothers and 'I Heard It Through The Grapevine' by Marvin Gaye, its B-side, 'After The Lights Go Out', is lyrically superior. This song indicates the path Scott's writing was to take and its edgy, neurotic theme and fly-on-the-wall observations crop up repeatedly in the cream of Walker's subsequent work, most notably 'Montague Terrace (In Blue)' on his first solo album.

In the wee small hours of the morning, Scott broodily paces the floorboards of his flat as he reflects on a love that has turned sour.

Although he reasons that his former lover was 'just a girl whose memory is wiped away with time', daybreak finds him starkly acknowledging that he 'just can't seem to tear away her kisses from the night'.

'As the sun goes down my silent little room is growin' dim/And the man next door is saying what a lousy day it's bin/And the clock on the wall, I'd like to put its ticking to an end/In the room below, the girl is cryin' for her guy again/After the lights go out what will I do?/After the lights go out facing the night without you . . .'

This largely forgotten masterpiece contains all the bricks that Scott would use in the construction of some of his most brilliant examples of poetic architecture. Yet 'After The Lights Go Out' is actually the work of Stewart and clearly illustrates that he and Engel were sharing the same lyrical odyssey as well as drawing inspiration from one another. 'Those two were like peas in a pod,' remembers Allan McDougall. 'Both were blond, with the same classical good looks and had the same musical interests.'

Stewart was not only Scott's oldest and closest friend, but he also shared the latter's cynicism for the record business as well as his taste for modern jazz. He even possessed the same highly-strung personality and dry sense of humour. Scott's former schoolmate was a valuable addition to the Philips backroom team and it was he, more than anyone else, who deserved to be called the fourth Walker Brother. Soon after the group arrived in Britain there was even talk of drafting him into their ranks.

Unfortunately, Stewart's increasingly brilliant input ended abruptly when he was involved in a near-fatal road accident in Birmingham the following November. Always something of a daydreamer, he temporarily forgot that the British drive on the 'wrong' side of the road, stepped off a kerb and was mown down by a car coming from the opposite direction. Stewart suffered multiple head and leg injuries and was lucky to escape with his life.

Scott, who rushed to the hospital on hearing of the accident, paid the bulk of his friend's medical fees before Stewart returned to Los Angeles and a lengthy period of rehabilitation. He never returned to England and his departure, coming at a time when Scott's relationship with John was breaking down, must have deepened Engel's growing sense of isolation.

7 Through a Long and Sleepless Night

'Sometimes, I think when I get enough money I'll get the hell out of it all, take my guitar and go to Europe as an unknown – just to see the reaction.'

Scott Walker, 1966

THE PHENOMENAL SUCCESS of 'The Sun Ain't Gonna Shine Anymore' during the spring of 1966 caused Scott to become totally obsessed with his privacy – or, more accurately, the complete lack of it. No matter where he moved, the girls would descend on his latest flat and pound on the windows or shout through the letter-box as Scott cowered behind curtains that were permanently drawn night and day, and hung precariously from their rails as if torn across with great force. Engel's neighbours, not unnaturally, would quickly tire of the constant disturbance and organise petitions calling for the singer's eviction. Although by the time they came to be delivered he had usually fled the scene.

On moving into a basement flat in St John's Wood, Scott, in a determined effort to avoid being tracked down, ordered Brian Sommerville to address all mail to 'The Occupier'. In addition to making the totally spurious claim that a fault on his telephone meant it could not receive incoming calls – an ideal excuse for avoiding what he regarded as further invasions of his shrinking solitude – Scott took to wearing horn-rimmed spectacles in public, convinced that his changed appearance would help put fans off the trail.

Yet after a few tranquil days, Scott peered disbelievingly through his curtains one morning to find dozens of chanting girls milling outside on the pavement. John and Gary were experiencing identical problems in other parts of the West End. The fans seemed blessed with almost supernatural powers of detection.

The Walkers were not to know the astonishing lengths to which some girls would go to meet their idols. For example, a pop paper's innocent revelation that Scott lived in St John's Wood would lead to the area being flooded by Walkermaniacs who would carry out a systematic search of the surrounding streets. Shopkeepers, pedestrians and even passing motorists would be shown photographs of Scott and asked: 'Have you seen this man?'

Eventually, after days of fruitless enquiries, the girls would locate the newsagent where Scott bought his morning paper or the chemist where he purchased his vitamin pills and consequently discover the street in which he lived. Then it was simply a process of staking-out buildings liable to be harbouring a fugitive Walker Brother and finally, like Kirk Douglas's sheriff in *Last Train From Gun Hill*, they would get their man.

Following the discovery of his St John's Wood refuge, a shaken Scott insisted that the move to his next flat would take place at an hour when even the most deranged Walker fan would be safely tucked up in bed. Maurice King and Gary duly helped to transport his belongings to a flat in the Fulham Road, and the latter recalls that it was around 4 a.m. before the operation was finished.

'By the time we left, Scott was gettin' ready for bed and everythin' seemed fine. Then sometime the next afternoon he rang up and yelled: "They've found me! I can hear 'em screamin' outside!" He wanted me to get down there right away so I got up and went round as fast as I could. When I got there I found his flat was right next to the Stamford Bridge soccer ground and the screaming he thought he could hear was the cheering of all these fans. There was Scott, who wanted to be left alone, with forty thousand people outside his flat every Saturday. So he didn't stay there very long either.

'Then he used to experiment with various disguises. One warm, sunny day he put on this coat, a scarf which went up to his nose, some sunglasses and a hat. He said: "They're never gonna recognise me." As soon as we hit the streets everyone started starin' at him. He said: "How could they possibly do that?" and I said: "Because you're the only guy out here who looks like he's dressed for Alaska."

'Another time he bought a hard hat of the type they use on building sites. He thought it was great because it hid his hair, but when he put it on he just drew more attention to himself. If he had just walked out normally he might have got away with it, but the fans by this time were goin' around lookin' for someone in disguise.'

Scott's nerves were in tatters. He found the obsessive devotion of some fans greatly disturbing and had a secret dread that one day some exceptionally distraught teenager would set fire to herself outside his flat, rather like the monk whose self-immolation in protest at the Vietnam government's treatment of Buddhists was captured in one of the most famous photographs of 1963. But Scott could hardly count on Maurice King for support and understanding. King was a hard-nosed, abrasive character who could not be expected to have much empathy with a temperamental pop singer.

A Quotations guitarist, Graham Dee, was nicknamed 'Twitcher' because of an unfortunate nervous tic that occasionally caused him to jerk back his head and right arm without warning. The problem magically disappeared whenever he strummed his guitar, yet King was haunted by the thought of Dee's twitch manifesting itself during a mimed performance on a live television show.

'Maurice has got something for Twitcher tomorrow night,' a beaming King announced to the puzzled guitarist in the dressing-room one evening. 'What's that, boss?' asked Dee. 'Top of the . . .,' teased King. 'Pops!' answered Dee brightly. 'That's right,' smiled King, poking the guitarist in the chest with a drumstick. 'And if you fucking twitch once,' he suddenly roared, 'I'll knock your bloody head off!'

Scott, no doubt emboldened by the fact that he was the ace in King's pack, was the only person prepared to stand up to the man he called 'Boris the Monster'. Most pop stars of the mid-sixties were meek, trusting creatures who would quite obligingly have leapt off the top of the Post Office Tower on the instructions of their Svengali. Scott, however, would make no secret of his contempt for some of King's strong-arm tactics. Chris Welch, who was backstage at the Finsbury Park Astoria for the opening of The Walkers' spring tour, observed King tearing a strip off one of the group's roadies. 'That's my manager,' said Scott, loudly enough for King to hear. 'Offensive, isn't he?'

The Walkers had been playing two concerts a week for a couple of months now, and offers on the table included three weeks at the Paris Olympia and shows in America, Scandinavia and Holland. Yet there was no let-up in the exhausting schedule. Before The Walkers were plunged into their 27-date tour with Orbison and Glasgow raver Lulu, they first undertook an experimental week of cabaret at Stockton's plush Tito's club following three days of rehearsals.

Scott confided that he had never been so nervous, but the perfectly balanced show received the biggest ovation in the club's history after the band had rocked their way through 'In The Midnight Hour' before 'Summertime', which was 'the high spot of the evening' according to *Melody Maker*. 'I loved every minute,' Scott said later. 'I never enjoyed working so much in my life . . . They all listened, it was so nice for a change.'

The start of The Walkers' tour coincided with the news that EMI were to release an album of material Scott had recorded with John Stewart three years earlier. According to Barry Clayman, only an injunction had prevented Tower Records from releasing it as a Walker Brothers album in the United States. In Britain, the album was credited to 'John Stewart and Scott Engel, Original Members Of The Walker Brothers'.

The hastily-compiled sleeve-notes, which described the record as 'an indispensable memento of the boys' astounding success story', managed to confuse Stewart with John Maus, an error which various pop historians have faithfully repeated over the years. It is doubtful whether many Walker fans were taken in, however. Apart from having the word 'rip-off' metaphorically stamped all over the cover, one of the two smiling faces clearly belongs to the enigmatic Stewart.

EMI's blatant attempt to cash in on his burgeoning popularity deepened Scott's suspicion of the record industry. 'It's all a big, phoney mess,' he told Chris Welch – 'the people in it and the way it's put together. People are blown up into something interesting and they are nothing like as interesting as the stars of years ago.'

Scott told the journalist he disliked success and had no friends. 'I haven't always wanted to be a star anyway,' he protested. 'I've got a gigantic inferiority complex and think that everyone is lookin' at me, and now they are! I spend most of my evenings down at Ronnie Scott's. You find a lot of pseudos and hippies there but not as many as the "In" clubs. I go to the Scotch of St James about once a month and they all see me standin' there with my drink in my hand and say: "He's the one who doesn't like In clubs", and I feel such an ass and think, what am I doin' here?'

The sedate surroundings of Tito's in Stockton were a world removed from the frenzied atmosphere at the Finsbury Park Astoria where the British tour began on 25 March. Technically, Roy Orbison topped the bill, closing the show after Scott, John and Gary had completed the first set, but this tour really belonged to The Walkers, who were by now at the peak of their popularity. Yet what should have been a triumphant procession to all corners of the United Kingdom and Ireland degenerated into something of a farce, following a series of mishaps.

The second date was in Birmingham and when The Walkers' Rolls-Royce pulled up outside the Albany it was surrounded by the usual rampaging hordes as police fought to keep control. Unfortunately, Marlene Dietrich, the legendary film star, who was also staying at the hotel, swept majestically into the foyer just as the boys made a desperate sprint for the entrance. At this point, the thin blue line of police broke and the foyer was swamped by a tidal wave of teenagers, all maddened by a tantalising glimpse of their idols. Poor Ms Dietrich was trampled to the carpet where she lay spread-eagled with dozens of shoe marks covering her black dress. It must have been a particularly nasty moment for Maurice King, who was subjected to a remarkable stream of pithy Anglo-Saxon phrases from the German actress. Threats of legal action, however, were not carried out.

Then, following the show at Chester on 29 March, John, being pursued from the ABC Theatre towards the group's hotel by fans, tumbled down some steps and was knocked unconscious. Doctors advised a day's rest and, with Scott suffering a bout of flu, The Walkers were replaced by The Cryin' Shames at Wigan the following night. Orbison, who had injured his leg in a motorcycle accident, was forced to perform for the remainder of the tour with his foot in plaster. Then laryngitis sidelined Lulu for a week, although she was able to rejoin the show on 1 April at Edinburgh.

John's head injury was a salutary reminder of the risks The Walkers were running, but Gary Leeds remembers that, far from offering protection crash helmets only caused further weals and bruises, especially when girls tried to wrench them off. Reaching the sanctuary of the getaway car was a major problem with or without protective headgear.

'After one show we were gettin' into the car and this girl got hold of John by the hair. He yelled: "Let go! You gotta let go!" He couldn't get her off so I hit her full in the face. I don't know why I did that, I guess I just panicked. But it didn't even faze her; she just carried on screamin'. I don't think we fully appreciated the dangers. One night, right in the middle of our act, I heard this metallic bang just by the side of my drum kit – someone had thrown a horseshoe from the audience.'

But the worst moment came on a flight back from Douglas, on the Isle of Man, to Manchester Airport. Scott detested flying and had to be paralytically drunk before getting aboard a plane. He would refuse to fly first-class, saying: 'Why pay a thousand pounds to be killed, when you can do it for three hundred?' Perhaps mercifully, it was Gary, the qualified pilot, who noticed oil escaping from an engine when the plane was several thousand feet above Liverpool Bay. Displaying his usual lack of tact, he nudged Scott awake and said: 'I don't wanna worry you, man, but does that look like oil to you?' Scott peered groggily out of the cabin window and then sat bolt upright, the colour draining from his face. 'That looks like oil to me,' he replied in a strangled voice.

'I said: "It is, there's oil comin' out of that engine." He said: "No, it can't be." I was tryin' to think rationally, tryin' to figure out what would happen next. I reckoned that the friction would probably lead to a fire and at the same time I was wonderin' why the hell the pilot hadn't cut the damn engine out. Surely a warning light must have lit up in the cockpit by now? Scott put his hand up and called over the stewardess. I'm thinkin' he's gonna ask her to take a look, but instead he orders a large whisky. Just then the pilot announces that he's got a slight problem and he's closin' down one of the port-side engines. Scott asks: "What happens if it catches fire?" I say: "Don't worry, they've cut it out." But inside I'm thinkin': "If this thing catches fire, we gonna get ourselves blown up here!" '

The incident is confirmed by Graham Alexander, The Quotations' bass guitarist, who remembers that Gary appeared very authoritative and assured everyone that the plane could land on three engines. According to one version of the story, Leeds calmly read a book about an air crash as they came in to land at Manchester. The effect of the episode on Scott can easily be imagined. From then on, he would only fly under heavy sedation and preferably with a doctor (rather than Gary) by his side.

Towards the end of the tour, Maurice King approached Roy Orbison and asked him whether The Walker Brothers could close the show. 'Another town, another show, another dollar, hell, it's all the same to me,' replied the genial Texan. Scott and 'The Big O' are among a select band of pop musicians whose street credibility has remained undiminished by the passage of time, yet Engel had nothing in common with his fellow American. 'I met Orbison in the Playboy Club a few days ago,' he told *NME*. 'He was bein' very nice to everyone. Told me what a nice hotel he was stayin' in and how nice the people were to him. He got a bit too nice about everything for me and I left.'

Tales of madness from this period are legion. One night, having played a show on the East Coast, The Walkers were being driven back to London in the early hours by Bobby Hamilton when Gary insanely suggested a spot of night fishing. They eventually located the shores of Connaught Water in a thick mist and Hamilton, a keen fisherman, unloaded the rods he habitually carried around the country with him.

It was by now three o'clock and while Scott slept soundly in the back of the car, Hamilton, John and Gary cast their lines into the freezing waters and spent the next three hours waiting vainly for a bite. The ghostly mist could have come straight out of a Hammer horror film and they could barely see the surface of the water. When it cleared at about 6.30 a.m. the hapless trio discovered that they had spent half the night fishing in a large puddle.

Then in Glasgow The Walkers were invited to a country home for a shoot the following day. Having bought three automatic shotguns they proceeded to Edinburgh and were booking into a hotel when the manager said: 'You're taking a chance, aren't you? Four men armed with shotguns have just held up a security van in Glasgow.'

The chance of an epic publicity stunt was not lost on Brian Sommerville. While The Walkers remained in their suite, he rang the police, giving them a bogus tip-off. He then contacted the national press to ensure that various journalists were present when a cordon of police surrounded the hotel before moving in to arrest the 'robbers'. Released after questioning, The Walkers found themselves front page news and even Scott saw the funny side.

But the laughs, not that there had ever been many as far as Scott was concerned, grew fewer as the great perfectionist recklessly extended his workload while noting, with mounting annoyance, John and Gary's increasingly hedonistic lifestyle. 'I was working like a badger. The other guys were just enjoying things,' he remembered. 'And it really made me angry that people weren't digging the music as much as the image.'

It is easy to sympathise with Scott's frustration, even if his burden was largely self-inflicted. He was working closely with the record producer and arranger, finding songs and choosing musicians as well as taking the first steps to being recognised as a songwriter in his own right.

Yet Scott's compulsion to control his own destiny, or, some would say, an expanding ego, meant his pivotal role was not confined to the studio. He even instructed Hamilton on how to operate the lighting system on tour.

'We're gonna do a forty-minute show,' he'd tell Hamilton during rehearsals. 'If I am seen for more than two minutes out of the forty, you're sacked!' Although Scott was obviously joking, the underlying message was clear: the amount of time The Walkers would be seen by the audience had to be restricted to the bare minimum, thereby ensuring that the fans would be left panting for more. Hamilton says that Scott had 'forgotten more about road managing and tour managing than I'd ever learnt.

'He taught me more in two weeks than I'd learnt in the previous two years. Believe me, making sure he was seen for just two minutes out of forty was some problem, especially when two thousand kids had paid to see him. But Scott knew what he wanted and he knew which way to go. He was an absolute master at everything he touched. We never seemed to have enough time to explain the most complex lighting system in the country to the stage technicians at the various theatres. We would put the spot where Scott would be. It was either a pin-spot or a half-spot, no one ever saw the boys' feet or below their waists. The blokes operating the lights would have two hundred and ninety calls during a show and that's an awful lot of calls for two lads.'

Hamilton claims that on occasions The Quotations would spend up to fifteen or twenty minutes repeatedly playing the 'Land of 1,000 Dances' riff with just two small spotlights illuminating the blacked-out stage. Then Gary would stride momentarily into view and sit in darkness with just his bass drum illuminated. Hamilton would pop his head through the dressing-room door and shout: 'You're on boys!' while Scott and John were still drying their hair. He would then radio for a spotlight to hit stage right. As the light appeared, Hamilton would roll up his shirt-sleeve and extend his arm into the beam, twirling his wrist in a convincing parody of Scott's most famous gesture. The theatre would erupt. He would then withdraw his arm, run around to the other side of the stage and repeat the manoeuvre with his left arm. Again, pandemonium would ensue.

By now everyone in the audience would be on their feet. Suddenly a spotlight would pick out Gary hammering away on his drums. Then John would come shimmying into view from the left and seconds later, his arrival preceded by a twirling arm, Scott would finally emerge. Hamilton says that in two years he barely heard The Walkers sing because the screaming was so great. He doubts whether the fans saw much of them either.

'Sometimes the band just used to stop and the houselights would come on and we'd start all over again. The management would go berserk. All this teasing was Scott's idea. You never saw the three of them on stage at the same time as the spotlights would be constantly switching from one to the other. Sometimes we'd just do 'Land of A 1,000 Dances' and 'The Sun Ain't Gonna Shine Anymore' and then come off. That's how exciting it was – or how bad it was, depending on your viewpoint. "Great show Bobby," Maurice would say when it was all over. "It's a pity you forgot to switch the bloody lights on." '

Scott also had very definite ideas on how to deal with the press on tour: he simply adopted a policy of non-cooperation. Engel reasoned that if he refused the first twenty requests for an interview, but agreed to the twenty-first, the reporter would be so grateful for an exclusive that he would give The Walkers the best write-up of their lives. A constant queue of journalists outside the dressing-room door testified to the success of this ploy. The publicity the group engendered from having no publicity was tremendous.

Graham Alexander recalls that Scott would insist that no one, apart from the band and its management, was allowed into the dressing-room and could explode with anger if someone carelessly left the door open, particularly during those harrowing moments when he was summoning up enough willpower to go out on stage.

'He hated the very idea of strangers in the dressing-room. On one package tour, some promoter brought his wife and some friends backstage with the obvious intention of introducing them to The Walkers. As soon as they opened the dressing-room door Scott ordered them to "Get the fuck out!" The promoter said: "But I'm the guy who's paying your wages" but Scott just replied: "I don't give a fuck who you are, just get out." His anger was controlled, but the promoter sensed there was no point arguing with him so he left. Scott could be extremely stubborn. When he had an idea in his head he would stick to it, although it usually turned out to be very good.'

Perhaps Scott's attitude was shaped by a desire to protect his legendary privacy, yet evidence suggests a more calculating motive. One day Scott and Bobby Hamilton were gazing down at a group of fans from the safety of their hotel suite when Engel said: 'Bob, those kids down there think that when I go to the toilet it don't smell, right?' A puzzled Hamilton confirmed that was probably indeed the case. 'They think that if I wanted to, I could fly out of here like an angel and go down there?' Hamilton again answered in the affirmative. 'And they don't think that I get my willy out and have a wee?' Hamilton nodded his head. Scott looked at him intently: 'So if they ever see me on stage and I'm not lit right, that's blown it hasn't it?' he said softly. 'And they must never see us backstage, under any circumstances.'

If Scott's intention was to create an air of mystique around The Walker Brothers, his success has been spectacular. Almost thirty years after their chart début a legendary aura still surrounds the group. The biggest irony is that the Scott Walker image, though partially self-created, became an intolerable burden which Noel Scott Engel was unable to shed. As recently as February 1992, a British tabloid newspaper challenged its readers to produce a contemporary photo of the reclusive leader of The Walker Brothers.

Not surprisingly, all three Walkers were shattered by the time the tour finished at Coventry Theatre on 1 May and Scott immediately left for a fortnight's holiday in Spain with Graham Alexander. They flew to Barcelona and from there hired a taxi to take them 100 miles down the coast to the resort of Sitges.

'We spent a couple of weeks getting drunk and just lying in the sun. During the whole of that period only one guy, an English holidaymaker, recognised Scott, and even then he pretended to be someone else. When we returned, Scott told everyone that we had travelled down the coast on motorbikes. He might have thought the story was good for his image or he could have been deliberately goading Maurice King, who really worried about Scott taking stupid risks.

'Around this time I stayed with Scott at his St John's Wood flat for about six weeks. I got the impression that he didn't enjoy having a flatmate because he lost his privacy. Admittedly, it was his own flat, but I still found him rather selfish. He would play records in the middle of the night or suddenly insist that we go out at a very late hour.'

Back from holiday, The Walkers flew to West Germany to fulfil club and television dates from 28 May and then travelled to Denmark for two nights at the Carousel Club in Copenhagen, where they had the misfortune to check into the same hotel that The Rolling Stones had trashed the previous week and were refused admission by the manager, who had thought The Walkers were a circus act. On a happier note, Scott met his future wife Mette Teglbjaerg on this visit.

Scott and John were both attracted to the vivacious, dark-haired twenty-year-old, and tossed a coin to decide who would go out with her after the show. It was Scott who called correctly.

The group then left for Sweden and more concerts and television appearances, moving on to Holland and Switzerland and finally back to Germany. The Walkers were riding the crest of a wave and on their return to London, Philips, conscious that the group's next album was still some months away, responded to the clamour for fresh material by rushing the boys into the studio to record 'I Need You', a four-track EP.

This record, chiefly memorable for Scott's outstanding reworking of Randy Newman's 'Looking For Me', the story of a teenager pursued by a gang of street toughs, and 'Young Man Cried', a rare collaboration with Johnny Franz, also marked the arrival of Reg Guest as musical director. Over the next two years, Guest's influence on Scott became secondary only to that of Franz. During those heady years at Philips, Scott made full use of a remarkable array of talent at his disposal. Men like Raymonde, Guest, Peter Knight and Wally Stott were rightly regarded as the finest musical directors in the world.

Raymonde and Knight are now dead, while Wally Stott (of whom more later) has carved out a hugely successful career in America. Reg Guest, who is retired and lives in a large flat in Hove, near Brighton, is a cheery, avuncular 71-year-old who bears little resemblance to the lithe, cool jazz pianist who arranged some of Scott's finest moments on vinyl all those years ago.

Guest established himself as a sessionman-around-town during the 1950s, going on to play piano on dozens of hit records by artists as diverse as Frankie Howerd, Vera Lynn, Frank Ifield and Mandy Rice-Davies, arranging dozens of Top Ten records including 'Shout' by Lulu and Dave Berry's 'The Crying Game', and even cutting a couple of albums under the name 'Earl Guest' prior to joining Philips. 'I always thought I'd end up a millionaire, but somehow it never worked out,' he smiles ruefully. 'Yet when I look back at those old Walker records I realise that this was my life. I worked like a trojan, but I was intensely happy.

'Ivor Raymonde had gone to Decca, then one day Johnny Franz rang me up and to my surprise and delight asked if I would become his musical director. I was already doing a lot of arranging, but this was the kind of chance you grabbed. I'd played piano or organ on the Ivor Raymonde sessions and Johnny clearly wanted someone who knew how The Walker Brothers' sound was achieved. I liked Scott immediately and we built a good rapport. He was quiet, competent, and knew what he wanted. My attitude to Scott was to let him be Scott and not interfere with his far-out ideas. Spiritually, he was in some universe of his own and I never really found out what that was, but I let him be the way he was because as musical director I felt it was my duty to let him express himself.'

Guest's unconcealed admiration for Scott was evidently reciprocated. 'Reg is obviously brilliant, and one of the most underrated arrangers in the country,' Scott enthused. 'If only I could write music like that – he knows exactly what I'm thinkin'. It's the fault of so many arrangers today who profess to hate what they are doin' in pop, and the things they do, but he believes in what he's doin'.'

The Walkers' new arranger recognised an inescapable truth of which some of the group's more discerning fans were becoming uncomfortably aware: Scott's overall persona had grown to such an extent that John and Gary were now little more than passengers, in much the same way as The Beach Boys were beginning to be regarded as Brian Wilson's puppets. In the studio, of course, The Walkers were as manufactured a group as The Monkees proved to be six months later.

Officially, contractual difficulties were blamed for Gary's invisibility while John, on the first album at least, was effectively reduced to being a backing singer. The fact that John and Gary fulfilled essential roles on the road was forgotten as the music papers mischievously began speculating on whether Scott would go solo. Reg Guest confirms The Walkers' unusual set-up.

'I never quite knew what to do with Gary. He was supposed to be the drummer, but I never saw him actually play. John had a good voice and it must have been very frustrating for him to have to constantly play second fiddle to Scott.

'Sessions would start mid-afternoon. Occasionally, Scott would do his vocals there and then, but often he'd just work on the backing track and the lead would be put on later. A union rule meant you had to do the vocal at the same time as the accompaniment, so we sometimes used to pretend he was recording when, in fact, he was only rehearsing. Scott would do his vocal in the control room voice box. The musicians would see him mouthing away and they would be happy. After they'd gone he could spend some time working on the vocal.'

Scott Walker

The follow-up to 'The Sun Ain't Gonna Shine Anymore', Pete Autell's '(Baby) You Don't Have To Tell Me', was released on 8 July, the day that a whole edition of *Ready Steady Go* was devoted to The Walkers (a show chiefly notable for Scott's interpretation of The Beatles' 'We Can Work It Out'). Plans for an Australian tour were underway and the 'I Need You' EP leapt to No. 37 in the charts one week after release. The Walkers had the pop world at their feet, but the sweet cup of success was to prove a poisoned chalice.

8 In My Room

'I live the life of a recluse not out of choice or any mistaken notion that I am creating an image or sympathy for myself, but because this is the way I am.'

Scott Walker, 1967

EVER SINCE THE WALKER BROTHERS had arrived in England, seventeen months previously, John had accepted Scott's more dominant role without question, realising full well that his partner's astonishing voice could propel the group to stardom. Now, however, press criticism and the occasional barbed remark questioning his input – or the perceived lack of it – made him increasingly tetchy. Moreover, Maurice King's insistence that Scott and John should dispense with their guitars had further weakened the latter's already downgraded position. At one fell stroke, Maus, a decent guitarist in his own right, had been denied the opportunity to display the full array of his talents.

'I've been slated so many times,' he said bitterly. 'Andrew Oldham once said Scott was carrying me and Gary . . . which was pretty insulting. How does he know how well I can sing?' Maus was a natural stage performer whose thrusting hips thrilled pubescent girls and horrified their parents. To John's chagrin, one European critic said the music was great but he disliked the 'long-haired stripper', yet for such a tall man John demonstrated considerable grace on stage, which served to highlight Scott's own awkwardness.

Gripped by self-consciousness, Engel never fully mastered the art of natural movement, something that became painfully apparent during his later solo performances, when he sometimes seemed trussed to the microphone by invisible bonds. His most dramatic gesture was to fall on to his back during 'Land Of 1,000 Dances' and lie prone for a couple of minutes as the screams of the audience reached fever-pitch. John's extravagant on-stage persona may have been a subconscious attempt to divert the audience's attention from Scott, yet his insecurity manifested itself in the studio which was Engel's domain. 'I always feel odd about what I'm doing because of the comments that have been passed,' said John.

Only the amiable Gary seemed comfortable with the adulation and impervious to any criticism. He showered gifts on his countless girlfriends, startled diners at a swish restaurant by getting into a heated row with a bald-headed businessman over the length of his hair, and held drinking competitions with The Hollies at the Scotch of St James. On one memorable occasion, the drummer donned a gorilla costume and, egged on by Brian Sommerville, climbed into the ape cage at Chessington Zoo. Gary sat there in his costume, vainly trying to attract the attention of the passing public as a *Daily Mirror* photographer stood poised at the ready. Sommerville recalls that Gary's efforts to smoke a cigarette through the costume had to be abandoned because it was too dangerous.

'Then this couple came along with a young boy. The father was explaining that here was a gorilla and the boy was saying: "It's not, it's a man." He got a thick ear and the "stupid boy" bit from his father. Eventually, after a little more of this, Gary could stand it no longer and pulled out a magazine to read. The kid shouted: "I told you!" and got another thick ear for his troubles. That was the bit that got into the *Mirror* complete with an accompanying picture.'

Having obtained his pilot's licence in the States, Gary's occasional flights in a little Piper Cub attracted considerable publicity. One incident that failed to make headlines was when Leeds, having frightened the life out of passenger Brian Sommerville by looping the loop, smashed a wing against a car as he came into land, resulting in a huge insurance claim. More seriously, when Gary, this time accompanied by John, landed his plane at Radio London's Trophy Races at Brands Hatch, screaming fans pushed a television cameraman into the spinning propeller. The unfortunate man's clothes were torn off and he suffered an eight-inch gash in his back. Both Walkers were extremely shaken by the incident.

Gary attempted to consolidate his freelance activities by releasing a song called 'Twinkie Lee' as a follow-up to 'You Don't Love Me'. The song, which sounded terribly archaic, matched its predecessor by reaching No. 26, but *Melody Maker*'s guest columnist, Ric Rothwell of The Mindbenders, spoke for many when he judged it 'boob of the week'. It was the end of Gary's short-lived solo career.

In an effort to paper over the cracks, King and Clayman urged The Walkers to present a united front and Scott duly sought to assuage fan fears in an interview with Chris Welch at his new flat in Dudley Court, near Marble Arch. Crouched on a bed, his eyes obscured by those ubiquitous shades, Scott rather unconvincingly assured Welch of the group's solidarity. 'It's a thing that bothers me,' he explained, 'this vicious outbreak against the other two guys . . . The point is people think I am trying to hog the whole thing, but I'm not. The others can have the whole bloody thing!' A later remark, however, is more revealing. 'Say, Gary keeps turning it on that we'll never split up doesn't he?' said Scott. 'I think he's having hallucinations. I never see the cat!'

'(Baby) You Don't Have To Tell Me' was released, backed by Stewart's 'My Love Is Growing', against a background of simmering unrest. Although the record leapfrogged above the 'I Need You' EP into the upper reaches of the charts, and its big production faithfully follows The Walkers' winning formula, the song itself is rather weak. The record that had preceded it, of course, was an impossibly tough act to follow, yet in retrospect '(Baby) You Don't Have To Tell Me' does seem an ill-advised cover.

Gary Leeds maintains that the choice of material was a democratic decision, with everyone allowed to offer an opinion on what was put out. Even so, the views of Scott, which almost always mirrored those of Johnny Franz, naturally carried the most weight. Had '(Baby) You Don't Have To Tell Me' been the group's first single, its eventual chart placing of No. 13 would have been considered highly respectable. Instead, coming in the wake of three classic singles, it was classified as a failure, not least by Scott himself.

Yet this mediocre single was followed by 'Portrait', which is generally regarded as the group's finest album. Scott laboured long and hard in the studio that summer, often not returning to Dudley Court until the early hours. Apart from travelling the short distance to the studio, he rarely set foot outside his flat. When Scott had guests around he would invariably order food from the Lotus House, and on one occasion his monthly account topped £800, a sizeable amount of money in the mid-sixties.

Engel's increasingly preoccupied frame of mind was attributed to the amount of effort he was putting into the new album, so his apparent suicide attempt on 15 August shocked everyone. What prompted Scott's actions that Monday evening remains a mystery. What is known is that when Brian Sommerville rang earlier in the afternoon he found the singer 'very agitated. He had some business problems on his mind'. It was probably on Sommerville's suggestion that Bobby Hamilton called round a few hours later.

'I rang the buzzer downstairs but got no reply, so I went around to check that his Mini was there. It was, so I knew he was in. I managed to get inside pretty quick. Those kind of security systems were useless: whatever bell you pressed the buzzer would go and then the door would open. I went upstairs and rang his doorbell – no response. Then I looked through the letter-box and saw him lying on the floor.'

The sight of Scott's prostrate form drove Hamilton into action. Cursing wildly, he unleashed a stream of desperate kicks at the door, which eventually flew open. As Hamilton burst inside the flat an overpowering stench of gas hit his nostrils. Scott did not actually have his head in the oven, but was lying close by. Coughing and spluttering, Hamilton dragged the unconscious singer out on to the landing, where several neighbours helped in the battle to revive him.

'You stupid bastard!' screamed Hamilton as he slapped Scott's face in an effort to bring him round. 'This ain't gonna do your bloody voice much good! Now they're gonna have to take you to hospital and pump you out!' Scott, who by now was semiconscious, moaned: 'Leave me alone, leave me alone. I don't wanna go to hospital.' Yet Scott was hardly in any state to demur and was whisked into St Mary's Hospital, Paddington, from where he was released the following day after treatment. Hamilton recalls that his initial emotive reaction on finding Scott was proved correct. Engel's throat was so sore that he was unable to sing for several days.

'I just cannot accept that it was intentional. He wasn't the kind of guy to do something like that on purpose. Scott knew I was coming that night. If I said I would arrive at 8 o'clock then he'd know that his buzzer would ring at eight.'

A classic 'cry for help', perhaps? The incident remains unexplained as Scott, who recovered quickly, trenchantly refused to reveal the cause. Indeed, the subject appears to have become taboo in the Walker camp and was never discussed again. Here is what Scott told Chris Welch at the time: 'I've been seein' the right doctor, and gettin' tranquillisers,' he said. 'I get very excited about things and they are trying to calm me down. The other guys are tryin' to help me.'

Pressed to elaborate on the cause of the suicide attempt, Scott replied: 'That was it – a lot of pressures and a personal problem. I think it all woke a lot of people up, includin' myself . . . But pressure wasn't the only reason. Nobody has the right reasons and I'm not tellin' anyone the right reasons.'

Brian Sommerville had earlier found Scott fretting over some 'business problems'. Certainly, over the previous weeks Engel had worked incredibly hard in the studio. The 'Portrait' album was set for release and sales of the latest single had been disappointing. The failure of a record to break into the Top Ten may seem like an absurd reason to try and kill yourself, although people have been known to commit suicide for far less.

Scott, however, hinted that there was something else: a 'personal problem' which he refused to disclose. A couple of weeks earlier the *Daily Mirror* reported that Scott had made a marriage proposal to Irene Dunford which she rejected, leading to the headline 'The girl who said no to Scott Walker'. 'I did not take him seriously because he was so unstable at the time,' she says.

'Whenever we were out at a restaurant he had this annoying habit of cupping his hand over the side of his face and talking through the corner of his mouth as if he was afraid people were trying to over-hear. I took his proposal with a pinch of salt – it was after he'd consumed a couple of bottles of wine – although he did seem quite serious. I think he liked having me as an emotional prop.'

Irene's rejection of Scott's light-hearted 'proposal' gave rise to the far-fetched rumour that King had forced the singer to sign a deal whereby he would forfeit £50,000 if he married within the next three years. It is equally unlikely that Irene's decision was the cause of the suicide attempt. A more probable explanation is that Scott's black depression arose from a combination of factors.

'I'd developed an attitude of almost hate at what was going on around me,' he revealed some years later. 'I held it against anyone who appeared to be denying me my life, my privacy. Not only my fans . . . but also my friends. It was a very bad period. I thought everyone was trying to destroy my life. I had this idea that the press were people who misquoted me; fans were the ones who wouldn't stop ringing my phone, smashing my door and making me move flats. Then there was the man who was my manager – making me do it all; the agent who wanted my money; and the record company was sucking my blood . . . It was very immature of me. But to someone going through a paranoic stage it all seemed to make sense.'

At the time Scott told *Fab 208* magazine that he had suffered a very distressing period when: 'I had rows with just about everyone and everything went wrong.' Mary Arnold claims that the incident arose out of a sense of isolation. Although Scott craved a solitary existence, there were occasions, particularly during pressurised periods, when he was overwhelmed by loneliness.

'It was Scott's way of seeking attention. He was very temperamental and felt that people only talked to him because of who he was. After I married Maurice in May 1966, it took Scott about a year before he would even speak to me. He was quite upset when Maurice got married because he wanted him there all the time.'

Jonathan King, who says that Scott was involved in a series of apparent suicide attempts in the mid-sixties, eventually tired of rushing to his friend's hospital bedside. After the Dudley Court incident, King walked into Scott's room at St Mary's and sat down on the end of the bed with a fed-up expression on his face. 'This has got to stop,' he said sternly. 'Why?' asked Scott. 'Because it's fucking irritating!' replied King with feeling. 'I can't keep on having to dash to your bedside. You can do one of two things: either commit suicide properly, in which case I'll never be pestered again, or you've got to stop.'

Scott gazed incredulously at his bedside visitor for a few seconds, then burst into laughter. After Engel's release from hospital, the two men spent a fortnight in Sitges where the singer managed to get the teetotal King blind-drunk on tequila. The suicide attempts were never repeated and King believes Scott's actions were indeed a cry for help.

'He was maturing and had much more to cope with than most people because he didn't come from a settled background. Scott really envied my stable background and virtually became part of the family. Those of us who have a happy upbringing are lucky to have foundations laid down for us. Scott was one of those unfortunate people who had to start building on sand.'

However, the possibility of an accident, which Scott may have been too embarrassed to disclose, was not ruled out by some. Gary Leeds says: 'Mechanically speaking, Scott was a bit of a disaster area. He couldn't even change a plug.' Some sceptics, noting the imminent release of The Walkers' crucial second album, suspected a publicity stunt, yet Sommerville's testimony rules this out.

'He knew exactly what he was doing. He closed all the windows, put towels down by the door and turned the gas on. One of the roadies found him and called me. I was round there in minutes and, because it was me who called the ambulance, everyone assumed it was a stunt. The press went potty, Maurice King hit the roof and accused me of setting it up. Scott went to hospital and was kept in overnight. I went to see him the following day. He told me the reason he did it in the strictest confidence. All I can say is that it was over and done with straightaway and had no permanence in his life. It wasn't anything to do with the music or a relationship.'

As stardom was still a giggle to John and Gary, the fact that Scott found it increasingly intolerable was something his fellow Walkers could never understand. Surely it was fun to shoot the breeze with the likes of Paul McCartney or Eric Burdon down at the Cromwellian, laugh at your latest picture in *Melody Maker* or be given the best table in a restaurant by a fawning head waiter who invariably supplied a complimentary bottle of champagne? Then, to be pursued by nubile teenage girls every minute of the night and day was the dream of any red-blooded male. This was, after all, why young men formed pop groups in the first place, wasn't it?

Scott's reclusive nature and paranoid tendencies had become apparent to Maurice King within weeks of signing the group. Alarmed by an early example of John and Gary's extravagance, he told them sharply: 'You'll have to cut down on spending – it's no use, you'll both have to live as hermits, like Scott.' Engel, of course, was never quite the recluse of legend, although he did occasionally shut himself away behind drawn curtains, playing Mozart at full volume while devouring the works of Dickens, Hemingway, Dylan Thomas and Sartre. Scott told journalists that his eyes were light sensitive ('Everyone's on this daytime kick, it's awful') but a more likely explanation is that the drawn curtains were simply a device to hide himself from prying eyes. Scott just could not come to terms with the obsessional fanaticism he inspired.

Quizzed on their personal ambitions, the answers The Walkers gave *Fab 208* are extremely revealing. 'To become an international entertainer in all fields,' John grandly announced. 'An international star,' agreed Gary. 'To become a human being,' said Scott soberly.

Already developing an interest in health and physical fitness which would develop into something of an obsession by the mid-seventies, Scott was actually a fresh-air fiend who would have liked nothing better than the occasional leisurely stroll around London's landmarks. By the health-conscious eighties he had become a keen cyclist, but back in the sixties Scott's chronic fear of being spotted and pursued by fans effectively imprisoned him inside his flat, and what began as natural shyness developed into a persecution complex.

'On sight, people hate me,' he said. 'They're afraid of me and I'm afraid of them. But they don't know that, because I'm cool. .... I don't get lonely for people ... but sometimes I get lonely for a particular person.'

By nature a wary individual who kept strangers at a distance, Scott now feared that most of the individuals who approached him were only interested in his celebrity status, which in some cases was undoubtedly true. He was also distressed at the way stardom altered people's perception of him. Jonathan King was one of the few people Engel felt he could trust.

'I don't have a great many friends here, but then I never get close to people,' admitted Scott. 'I know people and I say: "Hi, how's things?" But I don't really care how things are, and I know they don't really care about me either. It gets kinda lonely, only there is no solution to the loneliness. To stop being lonely you have to share your life and your mind with people, and I can't do that.'

Incarcerated in his flat by day and often too tense to sleep at night, Scott sought solace in the works of French existentialist Sartre, Genet and other true artistic free spirits capable of shaping their own futures while he struggled to come to terms with the present. Existentialism preached freedom of the individual and was clearly highly attractive to someone like Scott, whose own existence was governed by such petty restrictions as recording deadlines, record sales and interview requests.

Although The Beatles had demonstrated conclusively that pop stars could write their own material, Scott, like most musicians in 1966, was only just beginning to expand his creative horizons. Yet what put Engel ahead of the rest was his major role in the studio at a time when the Fab Four were still largely answerable to George Martin.

Ensconced in the Philips control room with Johnny Franz, routining material, arguing over arrangements and listening to playbacks, Engel was arguably the first pop musician who sought total control over his work. His songwriting method rarely varied: he would compose his lyrics first and add on the melody afterwards. By 1967, Tony Gilbert of The Quotations was teaching Scott to read music, and after laying down a rough vocal on a tape recorder Scott would routine the material for Johnny Franz, perhaps using his own guitar. Then, in the studio, Scott's embryonic songs would take on a life of their own.

As his songwriting developed, so did the need for solitude. 'I must have privacy, I must have quiet to work' said Scott. 'For my music is my life and I must occasionally remove myself from everyone, even my friends.'

News of the Dudley Court incident spread quickly and Scott's flat was besieged with gifts, flowers and letters of support. When Engel strolled into Ronnie Scott's the following Saturday, he was surprised and even a little touched by the genuine warmth of his reception.

Graham Nash jokingly offered him 'a shilling for the gas meter' while it was rumoured that someone else, much to Scott's own amusement, pushed through his letter-box an electricity board brochure bearing the hand-written legend: 'Use electricity – it's cleaner'.

Engel was less enamoured with the response of some fans who, having obtained his address from the papers, did not exactly aid recuperation by constantly pounding on the door and making sleep impossible for almost a week. It was time for Scott to move again. This time to a flat in Portman Square.

By the time Chris Welch met up with Scott at the Scotch of St James the following week, the singer was cheerful, funny and bursting with enthusiasm over the 'Portrait' album and the future. 'I'm writing surrealist songs and using surrealist arrangements,' he revealed. 'We had two different arrangers on this album, but there'll only be one on the next, which will be Reg. I've written half of the songs for the album. They are violent and surrealist – you gotta hear 'em.'

In spite of Scott's personal problems, the summer of 1966 was a richly creative period. Sitting in a quiet corner of the club nursing a Scotch and Coke, he bemoaned the fact that it was too late to include his newest songs on the album.

A couple of days earlier, Scott insisted on using the sound of an enormous pipe organ on his latest composition. 'Scott,' laughed Johnny Franz. 'You're mad, but go ahead.' Engel duly dragged Franz and Guest down to the Odeon cinema in Leicester Square, where an unearthly organ refrain was recorded and ultimately used on Scott's 'Archangel' (a B-side to 'Deadlier Than The Male') a full six months before Procol Harum's supposedly ground-breaking 'A Whiter Shade Of Pale'.

Scott also talked animatedly about the latest addition to the Walker 'inner circle', Barrie Martin, The Quotations' saxophonist. 'He's a very unusual musician and we have a lot in common,' enthused Scott. 'Barrie could be one of the biggest names in jazz.

Whenever he appears and does a solo, he brings the house down. He's 22 – the same age as me.'

Despite this glowing reference, Barrie Martin never did become one of the biggest names in jazz. Today he drives a black cab around the crowded streets of London, but at night he plays sax in a band called Atlantic Soul Machine, whose impressive live performances have earned them a large following. 'The cab-driving sort of took over from the music and I ended up being off the scene for about thirteen years – which I now regret,' he reflects, tucking into chicken and chips at a Farringdon café and striving to ignore the good-humoured ribbing of a group of fellow cabbies. 'I still enjoy playing, though, and I like to think I'm a far better musician than I was in the sixties.'

Martin can claim a thimbleful of immortality – the swinging baritone sax solo on 'Summertime'. The Walkers' imaginative interpretation of the Gershwin classic is, by popular consent, one of the strongest tracks on 'Portrait', yet Scott, with typical perversity, denounced it as one of the worst. 'Barrie Martin's solo was the only thing that came off,' he maintained. 'The bass player and drummer fell apart.'

The album kicks off with the brooding, melancholic 'In My Room', which assumed greater significance in the light of the singer's recent suicide attempt. The solitary image of Scott, hovering on the brink of insanity following marital breakdown, is palpable.

'In my room, way at the end of the hall/I sit and stare at the wall/Thinking how lonesome I've grown, all alone, in my room/In my room, where every night is the same/I play a dangerous game/I keep pretending she's late, and I sit, and I wait/Over there is the picture we took when I made her my bride/Over there is the chair where I held her whenever she cried/Over there by the window the flowers she left – have all died . . .'

'In My Room' is the work of the New York songwriting duo Pockriss and Vance, although Scott's credit indicates that he adapted the lyrics to stamp his own introverted personality on the track. Once again, Engel had embraced someone else's bleak vision and made it unmistakably his own.

This most neurotic of songs is followed by Scott's first composition, the upbeat 'Saturday's Child', whose party atmosphere and driving bass patterns, reminiscent of Ike and Tina Turner's classic 'River Deep, Mountain High', coat an underlying sombre message which can be seen as an attack on the prevailing hedonism of the times.

John takes lead on Louis Armstrong's 'Just For A Thrill' which provides an ideal vehicle for his underrated bluesman's voice, but is again overshadowed by Scott's performance on 'Hurting Each Other'.

Scott's treacly rendition of 'Old Folks', the Robison/Hill standard, was apparently included as the singer's tribute to his father, with whom he had recently been reconciled. Unfortunately, 'Old Folks' has not dated well, and today sounds like the type of sentimental twaddle that Val Doonican would have rejected as being too maudlin.

Scott and John's voices blend to superb effect on 'Summertime', which became such a show-stopper when performed live. Martin's soaring sax is what makes The Walkers' version so very memorable, though.

'All I can remember about recording it is that I was very nervous,' Martin recalls today. 'Nobody came up and told me to relax and say: "Look, you can do this eight, nine or ten times if you like until we think that it is right." After the first take they asked: "How's that?" I said: "That's fine." Scott asked: "Are you sure?" I said: "Yeah!" I know I could have done it a thousand times better, but I was so nervous that I just wanted to get out of that studio.'

'People Get Ready', Curtis Mayfield's soul/gospel anthem, opens Side Two, followed by 'I Can See It Now' which, with its sensitive lyrics enriched by tender harmonies, violins and flugel horn, makes it regrettable that Engel and Franz did not collaborate more frequently. (The latter blamed laziness on his part.) Leiber and Stoller's song 'Where's The Girl' is a prime example of Scott's excellent range, but the piece unfortunately has yet to be enshrined on compact disc.

'Living Above Your Head', a number recorded by Jay and The Americans, crops up on most Walker Brothers' compilations; John's confident delivery on Leiber and Stoller's 'Take It Like A Man' betrays no sign of his discomfiture in the studio and Tom Springfield's 'No Sad Songs For Me' provides a suitably downbeat finale to the record.

The record sleeve was the work of top photographer Dezo Hoffman and the serene expressions of Scott, John and Gary give no hint of the personality and ego clashes that would tear the group asunder in just nine short months. 'Portrait' is the polished work of a group at its apex and, propelled by rave reviews, cruised to No. 3 in the charts.

The completion of a short tour, taking in dates at Southend, Dover, Morecambe and Hull, left Scott free to indulge in some extra-curricular activities on the record production front. He produced a John Stewart song called 'Light' by Finders Keepers, a Wolverhampton group, as well as working with a Merseyside outfit called Carol and the Memories.

The session that produced 'Light' proved considerably arduous for Finders Keepers. Scott infuriated the sessionmen by sitting in the studio's control box twiddling knobs and asking for more bass or drumming for hour after hour. When the group heard the finished product they could not believe it was the same song. But Scott's efforts were in vain. The record flopped, and Finders Keepers were lost in the archives of oblivion.

There was no let-up in The Walkers' murderous recording schedule. With their autumn tour of Britain less than a fortnight away, The Walkers revived Gene McDaniels' 'Another Tear Falls', another Bacharach-David composition, complete with a menacing Reg Guest accompaniment. This powerful vocal drama, arguably the most underrated of The Walkers' singles, disappointingly ground to a halt just outside the Top Ten. Scott blamed himself for the relative failure of both this disc and its predecessor, and bitterly regretted his expansive use of woodwind and orchestra against the advice of Franz and Guest.

The truth of the matter, as Scott would shortly acknowledge, was that the fickle British record-buying public was wearying of The Walkers' sound. Eric Burdon, when appearing on the *Juke Box Jury* panel, criticised the repetitive nature of the records and his views were echoed by Tom Jones in *Melody Maker* ('After their first hit it's like we're getting part two, then three, then four'). Keith Altham believes that Philips' reluctance to change a winning formula hastened the group's demise.

'Johnny Franz was a very accomplished musical director, but those kind of people tend to be a bit Frankensteinian. Although they help in the initial success of the band, they tend to have too much control for too long, because they quite naturally feel that they deserve to reap the reward of all the hard work they have put in.

'The actual development of an artist can be retarded by the record company's continual attempts to justify its own existence. I'm not saying that was necessarily true of Johnny Franz, but it was certainly true of some of the people who were around The Walker Brothers at that time. Once the record company find a successful formula they want to stick with it and consequently this quasi-Spector sound was over-used.'

The B-side of 'Another Tear Falls' reveals a delightful surprise. The hauntingly beautiful 'Saddest Night In The World', John's first songwriting success, is a bleak depiction of the aftermath of a broken love affair set in the rain-drenched streets of London's West End. Tenderly sung by Scott, this evocative slice of melancholy would not have been out of place on 'Portrait'. John's sporadic flashes of inspiration tantalisingly hint at the presence of a talent that could have developed alongside Scott's, yet his songwriting failed to progress in the way that, for instance, George Harrison's did in the dying days of The Beatles.

King and Clayman were busying themselves with the final preparations for The Walker Brothers' first headlining tour of Britain, which was due to open at the East Ham Grenada, when one of Scott's typically impulsive gestures hit the front pages. John Lennon had horrified Beatles' fans by having his hair cut for his role as Private Gripweed in Dick Lester's satirical oddity *How I Won The War*. A Beatle cutting his hair was big news and *Disc & Music Echo* lightheartedly carried an artist's impression of how Scott would appear with his locks shorn. Engel apparently took one look and tore round to a nearby barber's for a short-back-and-sides. 'This is the real me. This is how I want to be,' he told a shocked Irene Dunford.

Maurice King was livid. The lead singer of The Walker Brothers resembled a fugitive from a chain gang – with a major tour less than a fortnight away. Scott, who claimed he had always secretly yearned to wear his hair short, gleefully discovered that he could travel around his West End haunts virtually unmolested.

The show had to go on, despite the mutilation of Scott's barnet, so The Walkers duly assembled for rehearsals at the East Ham Grenada on 1 October. This Arthur Howes package tour also included Dave Dee, Dozy, Beaky, Mick and Tich, The Troggs and a young Irish singer called Clodagh Rodgers, who would later chalk up a series of chart hits, including the aggravating 'Jack In The Box' which she performed at the 1971 Eurovision Song contest.

The blonde teenager and her manager arrived at the theatre just as The Quotations were completing their rehearsal, and it quickly became apparent that Miss Rodgers was under the misapprehension that this was her backing band. She therefore commandeered The Quotations who, surprised though they were, good-humouredly agreed to accompany her during the rehearsal.

Just then, Scott's scowling visage appeared. He strode on to stage and quietly asked Miss Rodgers what she thought she was doing. Her tart reply provoked a testy response from Scott that surprised on-lookers. 'No way!' he exclaimed. 'These guys play with us and no one else.' Miss Rodgers promptly told Scott what he could do with his band before flouncing off-stage and off the tour as well.

Scott's outburst deeply embarrassed The Quotations, who revel-led in the camaraderie fostered on the road whereby groups would occasionally swap instruments or even an occasional guitarist or drummer during emergencies. Scott's prima donna-style tantrum was probably the result of first-night nerves. It can hardly have endeared him to Arthur Howes, though.

Picture the scene outside the theatre that night. A girl is standing on the pavement. She unfurls a large portrait of The Walker Brothers, screams loudly once and walks up the road. Nearby two thirteen-year-olds are sobbing uncontrollably as they support each other.

Once inside, the safety curtain bounces back to a warm-up chorus of 'We want Scott'. Following an inaudible announcement, the cur-tain rises and The Quotations launch into their fifteen-minute set which includes 'I'll Go Crazy', 'Little By Little' and 'At The Club'.

You are sitting in Row BE. Row BD is filled with one snogging couple and a team of obvious contenders for the World Screaming Championships. They take an instant dislike to the comedian-com-père as he struggles against impossible odds. You just manage to catch one line above the rising crescendo: 'Your face is like a million dollars . . .' 'Because it's green and crinkly!' chorus Row BD scorn-fully. One of its smallest occupants stops shouting, 'We want Scott!' and starts chanting, 'Get off, you silly bastard!'

Eventually the hapless comedian shouts: 'Dave Dee, Dozy, Beaky, Mick and Tich!' The group can only be heard during short lulls in the screaming. After a short break, during which ice-cream and or-ange drink repair sore throats, The Quotations reappear at the start of the second half. The screams rise at least two octaves for the appearance of The Troggs. The noise, both off-stage and on, is un-believable.

At last, The Walkers. At this point you realise that all the previous screaming was a mere rehearsal. Now you can actually feel the girls' breath like a force 10 gale on your neck. One of Row BD shrieks: 'I can't bear to look!' The one behind you keeps whacking your head with her rolled-up programme. Everyone is on their feet, but grim-faced security men with flashing torches soon put a stop to that. One girl is carried out unconscious.

'Scott! Oh God!' shrieks the girl with the deadly programme. During universal pauses for breath it becomes obvious that The Walkers can sing well and that The Quotations are doing an excellent job backing them, but mostly it is impossible to hear anything, or see much either.

They sing 'Land Of 1,000 Dances', 'I Need You', 'Another Tear Falls' and many others. A bright-pink-suited Gary takes over the mike for 'Twinkie Lee', with Scott supporting him on drums. Then suddenly they are gone, the lights come on and it is all over.

Dazed and drained, your ringing ears filled with the sound of sobbing females, you lurch towards the exit and totter off into the East London night . . .

9 I Don't Want To Hear It Anymore

'It was not solely my decision to break up The Walker Brothers, but for the first time in some years I feel free. I'm gonna do what I wanna do.'

Scott Walker, 1967

THE CRAZINESS WAS STARTING ALL OVER AGAIN. At Chester, scene of John's nasty fall the previous spring, The Walkers were only able to escape from the ABC Theatre by disguising themselves as policemen. The group walked off-stage at Bristol's Colston Hall in protest at the lights being turned out during their act and ignored the theatre manager's pleas to return. Police reinforcements had to be called in to usher out the angry fans.

Then, backstage at Manchester, John, his tongue loosened by liberal quantities of Whisky and Coke, publicly described Scott as 'moody, irresponsible and a pain-in-the-neck' during a lengthy tirade which was little more than a heavy-handed attempt at self-justification. 'My pet bitch is being compared to Engel,' said John belligerently. 'He's like a lead weight.

'I never sing the melody line, true, but nobody thinks of the harmony part, which is a more difficult job than people imagine. They seem to think that I'm nothing more than a backing track – but we all play our part.' In virtually the same breath John even offended Gary by describing his solo records as 'distasteful'.

This petty backstage bitchiness, fuelled by the fact that Clayman was sympathetic to John's viewpoint while King refused to hear a word against Scott, forced the growing divisions in the Walker camp ever wider. 'Maurice thought the sun shone out of Scott's backside,' recalls one former associate. Yet Scott, who now found the prospect of a solo career appealing, balked at the thought of going on stage without John and Gary. 'To tell you the truth, man, the idea of being on stage frightens me,' he admitted.

Scott could still laugh at Gary's clowning and the fact that he continued to speak fondly of the drummer suggests he was reassured by his presence. After all, had it not been for Gary's dogged persistence, the group would have disintegrated soon after arriving in

England. Even John, whose open dissatisfaction was turning him into Scott's chief protagonist, remained a vital emotional crutch. The trio had been through so much together and Scott found the idea of breaking free from The Walker Brothers' shackles both exciting and alarming.

On 22 October, Scott collapsed in the BBC dressing-room at Shepherd's Bush during rehearsals for Sunday's *Billy Cotton Show*. After Engel received medical treatment and was whisked back to his Regent's Park flat, Maurice King said the singer appeared to have suffered an allergic reaction to some tranquillisers he had taken. According to Gary, this did not placate Billy Cotton's son, who was so incensed by The Walkers' non-appearance that he vowed they would never appear on the BBC again.

Normally, Maurice King would have laughed off such a threat, but Bill Cotton happened to be the BBC's Head of Variety and an exceedingly powerful figure to boot. Cotton himself has no recollection of this incident, but Gary insists that the unofficial ban lasted until late 1975, when producer Robin Nash had to overcome initial resistance before the group was allowed to appear on the *Vera Lynn Show*.

Despite his collapse at the *Billy Cotton Show*, Scott had recovered sufficiently that night to take to the stage at Chiswick, and the remainder of the tour included dates at Newcastle, Sheffield and Coventry before appearances in Scotland and Ireland. An air of frivolity hung over the final show at Ipswich Gaumont on 6 November, where The Walkers' plans to surprise their fans were vetoed by Brian Sommerville.

'They were going to squirt water over the audience and drop their pants or something. I said: "It may be your last night, but it's the audience's first and only night and you have to behave like professionals." The one advantage I had was that I used to wear a suit with collar and tie and I didn't smoke pot, which people couldn't understand. This meant that when I wanted to read the riot act they sat up and took notice. Needless to say, they didn't go ahead with the idea.'

When The Walkers ran off stage at Ipswich it was expected to be their last British appearance for some months. The expiry of work permits meant that the group was unable to undertake live engagements and would have to tape all television work right up until the following April. However, the permits were extended to enable them to appear in a charity show in aid of the Cinema and Television Benevolent Fund at the London Palladium on 29 November for the Royal Gala, which was televised the following week.

After the show was completed, The Walkers, in company with their fellow artists, were lined up backstage to be formally introduced to His Royal Highness the Duke of Edinburgh and, moments later, Her Royal Highness Princess Margaret. Photos of the group grinning sycophantically at the Duke are deceptive.

When the Princess came down the line she paused in front of Scott and invited him to a party the following Saturday. Maurice King, who interpreted Scott's silence as a sign he was overwhelmed by this momentous offer, awoke the singer from his apparent trance by nudging him sharply. 'Yes Ma'am . . . thank you Ma'am,' grinned Scott, to King's obvious relief. 'Splendid,' smiled the Princess and moved a few paces along before adding, as an afterthought: 'Oh, and do bring your two brothers as well.'

King waited until the beaming royal personage was out of earshot before turning to Scott and gleefully rubbing his hands together. 'That's great,' he chortled. 'Just think of the publicity!' But King's triumphant grin died on his lips as he caught sight of Scott's sombre expression. 'I hope you enjoy yourself, Maurice,' he said coldly. 'Because I'm not going.' Not for the first time in their volatile relationship, King was heard to splutter: 'Are you bloody mad or something?' 'I don't have to do something I don't want to do,' said Scott obstinately. Despite King's pleas and threats, he refused to reconsider.

Barrie Martin and Graham Alexander, The Quotations' bassist, were by now among Scott's closest friends, and the former would spend hours sitting with Engel at Ronnie Scott's, totally absorbed in the music. Scott had told the press of his affinity with Martin, yet the pair irrevocably fell out over an incident at a show at the Swedish town of Malmö, one of a handful of hastily-arranged Scandinavian dates during The Walkers' enforced idleness in Britain.

Martin recalls that shortly before the show was due to begin, Scott declared that he was unable to perform owing to a heavy cold and sore throat. 'So that was it. He refused point-blank to go on, even though it was suggested that all he do was play guitar. The show went ahead with Gary and John, but all those Swedish kids were terribly disappointed. Let's face it, Scott was the most popular of the three and nearly everyone who was there had come to see him.'

Scott's decision also disappointed the Quotations, who recalled how Roy Orbison had soldiered on during the spring British tour despite a family bereavement and having a leg encased in plaster. Back at the hotel, when someone sought Martin's opinion on Scott's non-appearance, the tall saxophonist from north London, who was never afraid to speak his mind and tended to call a spade a bloody shovel, replied that the singer was 'out of order'.

'He could at least have played his guitar. As far as I was concerned, what he did showed a lack of professionalism and I let my feelings be known to the band.'

Back in London a couple of weeks later, Martin and The Quotations' trombonist Tony Gilbert accompanied Scott to the Lotus House one evening. At one point during the meal Martin briefly left the table to go to the toilet, and when he returned the atmosphere had turned positively chilly. As the saxophonist sat down Scott glared across at him and asked quietly: 'Is that right that you thought I was out of order back in Malmö?'

'It was obvious that Gilbert had told him what I'd said and Scott really seemed to take it to heart. His idea of a friend was someone who never criticised. I said, "Look, I was on that stage and I could see the disappointment written all over those kids' faces. Of course you're a great singer, but they would have been satisfied just to have seen you up there. You're their idol and God knows how long they'd been looking forward to seeing you. They weren't interested in your singing so much, they just wanted to see you." '

This was quite a speech from the saxophonist, but Scott's grim expression indicated that it had not been well received. 'I don't think you should criticise me,' he said icily. 'I'm sorry, but I think you're wrong,' countered Martin. Scott, whose much-professed dislike of 'phoneys' must have made him seem like the Holden Caulfield of pop, was badly wounded by Martin's home-truths. The two men never socialised again and although Martin remained in The Quotations for a couple more months, his relationship with Scott became strictly business from then on. Engel's prickly reaction may have been the result of heightening tension backstage where little cliques were forming and the atmosphere was heavy with conspiratorial silences.

Scott's humour was not improved by the unearthing of yet another skeleton in his closet. This time Liberty released an EP of songs he had recorded as an eighteen-year-old. *Melody Maker* declared that the tracks served as a 'fascinating insight into his vocal development', but Scott did not share its enthusiasm.

Small wonder then, that he yearned to temporarily escape the various pressures encroaching on his life. Engel told a surprised *Melody Maker* reporter that once the tour ended he intended to enter a Benedictine monastery to study Gregorian chant. 'Reg Guest and I are hung up on the Gregorian chant,' revealed Scott. 'It's one of the earliest forms of music and . . . when I play it softly it just takes me away from everything.'

Sure enough, a couple of weeks later Scott entered Quarr Monastery on the Isle of Wight, for what he anticipated would be a blissfully relaxing ten days. Engel, who was taught the Gregorian chant by Father Alham Dean, afterwards pronounced the monks to be the 'coolest' people he had ever met. He was given his own cell with a table, hard chair, a sink and a bed and three square meals a day consisting of home-grown food from the monastery garden. Scott did not have to wear a habit, although the music papers had fun depicting him in one.

But this new-found tranquillity lasted a mere couple of days after the press revealed his whereabouts. The bewildered monks found themselves inundated with telephone queries from giggling girls, some of whom even hammered on the monastery doors. Sunday mass was turned into a fiasco when dozens of Walker fans invaded the chapel. Scott, mortified at being the cause of this disruption, reluctantly cut short his stay, although it is probable that he made clandestine return visits over the next couple of years.

The following August, Scott rushed to a Liverpool hospital to visit Father Dean who had suffered a heart attack. Before Engel fled Quarr, the monk had handed him a large key and said he was free to return to the monastery whenever he wished. Scott was captivated by this concept of freedom and carried the key with him as a lucky charm for a number of years. It can quite clearly be seen dangling around his neck on the cover of his 1969 album 'Scott Sings Songs From His TV Series'.

Back in London, the widening schism between Scott and John was highlighted by the release of the 'Solo Scott, Solo John' EP on 9 December, containing two tracks by each. John's slow version of Bobby Hebb's 'Sunny' (a Top Twenty hit for its composer the previous September) seems rather unimaginative, while 'Come Rain Or Shine' suffers from a lacklustre arrangement which Maus himself directed, during Johnny Franz's temporary absence from the studio.

Franz, possibly due to his childhood disability, disliked walking and always parked his Rolls-Royce within a stone's throw of Stanhope Place. He developed an almost obsessive fear of traffic wardens and virtually the only time he left the studio during recording was to go and feed the parking meter.

One afternoon, during the recording of 'Come Rain Or Come Shine', Maus and Franz disagreed on the form of Reg Guest's arrangement, neither being prepared to give an inch. Just then, Franz suddenly remembered his meter was overdue and bolted out of the control room in a panic, leaving John to record the arrangement and ensure it was 'in the can' by the time of the producer's breathless return. Listening to the record, John's piece of quick-thinking opportunism appears ill-judged. The two songs hardly enhanced his reputation, particularly when compared to Scott's offerings on the other side.

'The Gentle Rain' (from the film of the same name) is a straightforward middle-of-the-road ballad sung by Scott in his Jack Jones style. An indication of the schizoid nature of his future career, it was accompanied by something completely different. 'Mrs Murphy' is the first of those grimy, kitchen-sink slabs of social melodrama that Scott would come up with from time to time. Once again, the listener finds Scott eavesdropping on neighbours gossiping in the hallway outside his down-at-heel flat about a young married woman and her affair with a teenage boy in the same block of flats. We have travelled this way before, of course, and will do so again, but the tableau is no less fascinating.

The scene abruptly switches from local gossip to number twenty-two, where the boy who apparently fathered the child lies stretched on his bed, 'thinking of a dream he had'. Although Scott's overheard conversation began with small-talk, he now holds the listener's rapt attention as he cuts back to the tut-tutting neighbours discussing the affair.

'Mrs Murphy' is a graphic illustration of Engel's obsession with the type of lowlife he first encountered when living out his Jack Kerouac fantasies by hitch-hiking across the United States as a teenager. Yet his overheard conversations still manage to convey sympathy for what Tennessee Williams, one of Scott's literary heroes, described as the 'fugitive kind'.

As if to demonstrate the diversity of Engel's talents, Philips released 'Deadlier Than the Male', the title track from a James Bond-style film, on the same day. Another Engel/Franz composition, this number is a fairly blatant reworking of John Barry's 'Thunderball' and Scott, who walked out halfway through the film's première, was incensed that Philips promoted it as a Walker Brothers single. It is a pity that the soaring 'Archangel', complete with doomy organ refrain built around a Bach fugue, was relegated to the B-side as the record failed to make the Top 30.

Scott may also have had cause to regret the January release of 'Stay With Me Baby', The Walkers' cover version of the Lorraine Ellison original. Scott and John give a powerhouse performance with the latter right at the top of his range, but the song, which Scott declared had to be No. 1 in order to keep the group together, was clearly not Top Ten material, or even Top Twenty as events turned out.

Again the B-side, Scott's haunting 'Turn Out The Moon', is infinitely superior. Franz and Maus apparently wanted to release 'Everything Under The Sun' (which would later provide a strong opening to the 'Images' album), but as Scott himself gloomily reflected: 'Engel put his foot down and came up with another miss.'

The record's sluggish performance was not helped by the fact that the group was unable to promote it. Two thousand girls turned up at Heathrow Airport on 15 January to see The Walkers off on their world tour which would take in Singapore and Japan as well as Australia. The relative failure of the last few singles had seemingly not dented the group's popularity. Screaming fans chased the boys across the departure lounge and forced them to seek refuge in a toilet. By the time The Walkers' plane started taxiing down the runway there were so many girls on the roof of the terminal that Heathrow security men feared it would collapse.

Scott's fear of flying had increased to such an extent that he would start to shake at the mere sight of a plane, and his obvious terror had spread like wildfire through The Walkers' entourage. Some of The Quotations managed to get drunk before leaving the departure lounge while John, who had always listed flying as one of his hobbies, looked ashen-faced. Gary Leeds remembers Scott's desperate suggestion that a handful of sleeping tablets washed down by copious amounts of brandy would make them sleep until Australia.

'The three of us were real nervous and ready to try anything, I guess, so we took these barbiturates and drank some alcohol, hoping it would knock us cold. As the plane was taxiing down the runway we could already feel ourselves going under. All of a sudden the damn plane turns round and starts taxiing back in. There had been some hydraulic failure. We were so far gone that we had to be carried off. There we were lyin' in the lounge with all these people lookin' at us. It was unbelievable.'

This false start proved an ominous portent. Whatever hopes Scott and John had of sorting out their differences faded on the tour Down Under, which only served to illustrate how far they had drifted apart. The two men simply had nothing in common. John, possibly as a result of his privileged upbringing, was deeply materialistic while Scott, who once described money as 'this monster that offends me' clearly was not. 'Me, I like having money so that I can spend it,' said John matter-of-factly.

While Maus flaunted his expensive sports cars and talked endlessly about his large house, two alsatians and attractive wife, Engel preferred to browse through an art gallery and discuss the music of jazz musician Roland Kirk. If John, in his fur coats, brown shades and cuban heels was the archetypal rock-'n'-roll animal, Scott, with his more down-at-heel look and self-effacing image, resembled a jazzman.

Music had been their common bond, yet the 'Solo Scott, Solo John' EP and forthcoming 'Images' album demonstrated growing incompatibility. For a couple of months Scott had been darkly hinting that 'outside forces' had been endeavouring to split the group – no doubt a reference to King and Clayman, whose own once sound partnership was now looking decidedly rocky. On the world tour these undercurrents of unrest manifested themselves in the dressing-room as well as on stage.

To all intents and purposes, however, it was business as usual as pandemonium reigned. When the tour, which also featured Roy Orbison and The Yardbirds, opened at Sydney Stadium, seventeen teenage girls were taken to hospital after collapsing in 90 degree heat. Surrounded by scenes of mass adulation, The Walkers ploughed on through New Zealand and on to Japan before returning to California to spend a few days with friends and relations. Scott, who took the opportunity to see Buddy Rich and Art Blakey in a Hollywood club, told his mother that the group was probably finished.

Such was the pace of change in the 1960s that the British pop scene The Walkers returned to that February bore little resemblance to the one they had left.

Scott Walker

The Monkees dominated the pop pages and Micky Dolenz caused a furore by candidly admitting that the group did not play on their hit records. Moreover, psychedelia was all the rage and the pop papers were littered with references to LSD, freakouts and acid trips. Against this multi-coloured backdrop, The Walkers and their over-wrought ballads suddenly appeared ridiculously archaic. The Jimi Hendrix Experience, who had just had a big hit with 'Hey Joe', joined Cat Stevens and Engelbert Humperdinck on what proved to be The Walkers' farewell tour.

While Scott applied the finishing touches to 'Images' at the Philips studio, King and Clayman fiercely denied rumours of an impending split, and plans for a summer tour of Japan followed by a week's cabaret in Las Vegas and another visit to Australia, New Zealand and the Far East suggest that they still harboured hopes of a reconciliation between Scott and John. The former, who was said to be planning a solo trip to Moscow to study the music of Shostakovich and Borodin, raised a few eyebrows when he turned up late for the première of *The Bible*, John Huston's sprawling Old Testament spectacular, at Leicester Square, walked up an aisle and enquired loudly: 'Has God been on yet?' He was asked to leave.

The Walkers had one shot left in their cannon. 'Images' virtually emulated the success of its two predecessors, yet the presence of three Scott Engel tracks and two from John Maus convey its somewhat fractured nature.

'Everything Under The Sun', on which the Engel and Maus voices complement each other perfectly, was co-written by Bob Crewe, and Michel Legrand's 'Once Upon A Summertime' ('my favourite number of all time,' said Scott) is followed by Engel's quite extraordinary 'Experience', a beery, Germanic romper which reveals a deliciously subtle humour and conjures up images of stout, rosy-cheeked bürger-meisters dancing on wooden tables.

This song, possibly a 'Tales Of Hoffmann' pastiche, is, perhaps, the first real example of Scott's classical influence. By 1967 he was heavily into Mozart and would subsequently discover Bach, Beethoven, Brahms, and Viennese atonalists like Schoenberg. John's lazy rendition of 'Blueberry Hill' reflected his continuing preoccupation with blues and soul, while Scott's brooding 'Orpheus', with its jagged, sexually explicit lyrics, would lead to absurd charges of misogyny in later years.

'Deadlier Than The Male' cannot seriously be held as evidence for the prosecution, being the theme for a film of the same name. *Hot Press* writer Joe Jackson, however, has observed that in 'The Amorous Humphrey Plugg', one of Scott's most memorable compositions on his second solo album, the song's female characters are reduced to little more than stereotyped receptacles for male lust. Yet a song like 'The Bridge', which appears on the same record, demonstrates that Engel's insight into the female psyche could be unusually sublime. Jackson could have quoted several other examples to demonstrate Engel's affinity with the opposite sex, most notably 'Rosemary' from 'Scott 3'.

The feuding Walkers' frontmen unite to close Side One with one of the all-time great versions of Ben E. King's 'Stand By Me', delivered with a blistering passion and intensity that perhaps only Scott and John could muster. 'I Wanna Know', the latter's first song on the album, is a pleasing footstomper, while Scott again takes lead on Legrand's 'I Will Wait For You' (the theme from *Les Parapluies de Cherbourg*) which could have come straight off his 1969 album 'Scott Sings Songs From His TV Series'. John's dreamy 'I Can't Let It Happen To You', which he composed on a tape recorder while sharing a hotel room with Gary, displays a sensitivity first revealed on 'Saddest Night In The World'.

But the highlight of the 'Images' album is undoubtedly Scott's 'Genevieve'. Even John, by now heartily sick of what he regarded as Scott's pretentious posturings, conceded that it was the best thing on the album. Scott said the song was about a mixed-up girl he knew and her 'pretty strange' ideas about love. 'I always write from experience,' he declared. 'It's the only way an artist can get any sincerity into his work.'

'Genevieve' can be seen as a statement of intent, Scott's first real attempt to achieve the Schubertian ideal of marrying words, orchestration and melody into perfect harmony. As if to provide further proof of Engel's chameleon nature, Tony Hatch's decidedly middle-of-the-road 'Just Say Goodbye' closes the album.

The enthusiastic reviews that greeted the album's release were overshadowed by the revelation that The Walkers' forthcoming British tour would be their last. Despite refusing to rule out the possibility of further cabaret dates and foreign tours, Scott conceded that the dwindling success of the group's singles meant that people had tired of the sound. 'The Walker Brothers are the hardest group in the world to record because we have such high standards,' he said. 'I'm proud of the sound we get because it's my baby, but the average person doesn't realise it is subtly different ever time.'

Engel's terminal boredom with his pop star role was thinly disguised in a spoof interview conducted by Jonathan King for *Disc & Music Echo*, in which the two men come across as pop's answer to Abbott and Costello.

> Engel: 'Why don't you ask me how my highly successful Australian trip went? Every other moron does.'
> King: 'Thanks. How did your Australian trip go?'
> Engel: 'Don't ask me. Ask me about the new LP.'
> King: 'I think it's great, fantastic, marvellous.'
> Engel: 'I knew you'd say that. Here's your money.'
> King: 'Seriously, what were your basic intentions when you recorded it?'
> Engel: '. . . We are trying to bring to the attention of the public some of the songs of the most talented composers around the world today.'
> King: 'Like Scott Engel, for instance?'
> Engel: 'No – really, I think it's about time a pop group started exploiting the wonderful music of Michel Legrand and some of the great Italian writers.'
> King: '. . . Lyrically, a lot of your own songs are highly surrealistic – is this a conscious pattern in your mind?'
> Engel: 'Yes, I'm warped.'
> King: 'Now specifically tell me about the idea behind "Experience".'
> Engel: 'It's my theory that the biggest problem in society today has to be with parents giving their children advice on things they know nothing about, as they've never experienced them themselves anywhere past their TV screens. This has a tendency to make their kids grow up to be as shallow individuals as they are, with a complete misconception of what's going on outside and around them.'
> King: 'Thank you Sigmund Freud.'

If Scott's professional life was in turmoil, any chance he had of relaxing in the privacy of his terraced house in Regent's Park had diminished. Wearied by the constant attentions of fans who forced him to wash his Marcos sports car at the unearthly hour of 2 a.m., Gary Leeds had sought refuge with Scott.

Unfortunately, Gary brought all his fans with him, along with his telescopes, Otis Redding records and endless coughs and colds. Scott awoke one morning to find fifty or sixty girls screaming through his letter-box and Bunny girls from the Playboy Club scampering all over the house, but this was nothing compared to the infernal noise of Gary's sitar. Inspired by his heroes, The Beatles, Gary wasted no time in endeavouring to master this intricate Indian instrument, and the wailing refrain that emanated from his bedroom drove Scott to lock himself in the bathroom. For all his diligent efforts, Gary's sitar made a noise reminiscent of a cat sliding down a blackboard.

The Walkers' farewell tour opened at the Finsbury Park Astoria amid a welter of rumours that the group was leaving Capable Management. John, accompanied by Clayman, had flown to New York ostensibly to discuss the possibility of a summer tour, but more likely to assess what success he might achieve there as a solo artist.

Back in London, much comment was aroused by Arthur Howes' decision to include The Jimi Hendrix Experience on the same tour as The Walkers and Engelbert Humperdinck. Hendrix, of course, with his manic guitar-playing, outrageous attire and druggy image, epitomised a new breed of rock star. Overnight, The Walkers had become as outdated as Fred Astaire and Ginger Rogers. These two worlds were destined to collide head-on with a shock of epic proportions at Finsbury Park Astoria on 31 March 1967.

While the audience screamed for Scott, John and Gary, nerves were being stretched backstage. Engelbert Humperdinck worriedly chewed cigars and ate eggs and beans in a transport café opposite the theatre until moments before the curtain went up. Hendrix and the Experience frantically washed their hair and searched for lost drumsticks. Scott sipped at a beaker of Coke and wandered rather absently around, talking excitedly about Buddy Rich to anyone who would listen.

Inside the Experience's dressing-room, Hendrix and his manager Chas Chandler listened gloomily to the chants for The Walker Brothers and wondered how on earth they could upstage the teen idols. Just then, Keith Altham, who had just finished interviewing Hendrix for *NME*, had a flash of inspiration.

'Jimi was already becoming famous as the man who played the guitar with his teeth so I suggested he go one step further and actually set fire to the thing. Chas said: "Great idea!" and Jimi started really getting into it. "Yeah, man," he kept saying. "Let's do it, let's do it." '

So, at the climax of the Experience's act, which had been greeted by the young Walker fans with a mixture of incredulity and amazement, Hendrix poured fuel from his cigarette lighter over the guitar and ignited it with a match. Even the guitarist seemed startled by the sudden ferocity of the ensuing inferno. Flames leaping up to ten feet forced the group to flee the stage, Hendrix nursing a badly burnt hand.

The guitar was left burning dangerously near the closed curtains and compère Nick Jones, who ran forward in a brave but misguided attempt to pick it up, also suffered burns to his hands. Order was only restored when an attendant rushed on and doused the flames with a fire extinguisher.

The publicity gleaned from one of those 'seminal moments in rock' was extraordinary. The Experience, who leapt back into the Top 30 with 'Purple Haze', were warned to 'clean-up' their act by tour organisers who felt it was too suggestive. 'The bosses are giving us hell,' chuckled Hendrix. 'They say we are obscene and vulgar. We refuse to change our act and the result is that my amplifier sometimes gets cut off at the funniest times . . .'

The shockwaves from Finsbury Park Astoria were enormous. Hendrix dominated the headlines to such an extent that it was difficult to believe The Walkers were on the same tour, let alone the headline act. Their farewell tour had been effectively hijacked and Scott was left uncomfortably aware that The Walkers epitomised an era in pop which was now passé.

The group's headlining performance on the *London Palladium* television show a couple of days later was the final straw. 'It's a nasty feeling watching a show like that,' said Scott disgustedly. 'I was so embarrassed . . . so full of shame for myself and the rest of the group.' Then, a few nights later, Scott, who had been celebrating the birth of Tony Gilbert's baby daughter rather too fervently, only appeared on stage when John and Gary were midway through the third number.

Scott's tardiness offended John's innate sense of professionalism and he refused to speak to the singer for the remainder of the tour. 'The final instalment came,' recounted Scott, 'when I started off late for a gig . . . we finished the act, but after that John wouldn't speak to me. This went on for a while until I started to wonder about being in a group with a guy who wasn't even speaking to me.'

A strained atmosphere hung over the rest of the tour. Scott, who would sometimes disappear for hours before a show, would occasionally be found in the lighting room just seconds before he was due on stage. This vanishing act played on John's nerves. He rarely saw Scott in the dressing-room; often his first glimpse of him would be when the singer suddenly leapt out on stage into the spotlight. After that one incident, he never missed his cue, but John fretted over the possibility that on another night Scott would again not make it. Gary strove in vain to improve relations.

'I found myself acting as a mediator between the two sides. John, I guess, fell for the oldest trick in the book – he started to believe his own publicity. He would get real upset and start throwing bottles around the dressing-room. He was probably thinkin' about the financial angle. Why split somethin' three ways when you can have it one way? One night Scott asked me if we were gonna break up. He said: "It's not workin' between the two of us is it?" We were in the dressing-room when the management announced the split. Maurice said Scott was stayin' with him and John was goin' off with Barry and what was I gonna do? I eventually got my band The Rain together and we had Maurice as our manager.'

The Walkers staged their last stand on 30 April at the Tooting Granada where the ubiquitous Altham found the backstage atmosphere suitably frosty. Even the presence of the visiting Shirley Bassey did little to break the ice. John sat glowering in a corner as Gary gamely attempted to keep the conversation going.

Scott, sitting in the opposite corner with his back to everyone, scrutinised his reflection in the mirror and slowly and deliberately clawed his face with his hands. He then started hugging himself as if he was cold and was distinctly heard to mutter: 'It's over . . . thank God, it's over.' As far as Scott was concerned, the three-headed Walkers monster had been slain. 'I've known Scott for four years and now I can't even talk to him,' said John plaintively.

'You see, when you're in a group you have to take other people's advice,' Scott later told *Melody Maker*'s Nick Jones. 'You have to listen to them and adopt what they say in a group policy. But that's the last time I ever listen to anyone! I want to be free. I know everyone thinks that Scott Walker's a difficult person to work with and only works when he wants. Well, that's right! I'm not singin' until I'm ready.'

Some silver-tongued photographer who wormed his way into the dressing-room that night was rewarded with a series of unintentionally comic snapshots which could have come straight out of the rock documentary spoof *Spinal Tap*. Scott and John sit side by side, steadfastly ignoring each other like two truculent infants as they glare stonily into the lens. A grinning Gary, his unbuttoned shirt revealing a scrawny torso, poses self-mockingly behind. In another shot Scott is rolling his eyes and pulling a face, clearly annoyed by the photographer's entreaty of 'just one more'. Rarely has the actual break-up of a pop group been so vividly portrayed.

'Scott and I both have strong personalities and Gary used to be in the middle,' John told the *Sunday People* in 1992. 'We split because Scott and I disagreed on what we should do. I recognise now that it was not the right thing to do. Who knows what we could have achieved if we had stuck it out together?'

Like so many of the great groups of the sixties, The Walker Brothers disintegrated amid a flurry of lawsuits and recriminations. Gary wearily recounts how the legal battle took eight or nine years to resolve – ironically by which time The Walkers were ready to reunite.

'Everyone was suin' everyone. When it was all settled we ended up paying a lot of taxes. It was the old story, I guess. You'd go round to see someone and found they were outta the country. Then you'd find out that you were on a far lower royalty rate than you thought. I wish we had stayed together. Scott hated bein' on his own and the alcohol was John's downfall. He seemed to have a lot of internal conflict with his family and ended up divorcing Kathy. John always had this thing about gettin' a big house in the country, whereas Scott wouldn't have cared if he had lived in a tent. The split worked out badly for all of us.'

Initially it was John who fared worst. Angered by his barbed comments at Scott and earlier avowed intention of going solo, hundreds of fans decided that Maus was responsible for the break-up and indicated their displeasure by marching from Baker Street tube station to Clayman's Maida Vale flat where John had sought refuge. Some reports stated that his car was vandalised.

John, for his part, privately blamed the split on Mette Teglbjaerg, Scott's new Danish girlfriend, who was by now his constant companion and would eventually become his wife. Shortly after the split, John was enraged to discover that one of his royalty cheques had been inadvertently sent to the Engel residence in Regent's Park. When he stormed around to confront Scott, Mette refused to let him in.

It was not until Mette briefly returned to Copenhagen that John was able to speak to Scott and recover his cheque. The two men patched up their differences over a drink, although the circumstances of the split left underlying traces of bitterness which lingered for several years. It was a sad and unseemly end to a group whose undoubted class had earned them millions of fans across the world.

The Walker Brothers, American interlopers on the dynamic British pop scene of the mid-sixties, were unique in more ways than one. Apart from coming across as hip Californian beatniks, their overall sound and image was both refreshing and innovative to the youthful British pop audience of the mid-sixties. Unfortunately, the Engel/Franz Wall of Sound, which provided a degree of sophistication to the records that even attracted mums and dads, ultimately led the group down a blind alley. While The Walkers appeared archaic to the dedicated followers of 1967 fashion, they were clearly too young and long-haired to attract the older Tom Jones/Engelbert Humperdinck audience. Thus their fate was sealed.

Even so, that trilogy of sixties albums is a fitting monument to what was indisputably one of the great groups of the era, whose work was occasionally blighted by ill-chosen covers. No 'All Time Great Singles' list would be complete without 'The Sun Ain't Gonna Shine Anymore' and 'Make It Easy On Yourself', and sandwiched between the death of Merseybeat and the birth of psychedelia is a period that will forever belong to The Walker Brothers.

10 Stand By Me

'I guess I am scared. I wanna get the right message across right now, without fallin' into black or white, like Sinatra or pop. That is very important to me, to establish myself as myself.'

Scott Walker, 1967

IN THE END, The Walker Brothers, a group which had swept all before them, went out with a whimper. Their final posthumous release, a flaccid version of the Phil Spector classic 'Walking In The Rain', came out on 13 May, backed by the appropriately-entitled Engel–Duncan song 'Baby Make It The Last Time'. *Melody Maker*'s caustic review of 'Walking In The Rain' indicated that the group had passed its sell-by date. 'Needless to say, The Walkers' version does little for the original except for sounding like typical Walkers records ... nothing about the record strikes one as at all adventurous or particularly imaginative. It will be a joy to hear The Walkers doing exactly what they want without quite so much melodramatic nonsense.'

The previous few days had seen Pink Floyd play at the Technicolour Dream all-night rave at north London's Alexandra Palace and the release of 'Sgt Pepper's Lonely Hearts Club Band'. The Walkers were clearly hopelessly outdated. Around this time, Scott produced a record by a new singing discovery, Nicky James, 'I Need To Be Needed' – a heartfelt plea that was ignored by the record-buying public.

While Scott found the prospect of a solo career daunting, he initially experienced a great sense of liberation and talked enthusiastically about his prospective début album, which was partly written at his girlfriend's Copenhagen flat that summer. 'It's uncommercial and difficult to understand but it's the feeler,' he explained. 'I'm writing my own, odd abstract stuff – I don't want the Tom Jones scene. I'll be skint if this LP doesn't work – but I won't switch to the old commercial scene. Never. I want to be first-class all the way too.'

John was also warming to the challenge of going solo, declaring that it would be like starting all over again, and Gary said he was recording material with Graham Nash, but first the pair of them were off to Morocco on holiday.

Compared with most skirt-chasing 1960s pop stars, Scott's love life appears to have been relatively straightforward. As Irene Dunford gradually faded from the scene (she would remain a friend until Scott left London in 1969), Mette became the most important woman in his life, but in the early days of their relationship Scott was by no means monogamous. 'Marriage itself is not for me, for I really don't believe I could be faithful to one girl,' he said.

Scott's love affairs tended to burn with a bright, fierce intensity, then quickly fade. He would perhaps live with a girl for two or three months before moving on. For a while, he moved into the flat of a German girl, whose knowledge of French enabled her to translate some of Jacques Brel's lyrics for him, and he was also seen in the company of a beautiful Czechoslovakian.

However, Scott's aesthetic appearance created a faintly androgynous image which still persists. Several of his fellow pop stars and quite a few writers assumed he was bisexual – or AC/DC as it was known then – simply because of his delicate appearance and the 'arty' and bohemian types he attracted. People would occasionally make snide insinuations about Scott and John, and when the former was apparently beaten up in Regent's Park one night, rumours spread that he was the victim of a gang of 'queer-bashers'. Barrie Martin remembers that Françoise Hardy, the French singer, was Scott's ideal woman. Like a lovestruck schoolboy, he had her picture on the wall of his latest flat and one night dragged Martin down to a club to see her.

'Another time, Scott and I were at Ronnie Scott's to see Joe Pass, the American jazz guitarist, and this guy who turned out to be George Shearing. I met someone I knew and they came up for a chat and I suddenly received these terrible vibes from Scott. He got really agitated as if to say: "You're with me and how dare you talk to somebody else?" He was very strange that night and when I heard rumours that he was AC/DC I wondered whether he had wanted more from me than just a platonic friendship.'

These rumours were fuelled by the fact that a member of The Walkers' camp, who lived with Scott for a time, was openly homosexual. Unlike some of his pop contemporaries, Scott was sympathetic towards the homosexual community and showed little inclination to dispel the rumours. Brian Sommerville suspects he may even have enjoyed the speculation.

'I can rule out the suggestion that Scott was gay. There was no chance of any relationship there. It used to amuse Scott because he knew what people said. He saw the perverse sense of humour side of it and was happy to play along with it.'

Jonathan King attributes the nudges and winks The Walkers attracted to the length of their hair. 'That whole androgynous look started in the mid-sixties but I don't think it was considered that important especially as we were all out pulling birds at the time. Everyone used to camp it up outrageously and it was great fun. The beauty of those days was that you could get up to all manner of things without any risks, although Scott never got into drugs and neither did I. As for sexual preferences, I'm sure he was completely hetero and has remained so.'

However, Scott's familiarity with the work of Jean Genet, the maverick French playwright and novelist, suggests a keen interest in gay culture long before the subject became fashionable. The reason Scott found Genet – a barely-educated orphan, petty thief, sometime male whore and irredeemable vagabond – so compelling probably had less to do with the Frenchman's sexuality and more with his resolutely two-fingered stance against a world which ultimately destroyed his ability to write by reducing him to the level of society's pet. Sartre excitedly hailed Genet as living proof of the existential hero – in other words, he chose to be a thief, he chose to be homosexual and he chose to be penniless and adrift.

When Edmund White, in his definitive 1993 biography of Genet, chronicles the writer's terrible sense of disenfranchisement, his tendency to teeter on the edge of life and his wish to sink, unseen, into the anonymous crowd, he could almost be writing about Scott. Genet, who fought hard to retain the freedom to observe from the outside, described himself as 'a fragment broken off from the rest of the world'. But for the French existentialists, freedom was something more precious than this. It meant the ability to select one's character and definition by the sum of one's acts, it meant being creative, regenerative and inventive – a philosophy with which Engel readily identified.

Electing to strike while The Walker Brothers' iron was still hot, John wasted no time in laying the foundations for his new career. He quickly recorded his first single, a Nicky James-Graham Nash composition entitled 'Annabella', and signed Columbia recording duo Sue and Sunny as his vocal backing. His solo début at Paris's Palais des Sports on 1 June was well received, and his first British concert at Torquay's Princess Theatre was followed by a handful of dates at other seaside resorts. There were also reports that John had been asked to write four songs by Italian producer Franco Zeffirelli – who had directed *The Taming Of The Shrew* – for his new film *Romeo and Juliet*.

Scott and John had both signed five-year contracts with Philips but, for a couple of months at least, the latter must have seemed potentially the best investment. 'Annabella', a sad song which sounded remarkably like 'Sunny' for several bars, was actually an insipid effort which only rose as high as No. 24, yet John was never able to improve on its modest showing. One of his own compositions would surely have fared better.

After a couple of months' silence, Scott slowly stirred. Announcing his intention to sing 'honest songs in a primitive way' he opted to launch his solo career on 6 August with a week's cabaret at Stockton's Fiesta Club, backed by a nine-piece band formed by Ronnie Scott. Engel, who called the Stockton engagement 'a warm-up', would also play Great Yarmouth and Blackpool.

Midway through rehearsals came one of those mysterious incidents that were forever punctuating Scott's accident-prone existence. The singer was taken to the St John and St Elizabeth Hospital after being found in a dazed condition near his Regent's Park home at 5 a.m. one morning.

Police said Engel had fallen, hit his head and cut his hands. Some reports stated that they were seeking his attackers (hence those 'queer-bashing' rumours), but the episode appears to have arisen from Scott's chronic insomnia, an obvious by-product of the continuing stress of being in the public eye. Scott, in an effort to tire himself out, would often embark on nocturnal rambles which, he complained, made him feel like Jack the Ripper.

On this particular night, he had taken five sleeping pills and some drink, but still could not sleep. Wandering out into the silent park he was suddenly overcome by dizziness and found lying on the path by a patrolling policeman. 'I never relax until I sleep,' Scott admitted. 'But I don't like to sleep because I feel as though I may be caught off-guard . . . I take lots of sleeping pills and drink a lot to relax and unwind. I have many faults, but I'm a human being.' These are poignant words which betray the deep-rooted fears and dark paranoia from which Scott could never escape.

Yet while the youth of London espoused drugs, free love and

psychedelia as they blindly answered the Summer of Love's clarion call, Scott boldly blazed a trail in another direction. The previous November, Jacques Brel, the 37-year-old Belgian troubadour, played a highly-acclaimed set at the Royal Albert Hall. The show was a sell-out and Scott, who was away touring at the time, bitterly regretted his inability to attend.

Engel was already immersed in European literature, music, cinema and art – indeed, it had been one of his prime motivations for leaving America – so the effect of Brel and his songs of fierce anger, black romanticism and world weariness was electrifying. 'It was one of the happiest days of my life,' said Scott, 'when a girlfriend gave me the first English translation I'd seen of Brel's lyrics.' He instinctively identified with Brel's cynicism and 'his rarely offering solutions yet stating the confusion so beautifully'.

Phil McNeill, in an *NME* article of January 1977, described the devastating effect of Engel's discovery: 'Nobody, not even Bob Dylan, or Jim Morrison or Lou Reed . . . has ever made more nihilistic, grandiose, debauched, schizophrenic, souls-in-torment, night-riding, heart-rending music than "My Death", "Amsterdam", "Jacky", "Next", "Mathilde" and Scott's own Brel-influenced tales of paranoia and loneliness.' What Scott did, in effect, was take Brel's work as a starting point and absorb the Belgian's influence into his own material which gradually expanded on each of his first four solo albums.

Brel, who was born in Brussels on 8 April 1929, remains both a figurehead and *éminence grise* of modern songwriting, despite a reluctance to either sing in English or, owing to his bitter opposition to the Vietnam War, perform in North America – or anywhere else after retiring from concert appearances in 1966. Though Flemish, he thought and conversed in French. After studying commercial law, he married and endured several years of interminable boredom in the family cardboard merchandising business until, nauseated by bourgeois convention, he made a new start in Paris as a singing composer.

Buck-toothed and lanky, Brel's acute lack of obvious mass appeal was thrust aside by impresario Jacques Canetti who presented him regularly at Pigalle's Théâtre Des Trois Baudets, where he was accompanied by his own chord-slashing on guitar and a small backing combo.

An instinctive sense of dramatic construction resulted in passionate performances that captivated an audience which grew considerably following 'Quand On n'a que L'Amour', his first record success.

Other domestic hits such as 'Le Valse De Mille Temps', 'Les Bourgeois', 'Les Dames Patronesses' and 'Les Flamands' gave vent to social comment via a wryly watchful, literate lyricism that remained intrinsically Gallic until CBS recording manager Nat Shapiro persuaded his superiors to release 'American Début' in 1957, which gave Brel a substantial English-speaking following. He was to stamp an indelible mark on the output of such diverse wordsmiths as Mort Shuman (a lifelong disciple whose collaboration on the hit play *Jacques Brel Is Alive And Well And Living In Paris* popularised his work in Britain and the United States), The Kinks' Ray Davies, Leonard Cohen, and David Bowie. It was Scott, however, who would become the foremost interpreter of Brel's work with the composer's full backing.

Brel's rejection of his comfortable, middle-class upbringing and subsequent bohemian lifestyle is uncannily reminiscent of Engel's, and the Belgian later revealed his own reclusive tendencies by withdrawing to the same Polynesian island as Gauguin. Brel eventually died of cancer in October 1978, a passing marked by a million-selling compilation LP and a posthumous burgeoning of his popularity.

In 1967, Brel instructed Shuman, the giant New York lyricist who translated his songs into English, to place all his work at Engel's disposal, which an awed Scott described as 'like taking a Picasso and changing it around a bit'. Despite speaking different languages, Brel and Engel would presumably have had much in common, so it is surprising that they never met. 'I don't know why, but I just don't wanna be disillusioned,' explained Scott. 'I think of him as being a certain type of person and I want to keep all the illusions I have of him.' Reports that the pair met up in Paris shortly before Christmas 1968, when Scott is supposed to have invited Brel to appear on his forthcoming television series, are without foundation.

On Saturday evening, 6 August, Scott, wearing a black mohair suit, with his hair brushed high, stepped nervously on-stage at Stockton's Fiesta Club to warm applause laced with a few girlish screams. Engel, acutely conscious that he was attempting to gain a whole new audience while retaining his young fans, immediately launched into a tearaway version of 'Gonna Travel On' to the accompaniment of Ronnie Scott's band.

Scott's customary stage-fright was obvious on the first couple of numbers, but as his confidence grew the shakiness diminished and he went on to convey sadness, sensitivity and occasional bursts of strength. Ronnie Scott's band sometimes overpowered the vocals, but for the most part they played sympathetically, and the renowned Engel diction was impeccable.

Scott's set showcased some of the Brel songs he was to include on his début solo album and some of the more aesthetic and poetically frank lyrics inevitably raised a few eyebrows. Apart from regular bursts of polite clapping, the Stockton audience listened in silence, yet at the end they rose as one to applaud and cheer the self-effacing figure who stood smiling shyly in the spotlight.

It was a triumphant moment tinged with emotion. Scott had produced an excellent performance laced with controversial new material and seemingly conquered his paralysing fear of going solo. 'He'll be another Billy Daniels, that kid,' a blunt Northern voice was heard to comment from behind a cloud of cigar smoke. Stockton's Tito's club audience had taken Scott to their hearts during his cabaret performances with The Walker Brothers. Once again he had not let Stockton down. 'The band is the best you'll ever hear,' Scott enthused to a journalist backstage. 'Ignore me – just listen to the band!'

The future seemed pregnant with possibilities, yet Scott simply could not stomach some aspects of the chicken-in-a-basket circuit. He flatly refused to sign autographs and make small-talk with queueing punters after his performances, arguing that he was paid simply to be a singer and entertainer. 'I will not have my privacy infringed upon!' he petulantly told Maurice King, who by now realised the futility of arguing.

For all the manager's bluster, some outsiders felt that Scott could wrap King around his little finger, which perhaps explains his decision to stick with 'Boris the Monster', as opposed to the more laidback Clayman. Not so, says Mary Arnold.

'Scott really needed a firm hand which is why he gravitated towards Maurice as opposed to Clayman. He was very demanding and wanted Maurice around him all the time. Maurice was a great frontman but not so good at organising. He'd often forget to book backing musicians for rehearsals which was one of the reasons why Scott, being such a perfectionist, ducked out of various concerts.'

The album that appeared in September had, as one latter-day

reviewer observed, definitely been conceived in a non-swinging part of London. Simply entitled 'Scott', the record's cover, depicting an anguished-looking figure wearing shades and scarf, his head bowed in deep contemplation, remains the definitive Scott Walker image – the quintessential tortured artist. The back cover has Scott in his lonely garret, pouting furiously as a mysterious girl hovers in the background. Keith Altham's sleeve-notes hailed Scott's gift of communication and the intensity with which he interpreted Brel's songs as approaching musical genius. A valid comment, perhaps, but the inclusion of a Keats quotation added to Scott's reputation for pretentiousness.

Many of the pop stars and writers who heaped praises on Engel in public were not quite so effusive in private, and his constant intellectual and classical references caused the same type of irritation in the late sixties as Sting's pontifications on all manner of good causes do today. Many fans, eking out a living in humdrum nine-to-five jobs, began to question why the man who seemingly had it all was so permanently bloody miserable. Stardom of this magnitude should surely be a fount of ceaseless happiness.

More surprisingly, the golden Engel baritone – or, more specifically, its occasional vibrato – was unfavourably compared with the more passionate delivery of Tom Jones. Freddie Winrose recalls that this sporadic tremor in Scott's singing voice was one of the reasons why Johnny Franz had dispatched the singer to Denmark Street.

'I probably worked with Scott for about eighteen months during the sixties but we never could quite get rid of that vibrato. Just when I thought we had it licked he'd disappear for a couple of months which was very frustrating. Johnny used to send him to me on the day he was due to lay down some vocal tracks. I would take him through my specially designed exercises and he would go off to record in the studio that evening.'

Nothing irritated Scott more than comparisons with Tom Jones, a singer whose histrionic style bore no similarity to his own more subtle approach. 'Every time I hear Tom Jones I want to jump out of a window,' he said acidly. 'I'd sooner hear somebody who doesn't claim to be a great singer, like Mick Jagger. I hear Tom Jones destroying a song, and yet he and I are always being compared as singers.'

By confining Scott to the same shelf as Tom Jones or Engelbert Humperdinck, the press revealed its own difficulty in categorising him. That all three singers differ appreciably in terms of range, delivery and material must be evident to anyone with even a cursory interest in pop music.

What principally set Scott apart from the others, of course, was his unique style of songwriting, which by now was becoming his *raison d'être*. In retrospect, his increasingly avant-garde approach to writing at this time indicates he was marching to a different drum than the rest of the sixties' pop culture, hence the often unconvincing and misleading attempts to pigeonhole him.

Flower Power and so-called mind-expanding drugs were two more of Engel's pet hates. 'I want to put over my own way of communicating aside from the psychedelic thing, because I don't believe those people convey real emotion,' said Scott.

'This album is to make people walk away crying. I'm writin' songs and I want to get more experience of life to put into them ... I can only write about the people and things that I know.' 'Montague Terrace (In Blue)', one of Walker's most impressive tracks which bestrides this first album like a colossus, is a prime example of his intimate writing technique.

The song is about a young couple Scott knew, who lived in a small rented apartment in London. 'They're very stimulating. They think along my lines,' said Scott. 'I love them very much. Well, as much as I could ever love anyone, that is.' The identity of this mysterious couple is unknown but, along with Jonathan King, they were Engel's closest friends at this time.

'Now it doesn't matter too much to them that the man upstairs is always making a noise and that the woman across the hall has a dubious profession,' said Scott. 'They are in love and that's all that matters – sometimes I go round to see them when I'm really down and just being there makes me feel better. Anyway, in spite of their surrounds they are always planning their dream house – a blue mews cottage in Montague Terrace.'

The song, with its lilting melody encased in Wally Stott's rich string arrangement, is a classic from beginning to end as Scott pads stealthily around a house awash with seething passions.

This time, Scott supplemented the genius of Reg Guest on the production side with the talents of fellow arrangement experts Wally Stott and Peter Knight, both of whom were classically trained and had worked for many years on BBC television and radio. This formidable trio placed Scott's vocals in lavish settings while his vivid interpretations of 'Mathilde', a thundering Stott arrangement topped by a quite astonishing display of vocal dynamics which bring Brel's *femme fatale* to life, the doomy 'My Death' and debauched 'Amsterdam', heralded the beginning of his Brel obsession and pitched the singer into a twilight world of drugs, whores and bums.

The hated straitjacket of commercialism was contemptuously tossed aside as Scott started creating the music he had always wanted to make. 'The people following me don't want sugar-coated rubbish,' he declared. 'A song such as Brel's "My Death" is an important song, a strangely aching song, and people come away itchy after hearing it.'

Traces of Scott's own country and western leanings can be detected on Tim Hardin's 'The Lady Came From Baltimore'. Engel's own 'Such A Small Love' demonstrates his growing confidence as a songwriter and 'Always Coming Back To You' memorably expands the 'First Love Never Dies' theme. 'Such A Small Love', a song notable for its macabre-sounding organ and oppressive atmosphere, is about a young man attending the funeral of his best friend and at the graveside he notices a girl who spent the previous evening with his friend. ('How you would have laughed if you could see us here . . .')

'She is crying, but he knows that the girl cannot really have known his friend's worth over the years,' explained Scott. 'Hence, "Such A Small Love" – such a small tear.' 'Scott', a potent mix of love, sex and solitude, is only slightly diluted by the presence of middle-of-the-road covers like 'When Joanna Loved Me' and André Previn's 'You're Gonna Hear From Me'.

Melody Maker, remarking on the aura of melancholy, 'a deliberate installation of sadness and a distillation of madness', felt the record made a completely unique contribution to British music. 'This is a triumph for Scott . . . and proves the rightness of his action in seeking after musical truth.' Helped by similarly glowing reviews, the album rose to No. 3, spending a total of seventeen weeks in the charts.

Its success was also a financial blessing for Scott, who always claimed he had emerged from the ashes of The Walker Brothers relatively broke. While Philips had obviously paid for The Walkers' recordings, the 'phenomenal' sums spent on gigantic orchestrations like 'Archangel' exceeded budgets and the balance was apparently met from Scott's own pocket.

'[The money] went because I wanted the group to become as big as The Beatles or The Rolling Stones,' he said. 'But it required us to act as big stars and big stars don't work every night in Britain. Apart from a trip to Japan we didn't work a lot abroad and percentages from recordings were low . . . Then there were bills for suits that got torn every night we played, hotel bills, big drink bills and entertainment bills. We came out with no money.'

Scott's lament was an all-too familiar refrain. Money may not have been his prime motivation, but he now realised that without it he would be unable to produce his kind of records. This re-evaluation explains why he readily accepted a one-off offer to tour Japan with The Walker Brothers at the end of 1967.

Following The Walkers' ill-tempered split, Bobby Hamilton had remained as John's road manager ('It was an easier life, to be honest') but Scott agreed to be best man at his wedding at London's Caxton Hall that September. The event was supposedly secret, yet thanks to Brian Sommerville over 3,000 fans turned up to catch a glimpse of The Walkers.

John, who was away touring, did not attend, but Scott and Gary looked resplendent in their best suits. Scott posed for photographs with the happy couple, but insisted that Gary made the best man's speech.

Fans who expected Scott to embark on an autumn tour were disappointed. Promotion of the album consisted of a handful of cabaret dates with Ronnie Scott's band and occasional television appearances including the *Dusty Springfield Show* on 19 September, when Scott performed 'When Joanna Loved Me' and 'Mathilde', appearing to almost collapse through nerves at the end of the latter. Four days later, Scott turned up on *Dee Time*, the Simon Dee show which was extremely popular. Pressed by Dee, Scott praised the attitude of his young fans, seemingly unaware that these were the very people he was beginning to alienate.

Apart from refusing to tour, Scott also announced that he would not be releasing a single, rather pompously declaring: 'I consider myself to be more of an album artiste.' Today, of course, the album is all-important, but back in 1967, when the singles market was huge, Scott's stance was unorthodox to say the least. *Melody Maker* readers' dissatisfaction spilled over in a series of vitriolic attacks which accused Scott of being 'exclusive' and 'selfish'.

Seemingly unmoved, Scott spent the autumn fulfilling cabaret and recording engagements and on 24 September flew to Moscow on a two-week 'cultural visit' to study Russian music and art. 'As an American, he has been told all the bad things about Russia,' said Brian Sommerville. 'Now he wants to go and find out about the good things.'

The visit was a disappointment. The Cold War was still chilly and Scott, who travelled with an official tour party, was not allowed the freedom to explore Moscow and Leningrad or meet Russian poets Yevtushenko and Voznesensky as planned. Red tape was the official reason this rendezvous did not take place, although Scott, with typical candour, later admitted that he had missed their meeting due to an acute hangover.

Back in London, Scott, under pressure from Philips, bowed to public clamour by agreeing to release a song from his planned second album as a single. Philips' satisfaction was short-lived. 'Jacky', Brel's romping anthem to megalomania, with its references to 'opium dens, authentic queers and phoney virgins', well and truly set the cat among the pop pigeons. Radio 2 listeners denounced 'Jacky' as 'a nasty song' and Simon Dee was not permitted to play the disc on *Midday Spin*.

As public criticism mounted, Scott's pre-taped insert on *Top Of The Pops* was cancelled along with appearances on *Dee Time* and Jonathan King's *Good Evening* show. The record's B-side, Scott's Spanish-sounding 'The Plague', was forgotten in the furore, receiving belated recognition when covered by Marc Almond a couple of decades later.

Scott, who promoted the disc with shows in Paris, Amsterdam and Brussels, anticipated the more hostile reaction in Britain. 'I put out "Jacky" because I felt it was so refined and beautiful, even if it stands a good chance of being banned and crushed,' he said. 'The song is about a man's reflections on his childhood . . . I'm not deliberately going out to shock with "Jacky" . . . I don't want it banned. I want it to be looked at, even though I do not think it will be a big hit.'

The BBC took one look and decided that the lyrics of the song made it suitable only for late-night listening. 'We haven't banned it, we're just not playing it,' said a terse spokesman. As a result, Scott was unable to promote the record at peak viewing times, although it still reached No. 22 in the charts. Maurice King ensured that over 40 teenage girls registered their disapproval of the ban by staging a picket outside Broadcasting House. 'I'm so disillusioned,' sighed the manager, articulating Scott's own feelings.

Although he had predicted both the ban and the disc's subsequent failure to breach the Top Twenty, Engel's first brush with the powerful Establishment left a bitter taste in his mouth. 'What sickens me is that you can show TV documentaries on prostitution or homosexuality and no one makes a murmur,' he told *NME*. 'Frankly, the hypocrisy over the censorship of this single horrifies me.'

One unfortunate side-effect of the controversy was that Philips would start regarding Scott's increasingly non-commercial output with deepening unease. The singer could generally count on the support of Johnny Franz, of course, but elsewhere his lyrics were subjected to nervous scrutiny. 'I can't tell you what a fight it was to make those first records, even though they were charting,' he told Richard Cook in 1984. 'It was like those people at Philips were just waiting to say, no more of this shit!'

Keith Altham asserts that Scott's pursuit of excellence was years ahead of its time: 'All musicians who had something to say were trying to gain more artistic freedom by wresting control from the people who had originally manipulated their successes, but Scott somehow burned with a greater intensity in that area.

'He was prepared to take on unpopular causes at a time when they weren't considered to be commercially in vogue and of course the record companies would listen to this and say: "The general public aren't going to wear this, Scott." He had to struggle against administrations that were always reluctant to make that extra step forward and take on something that was challenging and interesting.

'The fact he was a frontman who didn't have the ruthlessness of a Jagger, or a McCartney or a Rod Stewart also caused him problems. Things would have been a lot easier if he'd been more of a musician and had the creative outlet of playing. Having arrived on the scene as a teenage idol he then had to prove he was a singer/songwriter in disguise and people were less inclined to meet that metamorphosis.'

An embittered Engel pronounced himself weary of the pop scene, complained that he had missed too much in life and told one startled writer of his intention to work in a Copenhagen beer factory where he could meet 'real' people.

With the controversy over 'Jacky' still raging, the offer to tour Japan with John and Gary must have come as a welcome relief. A couple of days before Christmas, Scott again made headlines when he was rushed into the London Clinic with appendicitis after road manager Ralph Gurnett found him unconscious at his Regent's Park home.

When he awoke in the operating theatre, Scott refused to allow doctors to carry out surgery and discharged himself. He was fit enough to perform on the Frankie Howerd Show on 22 December.

Maurice King and Barry Clayman had signed the lucrative contract to tour Japan the previous spring, when the group was still together. Fearing the prospect of adding more litigation to the legal morass caused by The Walkers' messy split, they urged Scott, John and Gary to accept the offer. The Walkers needed little persuasion. Scott regarded the tour as a necessary evil and stated that his earnings would be ploughed into the making of his second album which was already taking shape.

John had suffered a disastrous six months in which his new single 'If I Promise' had flopped (a fate that would also befall his début album, 'If You Go Away'); he collapsed through nervous exhaustion in a *Top Of The Pops* dressing-room, and also managed to write off his Marcos on the Chiswick flyover. On top of this, his fairy-tale marriage to Kathy had run into difficulties and when John appeared on *Dee Time* in November, he met Julie Parker-Cann, the DJ's secretary, who would later become his second wife.

Gary, meanwhile, one of the most accessible pop stars of the preceding two years, had kept such a low profile that one of the pop papers organised a search for him. On being tracked down, Gary said his group The Rain would be releasing a single in the New Year. 'I've been sittin' back, watchin' the scene,' he said. 'I've been tryin' to assess which way the trend has been goin'.'

During the run-up to Christmas, the national press carried photos of a relaxed-looking Scott sitting in a Heathrow departure lounge with Mette, who was catching a flight back to Copenhagen. Scott's eighteen-month-old romance with the girl he had met on a Walker Brothers tour was finally revealed to the world and the singer, so often surly and evasive when questioned about his private life, seemed to have been transformed into a kitten.

'She completely transforms me when we're together,' he purred. 'I'm very self-indulgent and self-centred. It's my biggest fault and I'm only too aware of it. But when I'm with Mette I find myself doing things for her . . . There's a very childlike quality about this girl that changes my outlook and personality.'

Hard-bitten Fleet Street hacks, while not exactly sobbing into their notebooks, were apparently so moved by this tender little scene that the fact Scott had persuaded Mette to return home to face a shoplifting charge was mentioned only in passing. Their attitude actually shows how news values have changed over the last 25 years. In retrospect, Scott was lucky to be around when the press displayed a modicum of discretion.

TV director Barry Cawtheray, who was directing a film documentary of the tour of Japan, related the following in *NME*. One miserable Saturday morning in late December, Gary Leeds sat hunched in the back of Maurice King's vast Pontiac as it swept down a south-west London street. Sniffing dolefully, the drummer pulled a small bottle from his jacket and administered a dose of nose drops to combat the bout of 24-hour flu which gripped him. The car pulled up before a modern apartment block where Scott shared his new home with Gurnett, whose six-foot, eighteen-stone frame proved useful in repulsing any unwanted callers.

Gurnett, who Scott dubbed 'Big Louey', was a genial, unflappable character who had even retained his sense of humour on discovering a girl attempting to enter Engel's flat through the chimney. Aware of Scott's vanity, which was indicated by the fact that he bleached his hair, Gurnett teasingly referred to the singer as 'International Cabaret Star'.

When King marched into the flat that morning, Scott looked an unlikely international cabaret star. He and Mette had enjoyed a riotous, drunken evening in the West End and had not managed to get to bed at all. At around 4 a.m. Scott, still reluctant to call a halt to proceedings, had dragged Mette off in the direction of Covent Garden, where he knew that certain pubs would continue to serve alcohol under a special 'porters' licence. 'But they figured we didn't look like porters so we had to split,' he told his disbelieving manager.

Between them, King, Leeds and Gurnett managed to bundle the rather dishevelled Engel into the Pontiac and set off for Heathrow Airport, where the two Walkers were frisked for drugs. The fact that the customs men were left disappointed is not surprising. Scott, while respecting other people's opinions, was personally against drugs and abandoned his own experiments with marijuana after discovering it gave him a sore throat.

'Flower power, I believe, is a lie,' he once said. 'It would be lovely if it were real, but the human race is so complex, it just could never happen. But for talentless people, full of vice, it's the easy way out, it's not living . . . I don't wanna see my fans walking around like drugged zombies. We must own up and face life.'

John, who had spent Christmas in Los Angeles, was making his own way to Japan, but aboard the plane Scott was reunited with Barry Clayman and Bobby Hamilton and introduced to the six-piece rhythm section of The Walkers' backing group which King had hired. Heavily sedated, Scott slept all the way to Copenhagen where he staggered drowsily into the arrivals lounge, declared the Danish people to be beautiful 'like children' and promptly fell asleep across two chairs, a black stetson pulled over his eyes, totally oblivious to the multi-lingual flight announcements, call chimes and crying babies.

Having changed planes, The Walkers and their entourage flew over the Baltic and Moscow across the Volga to Tashkent, enduring an uncomfortable couple of hours in a freezing airport building, where Scott gallantly attempted to converse with a group of women in their Slavic tongue.

From Tashkent the party flew over the Himalayas and India to Bangkok where they touched down in 89 degree heat. After refuelling, they crossed the Mekong River and toasted the New Year with champagne while flying down the regular civilian air corridor over South Vietnam where a truce was in operation. A brief stop at Hong Kong preceded the final leg to Japan's Osaka Airport, where a frenzied crowd of 2,000 fans waved banners proclaiming 'The Sun's Gonna Shine Again'. The Walkers enjoyed huge popularity in Japan, which still persists. In fact, their ten-day tour generated so much excitement in advance that a Tokyo camera crew flew to Los Angeles to interview Gary's parents.

The appearance of Scott on the aircraft steps, arms raised above his head like a conquering hero, triggered an explosion of flashbulbs and a crescendo of screams. On the way to the hotel Scott and Gary's police-escorted motorcade was overtaken by a car containing a waving John Maus, whose American plane had landed a few minutes later.

Following two concerts at the 2,000-seat Osaka Festival Hall, at which Gary sported a bright saffron jacket, dark red shirt and turquoise trousers, while John opted for a purple frock coat with white lace cuffs and Scott a more conservative black suit, The Walkers moved on to the Tokyo Hilton Hotel and two concerts at the giant Korakuen Stadium in front of 10,000 Coke-drinking popcorn-chewing appreciative young Japanese. The first show, which was televised later that night, featured most of the group's old hits including 'Make It Easy On Yourself' and 'My Ship Is Coming In'. The following night, over twenty fans were injured when a crash barrier collapsed at Nagoya City Auditorium.

Almost unbelievably, Japan belonged to The Walker Brothers, seven months after they had officially broken up. Any country which put Gary's 'Twinkie Lee' in the national Top Ten was clearly Walker-crazy. Much to his surprise and delight, the affable drummer found the Japanese preferred him to Scott and John, and chants of 'Gai-ree' formed a regular backdrop to the shows, recordings of which emerged on a live album on the Bam Caruso label nineteen years later.

The boys were taken on sightseeing tours of Kyoto, the ancient capital, a huge feast at the best Geisha house in the country was laid on in their honour and they even recorded a television commercial for chocolate, after Scott had taken charge of the sound session, worked out harmonies on a piano and even checked the pronunciation of certain Japanese words.

The final day of the tour, 9 January, was Scott's 25th birthday and the Tokyo Hilton was inundated with greetings, telegrams, cards and gifts. An end-of-term feeling at the last concert in Shizouka at the giant Sumpu Kaikun Stadium was highlighted by Johnny B. Great's rendition of 'I Do Like To Be Beside The Seaside' and at the end a near-riot broke out in the audience when fans clambered on stage, reaching out tearfully as The Walkers were presented with gifts and huge bouquets.

Scott's final 'thank you' speech marked not only the end of the tour but seemingly the end of The Walker Brothers, so it was a slightly subdued party which returned to Tokyo, munching slabs of birthday cake. Everyone went off in different directions; the English musicians caught a direct flight back to London while John journeyed on to Hawaii for a holiday and Gary cut a single with top Japanese band The Carnabeats under Scott's direction. After attending an awards ceremony the next day, Scott and Gary departed for Los Angeles before returning to Britain and markedly different fates.

When their plane stopped for re-fuelling at Honolulu, Scott went for a short walk to stretch his legs and gather his thoughts. The Walker Brothers had finally been laid to rest and a solo career stretched before him. As he reflected on the group's ups and downs over the previous three years, Scott suddenly caught sight of the un-mistakable figure of John Maus, glass of bourbon in hand, sauntering along a spit of white sand about 50 yards away.

'Hey man!' yelled Scott. 'Where ya goin?' John spun round and grinned, but did not stop. 'Guess I'll head back to the States!' he shouted. 'Gonna try and make it big back home!' With a final wave, he continued on his way. 'Good luck!' yelled Scott after the retreat-ing figure. He stood and watched John disappear among the palm trees, then turned and walked quickly back to the airport to board his flight for Los Angeles.

11 Black Sheep Boy

'I don't smoke. Clubs bore me stiff and food is somethin' to eat
and not to celebrate over.'

Scott Walker, 1968

A S FAR AS MAURICE KING WAS CONCERNED, 1968 was the year when
Scott would finally shed The Walker Brothers burden and
establish himself as a major star of international potential.
All the cards were stacked in Engel's favour: he was registered with the powerful Harold Davison agency and had, in Brian
Sommerville, one of the most astute publicists in the business. Moreover, the success of his first album indicated that many of the old
Walker fans had stuck by him. 'My plan was to convert the fans I
already had – and it seems to have worked,' he said. 'It shows that
something is gettin' through. And to a majority – not a minority!'

Scott's huge popularity was illustrated when *Disc & Music Echo*
readers voted him their Mr Valentine for the second successive year
(Paul McCartney was sixth) as well as the World's Top Male Singer,
while 'Scott' was second only to 'Sgt Pepper's Lonely Hearts Club
Band' in the LP section. In a message to his fans, Scott wrote that
these 'completely unexpected' results would 'encourage me to make
more public appearances in 1968'. Maurice King must have been
standing in uncomfortably close proximity at the time.

Engel's voluble manager, who dreamed of conquering Las Vagas
and earning a vast fortune, was confident that Scott's acclaimed
voice, handsome looks and all-round appeal would secure his own
television series, which in turn would lead to stardom in the United
States. While the first part of King's ambition was ultimately realised,
1968, with all its false dawns, flashes of triumph and unfulfilled
hopes, proved a microcosm of Engel's erratic career.

The year began with the news that Scott and Brian Sommerville
were applying for an injunction against an album simply entitled
'Scott Walker' – the result of Ember's latest raid on their vaults. This
time the record company had shamelessly unearthed a series of
demos recorded in Hollywood in 1959, including 'Too Young', 'Sun-

day' and 'All I Do Is Dream Of You'. Ember's boss Jeff Kruger, who said the record was one of the first albums ever recorded in stereo, made the usual noises about the tracks being of 'great historical interest', but what particularly infuriated Scott was that the sleeve-notes did not indicate that the album consisted entirely of old material. The record was eventually released under the title 'Looking Back with Scott Walker'.

As Peter Frampton of The Herd was hailed as the 'Face of '68', and Monkee Peter Tork wittered on about the merits of poverty, Scott was approached with an offer to make his first solo theatre tour of Britain in early March with Long John Baldry, who had just scored a No. 1 hit with 'Let The Heartaches Begin'. Plans for the tour fell through and Scott instead produced 'Spooky', the début single by The Rain, and a recent Top Ten hit in America for Classics IV. The record's spine-chilling, atmospheric feel was well received, but it was not the hit that Gary craved.

Scott was now consciously distancing himself from an increasingly alien pop world which revolved around the saccharine-laden songs of The Tremeloes and Love Affair. Apart from attending the Philips studio, he would only venture out to see jazz legend Coleman Hawkins at Ronnie Scott's or the latest Paul Newman movie. Instead of taking sleeping pills to combat his insomnia, Scott worked on his songwriting through the night until six or seven in the morning, then slept until three in the afternoon. 'What I am really is a glorified bum,' he said. 'My whole life revolves around my records . . . I only make just enough money to get by. I suppose you could call it a hand-to-mouth existence.'

Scott's fans would have been shocked at his relative impoverishment. His sole extravagance was the occasional bottle of expensive Mexican tequila. On one occasion, the singer marched angrily into Maurice King's office, demanding some money. Moments later he departed equally abruptly, seemingly content to have been given just five pounds, much to the relief of his manager who had nervously anticipated a demand for several hundred. When Scott decided to buy a new stereo set he found he only had £17 10s in his bank account and had to obtain an advance on his new album.

At this point, Scott's career entered its strangest phase, as he veered wildly from the role of tormented visionary to supper-club crooner. That April saw the release of 'Scott 2', complete with Brel songs 'Jacky' and 'Next' (the latter detailing the loss of a boy's virginity in a mobile army whorehouse), the content of which would still cause some of today's more timid Radio 1 disc jockeys to blanch. Yet within a week came the Tony Hatch/Jackie Trent ballad 'Joanna', pure MOR slush which predictably shot into the Top Ten and ironically remains Scott's best-known solo work.

The disc reaffirmed Engel's status as a sex symbol and inspired a fresh torrent of fan mail, yet the singer would have preferred just one letter praising his work and telling him that the song meant something to that person, than 100 requests for a lock of hair or a photo.

The fact that both album and single sold heavily indicated that Scott had managed to attract two wholly different types of audience. But would he maintain a foot in both camps or fall between two stools?

The much-maligned 'Jacky' opens 'Scott 2', the only Scott Walker LP which reached No. 1. 'Best Of Both Worlds', with its beautiful Wally Stott arrangement, is followed by Tim Hardin's country-tinged 'Black Sheep Boy' leading up to 'The Amorous Humphrey Plugg', the first self-penned composition on the record, and one of Scott's finest. Frustrated by his humdrum existence, Plugg glowers from behind the bars of his suburban cage and yearns to be free of screaming children, the blaring television and warring neighbours next door.

'I become a giant, I fill every street/I walk the rooftops I hunch-back the moon, stars dance at my feet . . ./Oh, to die of kisses, ecstasies and charms/Pavements of poets will write that I died in nine angels' arms.' Alas, the spectacular vision that Plugg paints is a fantasy. He may speak grandly of 'buildings blazing in moonlight' but at the end of the day he is just another bored Londoner, struggling to eke out an existence for himself and his family.

However, Scott's 'The Girls From The Streets' is a rather overtly self-conscious attempt to emulate Brel. *Hot Press* writer Joe Jackson, in his comprehensive study of Walker lyrics, asserts: ' "The Girls From The Streets" pales badly alongside Brel's "Next". Brel's language is blood-stained and true to army life; here, Walker's is dipped into too much literary wine.

'Yet most damaging is Brel's influence, musically. To Brel, a song's melodic structure was too often little more than a limp support system for a lyric. Similarly in "The Girls From The Streets", Walker merely erects a concrete backdrop for his own self-conscious attempt to write concrete poetry – proof that if he could get it immaculately right, he could also get it abysmally wrong.'

Brel's melodic limitations were one of the reasons Engel stopped covering the Gallic composer's work following 'Scott 3', yet songs like 'The Girls And The Dogs' and 'Next' complement the singer's own 'Scott 2' efforts perfectly. On 'Plastic Palace People', cellos and violins create the rustling of falling leaves as Scott details the free-fall of a balloon in exquisite detail.

True to form, Engel said he was disappointed with the album, blaming its 'lack of continuity' on the fact that it was recorded spasmodically over a long period. According to Jonathan King, the pair were discussing the album over dinner one night when Scott remarked quite seriously: 'I'm afraid it's the work of a lazy, self-indulgent man.' Whatever he may have felt, 'Scott 2', with its myriad smooth backings, was a major step forward.

Maurice King undoubtedly felt the same about 'Joanna', but for vastly different reasons. This song, rather peculiarly backed by 'Always Coming Back To You' from the first solo album, was surely the big commercial breakthrough which Scott's career required. 'All Scott needs is one big hit and he'll be an enormous giant [*sic*]', beamed King. 'It looks as though "Joanna" is going to be the one.'

Mary Arnold remembers the battle that preceded the record. 'You wouldn't believe the difficulty Maurice had in getting Scott to record that song. He was purely interested in recording obscure stuff for his albums while Maurice wanted something more commercial. His attitude was that if Scott wanted to do things his way, he first had to establish himself and songs like "Joanna" would help him to achieve that. Maurice reckoned that the public didn't understand stuff like "In My Room".'

By June, 'Joanna' had climbed to No. 7 in the charts and established Scott in pop's first division, alongside the candyfloss of Gary Puckett and the Union Gap, Bobby Goldsboro and The 1910 Fruitgum Company.

Scott's growing reputation for controversy was enhanced by his appearance at the *NME* Poll Winners concert at Wembley's Empire Pool. Casually dressed in a black polo-neck sweater, cord trousers and jacket, Scott trotted on stage as the Mike Leander Orchestra launched into 'Amsterdam' and proceeded to anger some members of the audience with what they regarded as obscene hand gestures during his performance. He then walked abruptly off-stage after discovering that Lander had no arrangement for 'Joanna'.

Engel's mood-swings and deep, in-bred suspicion fostered a love-hate relationship with the press. Yet his natural eloquence, eminent quotability, subtle wit and widespread knowledge on all manner of topics must have made him a fascinating interview subject. Scott, who possessed a rich, languid tone which matched his singing voice, was prone to lengthy bouts of self-analysis, and some of his interviews were so intense and of such a frank nature that they almost amounted to confessions.

On the Robert Kennedy assassination: 'I thought: "Well, you can always rely on America. Now they will go on an absolute orgy of remorse and after a couple of weeks it will all be forgotten." ' What is the role of the church? 'Takin' money from a lot of poor people in poverty-stricken countries . . . I think the Bible is a load of crap.' On his unhappy childhood: 'People lied to me all the time. I have had this terrible thing throughout my life.' And on his own creative driving force: 'I feel it is my duty to uncover hypocrisy everywhere and to throw it in people's faces.'

Considering he was such a sensitive soul, it is not surprising that Scott was wounded by criticism from fans as well as journalists, and eventually stopped reading the trade papers altogether, apart from *Melody Maker's* jazz pages. Curiously, after Nick Cohn of *Queen* magazine accused Engel of being 'self-pitying and self-indulgent' the singer carried the article around in his wallet, saying the piece was 'artfully' written and that he hoped to meet its author. On 22 June, *NME*'s Nick Logan interviewed Scott at length in a pub opposite the Talk of the Town nightclub, and returned to his office with a string of superb quotes including this bleak vision: 'All is lost anyway. We were doomed before we started.'

Logan's article was well-balanced and thought-provoking, but the following week Scott took the quite extraordinary step of writing in to complain that he had been 'made to look the Great Deliverer of the human race'. Protesting that: 'I am no modern day Don Quixote attempting to battle windmills', Scott babbled: 'I may talk in riddles . . . as I chase my thoughts like a madman . . . and I beg Mr Logan's forgiveness if I didn't make myself clearly understood.'

The author of this letter clearly possessed the sensitivity of a hot-house flower and the bulk of its contents must have passed over the heads of most *NME* readers. 'I prefer to work as a formalist,' Scott explained, 'waiting for my speck of dust to shine (not a formulist as Mr Logan points out, there's a vast difference between the two).'

Scott was rarely out of the headlines. That summer, he became one of the first pop musicians to make a stand on South Africa by declining a £10,000 offer to perform before a segregated audience. 'Nobody will force me to perform in circumstances in conflict with my own conscience,' he declared.

When an angry South African promoter publicly challenged Scott to demonstrate his sincerity by halting sales of his records in the Republic, Engel countered: 'Firstly, I can't tell any record company where they can or cannot sell their products. Secondly, if people of every race in South Africa buy records made by me I am happy, not because of royalties, but because it means they are gettin' some pleasure and joy in a country where apartheid creates only misery and hate.' This blistering salvo drew no response.

Engel, as we have seen, mistrusted Flower Power, saying he wanted people to 'face the realities of life and not escape them'. Yet like any intelligent person with an above-average awareness of world affairs, he worried about the state of the planet and, in particular, the escalating conflict in Vietnam.

That spring, it appeared as if Robert Kennedy, the Democrats' nomination for the American presidency, would travel all the way to the White House on an anti-war ticket. Kennedy, whose forthright views on racism led to him being described as 'the last white politician trusted by blacks', impressed even a hardened cynic like Engel to such an extent that he placed an advertisement in *The Times*, urging exiled American citizens to support the young senator's presidential bid. 'I think Bobby Kennedy is the only man with the right ideas about peace and war,' said Scott.

Two months later Scott began to lose interest in the presidential race, believing that Kennedy's victory was a formality. The subsequent events of 5 June, when the senator was assassinated within minutes of winning the Californian primary, must have been quite shattering for a man who always recoiled at the level of violence in his native land. 'I just hate America,' Scott bitterly told *Rave*. 'The assassination . . . just confirmed my opinions of the States, why I personally had to get out. I knew this could happen. There's so much inner tension in the people, such a fantastic pressure on society, loaded with demands that they can't give in to.'

The tragedy prompted Scott to declare he wanted to forget about being American. 'Sometimes it's difficult,' he said. 'Such as when US tourists happen to hear me speaking. They bang me on the back and say it's great to meet a fellow countryman. I usually tell 'em I'm British and just puttin' on a phoney accent to impress people.'

In 1976 Scott revealed that the policies of the Nixon administration were one of the reasons why he could not return to the States. 'When that sucker got into office, I rang up all my family and warned 'em what things were gonna be like,' he said. 'I just knew.' In the late 1960s, Scott talked determinedly of applying for British citizenship, but by the summer of 1969 Amsterdam was replacing London in his affections.

Scott performed 'Joanna' on *Top Of The Pops*, ITV's *It Must Be Dusty*, *Billy Cotton's Music Hall* and *Dee Time*, but Maurice King's optimistic forecasts of a spring tour did not come to fruition. Instead, while Davy Jones was assuring the press that he would remain a world star long after the dissolution of The Monkees, and Bill Haley and his Comets inspired a mini rock-'n'-roll revival, there came the surprise news that Scott was planning a summer tour of Japan with Gary Leeds and The Rain.

Once again the lure of the yen had proved irresistible. 'From the money I will get on this tour, I could last a whole year without makin' one concert appearance,' said Scott triumphantly. 'I'm prepared to over-prostitute myself to get any money to live on.' Engel's fear of performing was almost pathological, but as he had still to reap sizeable songwriting royalties, live appearances continued to provide the bulk of his income. In between tours, Scott lived frugally, determined to delay live performances for as long as possible.

Nevertheless, a series of special one-nighters – Scott's first live appearances since performing with The Walkers five months earlier – were arranged for Bolton, Birmingham, Bournemouth and Brighton. Scott, who was forced to cancel the Bolton date following an attack of German measles, gave no hint of nerves when he strolled on stage at the Brighton Dome on 21 June before a hushed audience of teenyboppers, and launched confidently into 'Jacky' to the accompaniment of Ronnie Scott's band.

With jacket open and tie loose, he delivered a powerful rendition of 'Make It Easy On Yourself' before the high spot of the evening, Brel's 'If You Go Away', which Scott sang perched on a stool, to the gentle accompaniment of his own guitar. After throwing himself into Jimmy Rushing's 'Baby Don't Tell On Me', in which he mockingly referred to his dance steps as his 'Tom Jones bit', Scott closed with 'Joanna' and 'Amsterdam'.

The Land Of The Rising Sun now beckoned and Scott braced himself for a fortnight-long tour with The Rain. Gary's band would perform their predominantly rock-'n'-roll set in the first half of the show before Scott emerged after the interval, to spread the Jacques Brel gospel. Gary and his merry men flew to Tokyo without any qualms, but Scott announced that he would travel overland on the famous Trans-Siberia Express, hoping to write his new album and fit in a cultural visit to Russia on the way. Yet two days after setting out on his Siberian adventure, Scott was back in Britain after Red Army guards confiscated his tapes and tape recorder at the Russian border. 'He acted so weird, they thought he was a spy,' says Gary.

'He turned up with all these tapes and cameras and stuff and wearin' those dark glasses. Then they found his vitamin pills and spent hours goin' through these medical books, makin' sure they were what he said they were. He wasn't gonna carry on after that. We ended up doin' the tour on our own.'

At first it seemed as if Scott would fly to Japan after all, but within a couple of days of arriving back in Britain he reportedly suffered a nervous breakdown, although Mary Arnold suspects this was merely a ruse to avoid the lengthy flight east. Scott was said to be suffering from severe psycho-neurosis after working too hard on his new album, which he wished to complete as soon as possible.

Following a fortnight's rest, he had recovered sufficiently to record two BBC television spectaculars at the Golders Green Hippodrome in north London. Screened in August, the first show, on which Scott performed 'Passing Strangers' with Kiki Dee, a singer he had long admired, was the pilot for his own six-part series the following spring, while the second, broadcast in December, featured jazz singer Blossom Dearie. After announcing that Lulu, the chart-topping Love Affair and Tommy James and the Shondells would accompany him on his autumn tour, Scott left for a fortnight's holiday in the South of France.

As it happened, Lulu pulled out after receiving a lucrative offer from Las Vegas, and Tommy James (who was unable to agree financial terms) ended up being replaced by The Casuals and Cupid's Inspiration, with The Paper Dolls, who had been ludicrously billed as Britain's answer to The Supremes, completing the line-up. There were reports that Scott would make his Hollywood début in a semi-musical, cast as a down-and-out. Like his planned musical *Cyrano de Bergerac*, with lyrics written by Jonathan King, this remained just a rumour.

During Engel's temporary absence from London, the pop papers focused on a swarm of Scott Walker lookalikes and soundalikes, ranging from established stars Steve Marriott of The Small Faces and The Herd's Peter Frampton to the now forgotten Barry Noble, Paul Slade and Dominic Grant. As these Scott wannabes vied for column inches, the ever-reluctant star appeared on the front cover of *Disc & Music Echo*, riding a Vespa scooter and looking tanned and fit, despite a recent mild bout of typhoid.

'I'm broke again and that's the only reason I'm doin' this tour,' said Scott, whose new pragmatism was beginning to sound like a mantra. 'Working in a theatre isn't nearly as bad as working in clubs – that really terrifies me because the audience is so close and it's such a claustrophobic atmosphere.'

Scott naturally included some Brel favourites in his live set but opted against the use of his own songs, insisting that he needed a 36-piece orchestra to perform them. Saying that he was 'obsessed' at getting his third album recorded, he confessed that he still did not have one song 'in the can'. 'I've written about four albums and then torn 'em all up again – it's madness!' he exclaimed.

There was a surprise in store for the girls screaming for Scott on the opening night at Finsbury Park Astoria. The singer's entrance was preceded by compère Mike Quinn, who gravely announced: 'A very special favour . . . he has prepared an act, and he says the words of the songs are worth hearing. Please do not scream. If you feel like applauding at the end of a song, go ahead.'

Scott then appeared, dressed casually in brown corduroy jacket, dark glasses hanging out of his breast pocket, and wearing a white shirt and black tie, and repeated the set he had performed at Brighton that summer to similarly rapturous acclaim. The audience diligently complied with Quinn's request, managing to restrict themselves to bursts of furious clapping mingled with one or two half-screams between each song. Scott did receive some criticism, however, for performing only six numbers.

The three-week package tour was Scott's first since The Walkers' British swansong eighteen months earlier – and it was destined to be his last. Engel could barely conceal his distaste at having to share the bill with bubblegum pop bands like The Casuals, and Maurice King felt strongly that his singer required a more sophisticated setting. Perhaps the worst moment of the tour came at Chester's ABC Theatre, when a telephoned bomb hoax caused the premises to be evacuated while The Paper Dolls were midway through their act.

Scott's reluctance to socialise and general aloofness annoyed the other bands, accustomed as they were to nights of heavy drinking and endless high jinks on the road. Of course, Engel's chances of a stimulating intellectual discussion with Love Affair and The Paper Dolls were about as likely as finding him cheering on Chelsea football team from the Stamford Bridge terraces. None of Scott's fellow pop musicians were overly philosophical.

Two days before the tour ended at Coventry, Suzi 'Tiger' Mathis, The Paper Dolls' lead singer, complained that the girls had never even seen Scott backstage, let alone spoken to him. After each show, Walker fans would crowd around the stage door to shower The Dolls with questions about Scott. What was he like? What did he say? Was he nice? The Dolls were kept as much in the dark as the fans.

'It's past a joke,' growled Tiger. 'The only person we ever saw him talk to was compère Mike Quinn.' Tiger's blunt views were possibly influenced by Scott's refusal to allow Ronnie Scott's brass section to accompany the girls, a stubbornness which had led to his public fall-out with Clodagh Rodgers a couple of years earlier.

Hankering back to the happy atmosphere which had surrounded a recent Herman's Hermits tour, Tiger bemoaned the stand-offishness of the show's leading star, whom she blamed squarely for the flat mood backstage. She was then made to look rather foolish when Scott invited The Dolls to join him for a drink and a game of cards following the final show. He was so charming and polite that Tiger found herself bitterly regretting those nasty tales she had told.

Rather sheepishly, she informed him of her press revelations. 'Oh dear,' sighed Scott, who must again have pondered the wisdom of agreeing to tour. 'I wasn't deliberately trying to be the star, but I regarded the tour as a job,' he later explained. 'I arrived on time for my job and went home. No one clamoured at the dressing-room door for my attentions and so I never seemed to meet them. If I put anyone off, I'm really sorry.'

After all this nonsense, Scott must have been relieved to disappear back into the studio and immerse himself in some serious work. He spent the remainder of the year at Philips, labouring over 'Scott 3', only emerging to appear at the Save Rave charity concert at the London Palladium alongside Madeline Bell and The Bonzo Dog Doo Dah Band, and to record his appearance on the Christmas edition of Cilla Black's show.

He also fulfilled a handful of Northern cabaret engagements before travelling to Paris just before Christmas to record Hal Shaper's 'The Rope And The Colt', the rousing theme of the French western of the same name.

Despite this hectic schedule, Scott somehow found time to produce John Maus's self-penned single 'Woman', which was released by Philips in mid-November. Back from his short-lived sojourn in the United States, John had re-signed with Maurice King, but the hit single he so desperately needed failed to materialise, although he soldiered on with the Carnaby label right up until 1970. Pressed for an update on his post-Walkers activities, John replied that he had spent months sitting on the floor of his Regent's Park flat, writing songs and downing bottles of wine. 'It's very cheap wine,' he added revealingly.

Meanwhile, The Rain, who had released an album in Japan the previous summer, also discovered that success in Britain was frustratingly elusive. After the failure of the ironically-entitled 'Come In, You'll Get Pneumonia', Maurice King lost interest in the band and a disillusioned Gary drifted back to California where he eventually took a job as a mortician.

Judging by his own comments, Scott also yearned to be free from the pop rat-race. 'Everything goes hand in hand in this business,' he said wearily. 'If you don't put out a single you are under pressure from the public who pressure my record company who pressure my manager who pressures me. That is the kind of tension which I can't abide and eventually it will be the thing that stops me.'

Yet as 1969 unfolded, the Scott Walker bandwagon appeared unstoppable. Faithful *Disc & Music Echo* readers voted him Top TV Artist (Male), and Top Male Singer (World) as well as their Mr Valentine for the third successive year. A startled Engel, who was unable to attend the awards ceremony at London's Seymour Hall due to a cabaret date in Birmingham, made one of the strangest acceptance speeches in history. 'Polls like this are frightening,' he said. 'You figure you've left it all behind you and then this happens. It's like a ghost rearin' up after you wherever you go. I figured about nine months ago some new meteorite would come along and wipe me from the face of the earth – but it didn't happen.'

Far from raising his spirits, these fresh accolades served as a painful reminder to Scott that he remained an integral feature on the pop landscape he wished to leave behind. Yet moves were afoot to establish him as an international star to rank alongside Tom Jones and

Engelbert Humperdinck. A six-part BBC television series, simply entitled *Scott*, would begin on 4 March with half-hour shows screened every Tuesday evening at 9.50 p.m., featuring guests whom Engel particularly admired.

First Scott had some unfinished business – that difficult third album which had drained so much of his creative energy over the previous twelve months. Finally released in March, 'Scott 3' confirmed that Engel's inspiration was now drawn almost entirely from classical music. Listing his main influences, he said: 'Beethoven, because he was the greatest expert in his medium who ever lived [Scott claimed to have six versions of every symphony], Shostakovich, because he was the last of the great symphonists and Brahms, because it is wonderfully intellectual music.'

Aware that the album would inevitably be compared with its chart-topping predecessor, Scott appointed Wally Stott, an orchestral arranger whose background was steeped in classics, as musical director. 'Working with Wally Stott on "Scott 3" was like having Delius writin' for you,' he said wonderingly.

By now, Scott's own anguished compositions were emerging from Brel's dark shadow. He is credited with ten of the thirteen songs on 'Scott 3', with Brel's 'Sons Of', 'Funeral Tango' and 'If You Go Away' (a high spot of Scott's live act which was included following an intensive campaign by Walker buffs) completing the line-up. 'It's Raining Today', a sublime melancholic tale of a wanderer's transitory love affairs, was inspired by Scott's hitch-hiking trip across the United States in 1959, while 'Copenhagen' was Scott's touching tribute to Mette's home town where they later lived (one latter-day reviewer said it was a good job she had not come from Deptford). 'Rosemary', which tells of an ageing spinster who has devoted her life to caring for her widowed mother and still fondly recalls a distant fling with a travelling salesman, was based on a girl Scott knew, who was unable to break free from her domineering parent.

'She hears a clock and it strikes like a hammer/Pounding the nails one day further in the coffin of her youth.'

The theme re-occurs even more savagely in 'Big Louise', 'a requiem for an ageing transvestite' who peers out from her 'fire escape in the sky' and tearfully reflects on the days when 'time sounded sweet'.

This latter track was Scott's personal favourite and apparently emerged exactly as he had intended. 'We Came Through' is a strident, 'Mathilde'-style military romp, which Scott said attacked people who put themselves on pedestals; 'Butterfly' was written as Scott watched a beautiful girl race across a French beach during an early morning rain shower. 'Like a butterfly lost in all this vast space. I tried to get close to Debussy or Delius. That fluttering feeling,' he said.

'Two Ragged Soldiers', inspired by a *Time* magazine article on New York's 'Skid Row', is an allegorical song about two tramps who weave fantasies around an empty bottle. The song is extremely compelling, but highlights perhaps Scott's greatest flaw: a tendency to glamorise his lowlife subjects. Anyone who has bedded down on Skid Row (or London's Embankment, for that matter) would hardly describe it as a glamorous experience.

'30 Century Man', which has Scott singing to the accompaniment of his own acoustic guitar, deals with the subject of suspended animation (a man is frozen alive and emerges 100 years later to shake hands with Charles de Gaulle, whom Scott felt would live forever); 'Winter Night' tells of a girl who has grown cold and indifferent to love, while the self-pitying 'Two Weeks Since You've Gone' (the B-side to 'Lights of Cincinnati') sounds semi-autobiographical.

Reviewing 'Scott 3' two decades later, Joe Jackson commented: 'In line with the ideal set down by Franz Schubert, the poetry, vocal melodies and orchestral accompaniment are so thoroughly integrated that the words interpret the meaning of the music just as the music interprets the inner sense of the words while the harmonies of the accompaniment add the necessary accents of light, shade, and colour. It is truly other-worldly.' It is surely no coincidence that Scott produced some of his most breathtaking work during this period of personal contentment. On tracks like 'Copenhagen' and 'It's Raining Today' Mette's presence is tangible. She is even pictured on the inside sleeve.

The record was another significant step in Scott's journey of self-discovery, but was Joe Public ready to travel that far with him? 'The Establishment have been tryin' to tell me for as long as I can remember that the public won't understand what the hell I'm talkin' about on record,' Scott told Keith Altham. 'I'm tryin' to prove they are wrong . . .'

Encased in an entrancing cover depicting Scott's brooding countenance mirrored in the pupil of a girl's eye, 'Scott 3' carries sleeve-notes of quite breathtaking pretension by Altham, which begin:

'Narcissus in Metamorphosis . . .' 'Fuck knows what it means!' laughs the author today. 'It sounds even more pretentious now than it did then. But there's this Italian surrealist's painting "Narcissus in Metamorphosis" in which he's admiring his own reflection in a pool . . .

'I was reminded of that when I went backstage after The Walkers must have had a terrible row [following their farewell British gig at the Tooting Grenada, in fact]. Scott sat staring into the dressing-room mirror clawing his face with his hands. Those sleeve-notes have haunted me ever since – Annie Nightingale once read them out on radio.'

The album's progress to No. 3 in the charts was another triumph for Scott over the sceptics, yet he fretted over its failure to reach the top spot to a neurotic degree. After much hand-wringing, Scott appears to have been browbeaten into the belief that the album's lack of commerciality prevented its progression to No. 1. 'The melody lines were too long and people were puzzled and got bored halfway through,' he decided. 'So "Scott 4" is gonna be much harder and tighter.' But before the album that would herald his artistic rebirth got underway, stardom on the small screen beckoned.

12 The Big Hurt

' "Scott 4" tried to link lyrics by Sartre, Camus and Yevtushenko
to Bartok modal lines, but nobody noticed.'

Scott Walker, 1976

QUARTER OF A CENTURY LATER, the notion of Scott Walker, one
of pop's most celebrated recluses, starring in his own BBC
television series (and a considerably successful one at that)
sounds as probable as Pink Floyd's Syd Barrett playing to a
packed Royal Albert Hall or Iggy Pop running for the American
Presidency. Although 'scared stiff' at having his own programme,
Scott seemed relatively relaxed in the confines of the BBC studios,
secure in the knowledge that all the shows were taped before a live
audience and any embarrassing blunders could be edited out.

Scott's confidence grew with every show; he moved well and
spoke naturally, introducing his guests with a smile and a few quick
words. The list of celebrities, which included jazz singer Salena
Jones, the Dudley Moore Trio, Tony Hatch and Jackie Trent and
Gene Pitney, was impressive, and coupled with the expertise of veteran producer Johnnie Stewart, who had known Scott since the early
days of *Top Of The Pops*, guaranteed 25 minutes of sophisticated,
polished entertainment every week.

In an obvious concession to an older and more staid audience
who might have taken offence at Brel's excesses, Scott's material
consisted primarily of safe cover versions like Bacharach and David's
'The Look Of Love' or 'The Impossible Dream' from *Man of La
Mancha*, although he did showcase some of his own compositions
from 'Scott 3', as well as a handful of Brel selections. Scott, express-
ing relief that he had survived the first two shows 'without dying or
fading or doing a Greta Garbo thing' appears to have been reason-
ably happy with the show, although he said he would have liked the
orchestra in closer proximity.

'Maybe it wasn't for the ultra hip, but I found it gentle enough
to help me enjoy Scott and fast enough to make me think that it was
all over much too soon,' commented Penny Valentine. Few disagreed

with her. The series received rapturous reviews and scored heavily over ITV's rival Tom Jones spectaculars. After it ended, Scottish and Irish viewers launched petitions for the series to be screened in their regions.

Unexpectedly, the sole dissenting voice came from Johnnie Stewart who, despite agreeing that Scott was a good singer, claimed his choice of material held limited appeal. The intricate writing efforts from 'Scott 3' were all very well, argued Stewart, but they were not box-office material and, more importantly, would not establish Scott as a star in America.

'If you are going to be a "name" artist you can't stay with "in the mind" songs all the time,' he said. 'You have got to do ballads and up-tempo stuff – the lot – much in the same way as stars like Tony Bennett and Frank Sinatra.'

Scott had been forced to endure Maurice King prattling on in a similar vein for four years. Grizzled showbiz veterans like Stewart or vocal tutor Freddie Winrose (who considers 'Scott Sings Songs From His TV Series' his finest album) simply could not accept that a lengthy residency at somewhere like the Flamingo Club in Vegas was Engel's very idea of hell. Always forward-looking, he found the prospect of regurgitating his greatest hits in front of an audience of stuffed shirts quite repugnant. During their first live dates in England, The Walkers' steadfast refusal to perform 'Love Her' was almost certainly down to Scott, who would have objected to performing a song recorded several months previously in California.

Although the likes of Stewart and Winrose were baffled by the singer's stance, it does explain why the notion of Scott 'doing a Tom Jones' and amassing a fortune by crooning safe ballads like 'Joanna' and 'Lights of Cincinnati' night after night, week after week and year after year in the gambling capital of the world was a complete non-starter. Instead, Scott harboured a secret ambition to produce Elvis Presley whose voice, he felt, was ideally suited to some of the old Walker Brothers material. 'I couldn't care less if I didn't get to sing another note,' said Scott defiantly.

The gulf between producer and star was evident from the first show, when Stewart vetoed Scott's plan to include 'Funeral Tango' (Brel's darkly humorous account of crocodile tears shed at a graveside) on the grounds of bad taste. 'What about all the sick people in hospitals?' he asked the astonished singer, who must have sensed in that instant the stressful conflicts which lay ahead. Ironically, although the subsequent album, 'Scott Sings Songs From His TV Series', reached No. 7 in the charts, it patently failed to match the sales of Scott's three solo albums, a fact which Stewart must have found highly perplexing.

'For me, the entire album is an exercise,' said Scott dismissively. 'People have been sayin' for ages that Scott Walker is a singer of standards, so let's see if he can sing 'em.' Clad in black, his blond hair cut short, Scott poses languidly on the cover; a pair of shades and the key from Quarr Monastery dangle from his neck. There is no sign of inner turbulence. He is the epitome of the pop star image he was hell-bent on destroying.

However, Scott suddenly found himself the target of a surprise attack in *Melody Maker* whose reviewer, concealed in a cloak of anonymity, described him as: 'An average singer with pitch problems who can sing a ballad well but not superbly, but who lacks the magic of the big league male singers.'

This diatribe was a bit over the top and evoked a shoal of indignant letters. Nevertheless, it suggests that the media's love affair with Scott was heading for the rocks. Jonathan King believes Engel's decision to branch out into his own TV series was a form of compromise.

'He wanted to make intelligent records but realised that a lot of those would not be commerical. Yet you had to be commerical to a degree to attract people who would then be prepared to listen to the more intelligent records. I think he enjoyed some of the commerical stuff although his heart wasn't really in it. Johnny Franz used to warn that he couldn't make all these self-indulgent records and I was very critical. If I thought a track was pretentious or uninteresting then I would say so, even if Scott adored it.'

After the series was completed, Scott left for a holiday in Greece, having grudgingly agreed to release Tony Macaulay's 'Lights of Cincinnati' as a belated follow-up to 'Joanna'. Engel claimed that his pleas to write his own single were overruled by Philips – on the grounds that his material lacked commerciality. The night before he was due to depart, Scott bowed to considerable pressure from Maurice King, Franz and several Philips executives and agreed to the release of 'Lights of Cincinnati'. 'Everyone was so gung-ho and anxious to get a record out at last. I said: "Fine – put it out. Don't bother me. Get outta my face." '

Although the often overlooked 'Lights of Cincinnati' is effectively the bastard son of 'Joanna', it is lyrically and melodically stronger and deservedly reached No. 13 in the charts. Even so, Scott found the song extremely boring and, on the couple of occasions he performed it on television, seemed to have trouble keeping a straight face. Explaining his decision to record the song, Scott said simply: 'I've gotta eat and pay the rent.'

Maurice King arranged six concerts for Scott to parade his varied repertoire that summer. He would play the Brighton Dome on 4 July and Blackpool ABC on 6 July before returning there three weeks later. Two shows would be given at each venue with Scott being joined by Tony Hatch and Jackie Trent at Brighton, and by The Rockin' Berries at both Blackpool dates. Engel would be backed by Ray Warleigh's seven-piece band which had already accompanied him in cabaret.

Scott was still based in London, although his trips to Amsterdam and Copenhagen were becoming more frequent. Mounting songwriting royalties meant that he could restrict his live appearances to three weeks a year and attend his local cinema at least four times a week. Scott's new home was a third-floor flat in St John's Wood, which he shared with a huge St Bernard puppy named Rasmus, who accompanied his master on at least one photo session. A shock was in store for Keith Altham when he arrived to interview Scott one afternoon.

'I remember getting out of the lift and knocking on his door. It opened and this furry monster – at first I thought it was a bear – came leaping through the doorway at me and sort of pinned me against the lift door on the other side of the landing. Scott came hurtling out on the other end of a lead saying: "It's OK, he's only a puppy." I remember replying: "Thank Christ for that, otherwise I'd have been down the bloody lift shaft or something." Who else but Scott would have this St Bernard in a third-floor flat in St John's Wood?'

Despite the artist's running battle with his record company, Scott's career had reached its artistic and commercial peak by the summer of 1969: within a couple of months he had released two successful, if vastly different, albums and enjoyed a moderately successful hit single as well as an acclaimed television series with the possibility of another to follow. Moreover, his fan club's paid-up membership of 16,000 was larger than that of The Beatles.

Less well-known were his independent production activities. That summer, Scott produced 'Ray Warleigh's First Album' – a promising début from the highly-rated young alto saxman – and 'Fallout' by jazz guitarist Terry Smith. Engel's versatility seemingly knew no bounds. 'Scott Walker has no rivals,' bragged Maurice King. 'He's streets ahead of anyone else, pro rata, for what he's trying to do.

'Tom Jones . . . is the biggest star in the world. But should Scott and I decide to push non-stop commercially, I believe he could be, and would be, much bigger than Tom. There are a lot of fine singers without an image; and a lot of stars with fine images and no voice. Once in a lifetime you find a combination of both – that is Scott Walker.'

A stirring tribute from a proud manager who clearly felt his protégé had the world at his feet. Yet by now King's refrain was becoming rather tired, and in persisting with it the manager was beginning to sound like a German general in 1918: one last push and victory would be assured. Even as he spoke, fate was conspiring to trigger a chain of events which would lead to the break-up of the King-Engel partnership and sever the slender umbilical cord which bound Scott to the world of mainstream pop, sending him spinning into a commercial void.

According to Mary Arnold – and her story is confirmed by two independent sources – Scott's incessant fight against censorship was placed in stark perspective by the shattering news that he had been conscripted to fight for the American army in Vietnam. Scott was horrified. The fear of being called up and having to put his life on the line for a country whose values he despised was one of the reasons he had left America in 1965. Now the demons from his own pit of hell had come to claim him at last.

Scott's phobia about flying had reached the point where not even a bottle of Scotch would get him aboard a plane. Yet in order to beat the draft, King and Engel would have to fly to New York and somehow convince the military authorities that the singer was unfit for active service. Any thoughts Scott may have entertained about making a public stand on the issue would undoubtedly have been dispelled by King, on the grounds that such a move would destroy his prospects of emulating Tom Jones's phenomenal success in America. The Welshman had, after all, publicly stated that 'a man should be prepared to fight for his country'.

While King busied himself with the travel arrangements, Scott shuddered at the prospect of performing at Brighton, but contracts had been signed and the show seemed set to go on. Scott was in a quandary. There was a limit to the number of sick notes his doctor could issue.

Mary Arnold says that, in desperation, Engel persuaded King to instruct the faithful Bobby Hamilton to stage a fake car crash on the road to the South Coast. The two men left London in separate cars and on a quiet stretch of road somewhere near East Grinstead, Hamilton duly smashed his Jaguar into a tree, later telling police that a broken track rod had caused the vehicle to leave the road.

He then took over the wheel of Scott's car and drove the apparently injured singer to East Grinstead hospital before ringing King to report: 'I've done it.' Arnold remembers how she and King were then forced to enact an elaborate charade in front of the press.

'Maurice, Bobby and me were the only ones in on it, so we all had to pretend how concerned we were. Even Maurice's secretary was left in the dark and the poor girl became really upset when she heard of Scott's "accident".'

However, Scott's reckless ploy backfired when doctors insisted that he should rest in hospital, which threatened to delay his crucial New York trip. 'Well, that's your own bloody fault then!' King bellowed down the telephone when Scott frantically revealed his predicament. After a couple of days, Engel discharged himself and the Brighton show went ahead with P. J. Proby.

Hamilton remembers things differently. He maintains that he and Scott were on their way to Brighton when the singer suggested a fake road accident on the spur of the moment. 'He said: "I don't fancy doing this concert do you Bob?" I told him that Maurice and all the other musicians would be down at Brighton and we had to go ahead with it. Scott thought for a minute and then said: "Let's have a car crash."'

Wrapping your own Jaguar around a tree may seem like dedication above and beyond the call of duty, but after letting Scott out on to a grass verge, that is precisely what Hamilton says he did. Engel even went as far as slashing his forehead with a piece of glass from the shattered windscreen to make his injuries seem more convincing. 'We were earning good money and I knew that Scott was in a position to buy me another Jag the following day,' says Hamilton.

The story of Scott's call-up initially appears suspect. Why, for instance, did such a publicity-hound as King not seize on the opportunity to gain acres of newspaper coverage for his star? Yet the manager had a very good reason for not going to Fleet Street. He apparently decided to try and convince the US Army that Scott was homosexual and therefore unfit for military service. Such a scam required signed statements from doctors in London's Harley Street as well as from lawyers in America, all of whom had to be paid off. King therefore told the British press that Scott had been offered 'an important dramatic role' in a major Hollywood film and was flying to New York to clinch a deal with 'top movie men'.

A couple of years after King's death, Mary Arnold was approached by an American lawyer who told her what had allegedly transpired in New York back in the summer of 1969. Having inspected the bogus written evidence and interviewed Scott, the draft board accepted that he was unfit for military duty and ruled that he would not be conscripted after all, putting him in the clear. But when the lawyer approached King for his money, the manager reverted to stalling tactics.

'He pretended that the record company had not released the money, but knowing Maurice he wanted to keep it for himself. After all, he'd got what he wanted and was looking to get home. I can't remember the actual amount involved, but I think it was around $10,000, which was a lot of money in those days. The lawyer checked with the company and found the money had been sent, so he marched up to Scott's hotel room and asked if he knew what was going on. He said he could tell from Scott's reaction that he didn't have a clue what he was talking about, so he went back to Maurice who eventually had to cough up. The guy said that if Maurice hadn't done so he'd have taken steps to ensure he never left the country.'

Although King had, in a sense, proved an unlikely white knight galloping to Scott's rescue, the singer was furious at being left in the dark over his manager's shady, behind-the-scenes manoeuvring. As Scott brooded in his room, he may well have recalled King's previous sharp practices and compared the manager's swish lifestyle with his own modest circumstances. 'When Scott found out about the money, it broke his heart,' says Mary Arnold. 'He lost his trust in Maurice.' Engel and King's clandestine New York mission may have achieved its objective, yet it left an underlying tension which led within weeks to an irrevocable split between the two men.

Scott's transparent relief at returning safely to London was matched by growing disenchantment with a manager who was still resolutely comparing him with Tom Jones. The singer's inner turmoil was highlighted by a shaky performance during his second show at

Blackpool's ABC Theatre on 27 July, which culminated in around twenty members of the audience demanding their money back and police being summoned to restore order. 'He was top of the bill, but he was absolute rubbish,' said one angry man. 'He sang the same song twice.'

Allegations of drunkenness were vehemently denied. 'I had a ferocious headache after the first show and took some pills the doctor prescribed following my road accident,' said Scott. 'Obviously, the two things didn't mix.' Engel insisted that he had performed Tim Hardin's 'Black Sheep Boy' twice in response to requests from the audience. Terry Smith, a member of Scott's backing band that night, believes it was an honest mistake.

'I remember being a bit taken aback when the number was counted back in. Some of us exchanged puzzled glances and there was a lot of scrabbling around for music sheets. I am sure the song was repeated midway through the set and was not an encore. Scott was such a perfectionist that everyone was quite shocked to discover he was capable of making a mistake.'

Considering Scott's huge respect for jazz musicians, he was probably more concerned about his band's quizzical reaction than the feelings of the audience. 'This whole thing has choked me,' said King. 'Once again, it's a case of a small minority spoiling things.'

On that fateful night, Scott had opened with 'Mathilde' and gone on to perform 'Stormy Monday', a hard blues number with Smith on guitar, as well as Brel's 'We're Alone'. Scott also combined 'Joanna' and 'Lights of Cincinnati', introducing them with the words: 'I'm now gonna sing a medley of my two hits in the past year. I'm joinin' 'em together because they are boring for me and they won't take too long.' Such a statement was not exactly going to endear him to the audience, or have them rocking in the aisles. The fact that Scott was perilously close to the edge was something no amount of subterfuge could hide.

Following the Blackpool debacle, King and his wife left for a much-needed holiday in the South of France, but the news that a letter from Scott's solicitors had arrived at Bickenhall Mansions sent them racing back to London. When King ripped open the envelope and read the letter's contents he paled visibly, sank into a chair and buried his face in his hands. Scott had ended their association after four tempestuous years. 'Not even Maurice could talk his way out of that,' says Arnold. 'His whole life was shattered; he had lost his prestige. Maurice was the kind of guy who wanted to make thousands not hundreds and he really believed there was no limit to what Scott could achieve. He was never the same man after Scott left him.'

Although King's brash and flamboyant personality remained a fixture on the London showbiz scene for a few more years, he never fully came to terms with losing Scott Walker, the pop singer who could really sing. King finally decided he had had his fill of temperamental musicians and bought a small supermarket near Old Street. 'At least baked beans don't talk back at you,' he remarked bitterly.

Always a heavy drinker, King gradually sank into chronic alcoholism and became ever more embroiled in the seedy London underworld. Finally, in June 1977, he was found dead in the flat above his former office, surrounded by empty whisky bottles and packets of barbiturates. The circumstances were never fully explained and an inquest recorded an open verdict.

Having shed the last link with his pop past, Scott cancelled a week's booking at Wythenshawe's Golden Garter Theatre and announced that from now on he would be known as Scott Engel. His new album, 'Scott 4', entirely self-composed and today regarded as his masterpiece, was at the time met with widespread apathy. The record failed to chart and was deleted soon afterwards, making it much sought-after by collectors who by the end of the 1980s were prepared to pay up to £40 for a copy.

The inner sleeve contains pictures of 'the unknown soldier' and Stalin, along with shots of a furrow-browed Scott and Johnny Franz poring over the control desk at Olympic studios (Scott's habitual studio was being refurbished). Artwork is credited to one John Constable. Scott is seen hunched over his guitar, routining material with arranger Peter Knight, while Wally Stott conducts from his podium. Scott's facial expression is one of grim resolution: he had learnt from past mistakes and this time would get everything right. This purposeful mood is encapsulated by the accompanying Camus quote: 'A man's work is nothing but this trek to rediscover through the detours of art, those two or three great or simple images in whose presence his heart first opened.'

The opening track is a splendid interpretation of the Bergman movie *The Seventh Seal*, an evocative Spanish-sounding opus in which a medieval knight stakes all on a game of chess with Death – and loses. Scott manages to encapsulate the apocalyptic feel of the picture which has plague stalking the land while God turns his back on the faithful. Yet the undoubted high spot is the desolate beauty of 'Boy Child' in which Scott retraces his steps back to childhood: 'You lose your way, a boy-child rides upon your back/Take him away through mirrors dark and blessed with cracks/Through forgotten courtyards where you used to search for you . . .'

Equally fascinating is Scott's bold foray into an Eastern bloc state to convey the crushed dreams of the Prague Spring of 1968. Clumsily subtitled 'Dedicated To The Neo-Stalinist Regime', the almost funky 'The Old Man's Back Again', with its irresistible growling bass line, is a bitter denunciation of the Russian invasion of Czechoslovakia: 'I seen a hand/I seen a vision/It was reaching through the clouds/To risk a dream/The shadow crossed the sky/And crushed it to the ground/ Just like a beast/The Old Man's back again . . .'

Scott, an avowed socialist, declared: 'Both sides were wrong. I don't like some of the things that are happenin' in Russia at the moment – it's neo-Stalinism . . . The Czechs, on the other hand, went about things the wrong way for a socialist state. What was done to them was cruel, but probably necessary in order to prevent the break-up of somethin' for which so many people have worked so hard and suffered so long. Socialism will not happen if there are dissidents within their own ranks . . . and neither will it happen if there's a dictatorship in the Soviet Union.'

In this song, Scott's most overtly political statement, his natural humanity even extends as far as the grim-faced soldier carrying out his orders that must be obeyed at all costs. 'I see a soldier/He's standing in the rain/For him there's no man to walk behind/Devoured by his pain/Bewildered by the faces/Who pass him by/He'd like another name/The one's he's got is a curse these people cry/Why can't they understand?/His mother called him Ivan/And then she died . . .'

Scott's characteristic realism enables him to see beyond the enforced jollity caused by the homecoming of a wounded soldier in 'Hero Of The War': 'He's a hero of the war/All the neighbourhood is talking about your son, Mrs Riley/Give his medals, hand them round to everyone/Show his gun to all the children in the street/It's too bad he can't shake hands and move his feet . . .'

The country-tinged 'Duchess' was inspired by Dion's 'Abraham, Martin and John' album, which Engel pronounced to be the best pop album he had heard. 'On Your Own Again', all 90 seconds of it, sees Scott at his most poetic, while his voice is at its confident peak on 'The World's Strongest Man' and 'Angels Of Ashes'. The presence of

Nashville-esque guitars on 'Get Behind Me' and 'Rhymes Of Good-bye' was virtually Scott's only concession towards contemporary musical styles.

Could this perhaps explain why 'Scott 4' was such a commerical failure following an unbroken run of successes? Jonathan King suggests that Philips had begun to tire of Scott's increasingly non-commercial output. The album was certainly not pushed as hard as its predecessors.

'Philips were getting fed up with him because they knew that it was getting difficult to break anything. Scott was becoming more intellectual and less commercial and also becoming more convinced that he did not want to be a celebrity. Unfortunately, there's this Catch 22 situation whereby if you don't want to be a celebrity you cannot have success even if it's non-commercial. In a sense, he was deliberately destroying his own success.

'It dawned on Scott what fame actually meant. It was a way of making huge quantities of money but losing out on every other level – creatively, intellectually, emotionally and even physically.'

The root cause of the album's failure seemingly centres on the splintering of Scott's fan base into three distinct groups at around the time of his television series. When Scott, who had bravely broken new ground on his preceding albums, extended the contemporary boundaries of pop still further, neither the teenyboppers nor the older, more serious fans and newer, middle-aged audience were prepared to follow him. The album received little promotion as Scott, still smarting from the Blackpool fiasco, showed no inclination to return to the stage. Some of the new songs were too intricate to be performed live anyway.

Years later, Scott admitted that his lack of management at the time of the album's release had not helped. Certainly, following Maurice King's summary dismissal in September, Engel effectively dropped from sight and gave no interviews on his latest work. His change of name may even have confused some would-be buyers, and perhaps the record's mixture of swirling strings, acoustic guitars and deep bass did not sit easily with the long-haired, denim-clad class of '69. Altham believes that Scott simply was not prepared to make the concessions that would have established him as an international art-ist.

'Scott was honest with himself and although he knew what he was doing wouldn't have a mass market he didn't care, it was something more personalised. Establishing a wider market for yourself requires an element of compromise. It's no good insulating yourself from talk-shows, interviews and photo sessions. Successful stars know how to gain the maximum exposure with the minimum of effort, but it really tore Scott apart emotionally to have to do things like that.

'In some respects he reminds me of Sting, another guy who came out of a three-man group as a face. Sting was saved primarily by the fact he was allowed to write and develop his own material right from the start. He didn't experience this Frankensteinian manipulation to the extent that Scott did. Sting is tougher than Scott, but then he didn't have to go through some of the shit that Scott did.'

Engel's dilemma was summed up by Chris Bohn's sympathetic *NME* article of July 1981. 'At a point when credible motives were becoming increasingly important to the newly polarised rock market, his unwillingness to disguise his MOR leanings alienated him still further from the "serious" quarters who had already firmly rejected him anyway ... Thus his penchant for full-blown orchestral arrangements – plus his TV show – bracketed him with the likes of Tom Jones, Jack Jones and Cilla Black.

'Keeping such company, there was no way Walker could have swayed the hearts or minds of dogmatic rock fans. To them he was just an MOR wimp – possessing his records was akin to carrying the plague.' Bohn perceptively suggests that Scott's preoccupation with Europe in a climate obsessed by Americana contributed to his commercial decline.

Chris Welch confirms this Walker backlash. 'A lot of people thought his solo stuff was twee and perhaps that's why his career began to fade. People did feel that his music was becoming a little too wet and wimpish. He was stretching audience loyalties a long way and the record-buying public can only take so much.'

Reviews of 'Scott 4' were mixed. *NME*'s Gordon Coxhill, a long-time Engel supporter, hailed it as his best yet, adding that Scott had 'outgrown his self-indulgent two-fingers-to-the-world phase ...'

Although *Disc & Music Echo* took the opposite view, their verdict was closer to public opinion: 'Judge it solely on song content and variety and you may be disappointed by yet another example of his self-indulgence. His songs sound annoyingly samey and only ingenious, inventive arrangements save them from total boredom.'

Disc was undoubtedly in tune with its younger, more pop-oriented readership. A couple of months previously the paper published a lengthy tirade by 'fourteen ex-Scott Walker fans' which ended prophetically: 'Don't underestimate our force/The end is nigh/ You're way off course/Your reign is over – goodbye Scott/Face it man, you've had your lot!'

'Those first three solo albums sold very well,' Scott reminded *NME*'s Phil McNeill in January 1977. 'When I made the fourth album I was livin' abroad . . . You gotta figure the state of mind I was in, in a foreign country, in total isolation . . . And a friend brought over some reviews and seein' things like "For Scott Walker freaks only and even heavy for them".'

Jonathan King believes that Scott was less worried about the album's failure than the other problems in his life. Nevertheless, those poor sales must have been a hurtful blow and the fact that the record was such a personalised piece of work would have deepened Engel's sense of despondency. In 1976 he remarked: ' "Scott 4" was all screwed up . . . I didn't have any management at the time . . . everybody I came to thought I was a nutcase.'

Back in April, Scott had dismissed comparisons with Tom Jones and Engelbert Humperdinck by pointing out that he worked harder on composing than any other aspect of his career. 'If I cannot prove myself this year, I will quit,' he said ominously. It was to prove no idle threat.

13 If You Go Away

'I had this thing once a year when I called everybody and said
I'm quittin'. The last time everybody said: "We thought you
already had." '

Scott Walker, 1970

DEEPLY UPSET BY THE ALMOST UNIVERSAL FAILURE of fans and critics
alike to understand 'Scott 4', Engel carried out his
threatened disappearing act. Turning his back on the
bright lights of London, his adopted home for the last four
years, he headed across the English Channel hoping to find solace on
the more enlightened streets of Europe's most laidback capital.

Accompanied only by Mette, Scott set up home in Amsterdam
and went to ground for the next six months while he waited for the
mental scars inflicted by the rejection of 'Scott 4' to heal.

There he was free to stroll or cycle along the tree-lined boulevards
winding beside the city's network of beautiful canals. A confirmed
Europhile, Scott loved the relaxed ambience and could visit the
famed Van Goghs at the Rijksmuseum without being pestered by
fans. For the first time in years he was able to enjoy something approaching a normal life.

Mette's mother, Dorte, who visited them there, says it was the
happiest she ever saw the couple. 'He couldn't go anywhere in England without being chased not only by girls but by their mothers as
well. Mette put up with their attentions but I think it got to her
sometimes. In Amsterdam they got some peace at last.'

Scott became unusually gregarious, throwing himself into a life of
bar-hopping. He'd meet a group of people, pour out his troubles over
a few drinks, and then move on. The next night he would go to a
different bar and meet an entirely new set of one-night acquaintan-
ces.

Later he told Tony Norman of *Music Now*: 'I could move
around, walk my dog, get smashed and just live a little. To me it's a
rare privilege to walk around without being stared at. People don't
know who I am there, so I've had a chance to get things sorted out
in my mind.'

Scott Walker

In an interview with *Melody Maker*'s Chris Welch in March 1970, Scott revealed just how close he'd come to drawing his solo career to a close for good. 'I had a period when I was going to quit. I felt a lot of people really had the needle for me. There was a legend or a myth that Scott Walker was a problem. People think I'm a doomy, depressed person. I don't know why. Perhaps it's the material I have been singing.'

Keith Altham had his own theory about Scott's withdrawal: 'I think people gained the impression that he retired from the fray because the stresses and strains had become too much. I just assumed that he had opted out, that he just didn't feel like banging his head against a brick wall and had taken the soft option – or perhaps it was the hard option.

'If you're a frontline person you have to be ruthless to stay at the top of the rock business and Scott just wasn't hard enough. He'd have been happier playing bass guitar in a band.'

Scott's insistence on living the life of a recluse rather than that of a pop celebrity gave birth to the bizarre rumour that he had become a London mini-cab driver which, considering his appalling motoring record, was about as likely as him sweeping around the English capital in a Rolls-Royce bearing personalised number-plates.

In one of the first interviews he ever gave, Engel admitted: 'I'm so nervous about driving. I've been in five accidents this year and been in hospital five times. I've nearly died and been inches away from going over a cliff.'

Barrie Martin, the one-time Quotation who, in an ironic twist, now drives a black cab, says: 'I couldn't even see Scott behind the wheel of a car let alone having to deal with the public. There's no way that Scott Walker was ever a taxi-driver, believe me.'

In fact, Scott's circuitous thought processes were along the lines of Altham's and led him to the unlikely conclusion that happiness within the music business lay in a return to his roots as a session player. Accordingly, he set about selling himself as a bass for hire: 'I wanted to join a group so I asked Alan Price and Georgie Fame. But Georgie didn't phone me back. I wanted to join Blind Faith as well, but I heard they got Rick Grech.'

Having no doubt read or heard the many stories of Scott's peculiarly fragile psyche, it is hardly a surprise that the hard-living Price and Fame declined the offer. They probably thought the phonecall had come from a prankster. Scott rather lamely added that he had not bothered following up his initial inquiry because his dog Rasmus, named after Mette's father, (Scott nicknamed the animal 'Nosey' after a teddy bear he had as a child) had been 'playing up that day'. Laughably, he also revealed that he did not even own a bass guitar anyway.

But Scott assured Welch that the worst was now behind him and while he revelled in his new-found release from fame, he also rediscovered the urge to write. Sitting in his flat, he would pick up his acoustic guitar and jot down ideas, many incorporating the characters he had met in Amsterdam bars and in his apartment block. He would hear his neighbours' footsteps, occasionally meet them on the stairs, and speculate on what kind of lives they led.

In September he left for a month-long trip to Greece, but it became a working holiday as he developed the songs around the loose concept of tenement life. And before the month was up he had cabled Philips in London, told them the musicians he wanted and announced that he was ready to record again.

Then came the disarming news that Scott was handing over the material to be rewritten by his new manager, a dapper Israeli by the name of Ady Semel. He had made his name with husband and wife one-hit wonders Esther and Abi Ofarim, who had scored a worldwide No. 1 two years earlier with their catchy ditty 'Cinderella Rockefella'.

Semel, whose own musical preference was firmly in the classical field, was in his mid-forties and as far removed from Maurice King as was possible to be. Always impressed by an intellectual, Scott no doubt warmed to this impressive, baritone-voiced blond who spoke no fewer than five languages and had a penchant for expensive suits and Mercedes cars.

Record company boss Dick Leahy, whose path would cross that of Scott and his new mentor five years later, remembers him well: 'He had the demeanour of a white Arab, effusive in a middle-eastern way with lots of hand gestures and body language. He was well-spoken and gave the appearance of being very cultured and caring.'

The one language Semel did not speak was that of journalists, who he mistrusted deeply. He did, however, realise that in his chosen line of work they were 'a necessary evil', although he insisted on sitting in on all Scott's future interviews and frequently took them over, much to the annoyance of music-press hacks, for whom getting an interview out of Scott was now becoming a difficult enough task without outside interference.

There is also little evidence that Semel had any musical skills of his own, but Scott insisted on the bizarre move of allowing the manager to restructure his new songs.

'I came back from Greece with the tunes and most of the lyrics done and worked on them with my new manager,' he told Tony Norman. 'He really stopped me going overboard on the songs which I have a tendency to do. He came up with some nice ideas, better ways of getting across my original idea.' Later he added: 'He acts as my censor, vetting all my lyrics and striking out the words likely to harm old ladies.'

After Scott made the decision to record again, the album came together remarkably quickly and was released in December 1970. In a mercifully brief sleeve-note, Semel gave his own interpretation of the work and his role in it: 'I've known Scott for over a year now, but can't really tell whether we think alike. We tend to respect, though, each other's idea of solitude and suspect, each in his own way, that "it might be lonelier without the loneliness".

'This is how we came to collaborate on this record, in an attempt to consider some solitary joys, some particular complaints (of an old-age pensioner, a kept cowboy, a resigned girl lover, a telephone crank, a landlady's grasp of an unneighbourly stripper, an immigrant waiter).'

Unfortunately, after the poor reception to his last entirely self-penned record, Scott was also persuaded, against his better judgement, to mix his own material with a selection of re-makes. While the tried and trusted Franz/Stott production and arrangement team worked on the original Engel/Semel material, the equally well-respected Peter Knight put together the cover versions that occupied most of Side Two. Years later, Scott would dismiss them as 'cornball shlock'.

Semel's classical music leanings are heard from the opening bars of Side One as the sound of a dripping tap merges seamlessly into a sombre cello solo, soon to be accompanied by violins and the happy voices of children in a playground. If the introduction laid Scott open to further charges of pretension, the salvo that followed more than made up for it.

'Little Things (That Keep Us Together)' skips along merrily, disguising a chilling lyric that describes how disasters including war, starvation and the crashing of a jumbo jet are somehow 'little things that keep us warm and close, keep us together and help us get by'.

With its Brel influence to the fore, it is perhaps the only song on 'Till The Band Comes In' not to have slipped into obscurity and certainly merits its inclusion on a number of subsequent compilations.

The tenement block lifestyle that had refuelled Scott's creative talent emerges loud and clear on the following track, 'Joe': 'As old Joe sat a-dyin'/The baby down the hall was cryin'/Somebody had a party goin' on.'

Again, the barbed lyrics are juxtaposed against the saccharine cocktail-lounge arrangement, as the old man who has outlived all his friends complains: 'There ain't no one left alive to call me Joe.' Even the fat boy who listened attentively to Joe's rambling tales has left to make his mark on the world but the old man knows the folly of such idealism. Speculating on where the boy might have disappeared to, the two themes are then neatly linked. Years before most people had heard of South Africa's notorious whites-only holiday resort, Scott sings: 'A postcard from Sun City/Was found layin' by your side/A kind of desert place/Where old folks dry away.'

'Thanks For Chicago Mr James' completes a strong opening trio. With its soaring chorus, it is perhaps the closest Scott had come to writing an epic ballad in the vein of The Walker Brothers' classic hits. Sadly, either Scott refused or Philips never saw fit to release it or any other track from the record as a British single and it remains a largely unknown gem.

The resigned lover referred to by Semel makes her appearance in the shape of his remaining charge Esther Ofarim, by now professionally and maritally separated from Abi. Although her interpretation of Scott's 'Long About Now' was her sole contribution, Scott was persuaded to include a 'with guest appearance' credit alongside the main title on the back sleeve title.

Scott's star might not have been in the ascendent, it is doubtful whether it needed boosting by such a remarkably prominent plug for an artist with just one chart entry to her name, but it seemed Semel had long-term plans for the partnership. Shortly before the album's release, he told the *Sunday Mirror*'s Jack Bentley that joint live appearances were already being planned, and revealed that one of the main reasons he was keen to manage Scott was to team up the two singers: 'I sensed an affinity between them. Another management interested in Scott obviously felt the same way because they tried to buy Esther's contract from me.'

The LP's next track 'Time Operator' poignantly imagines a cranky but lonely neighbour whose only contact with the outside world is through the telephone operator and the men who come to shut off his unpaid water and electricity supply. 'I'm not one to moan,' he wistfully declares; at least 'I made the bill for the telephone.'

Perhaps knowing that some would inevitably compare the song's sad central figure with his own hermit-like existence over the years, Scott could not resist an ironic reply: 'Still I'm not alone like all my/Neighbours say.'

By way of contrast, 'Jean The Machine' is the straightforward tale of another downtrodden resident, a Hungarian refugee 'with a voice like [Maria] Callas', forced to make ends meet by stripping in front of the house band at the local Palace. Over an authentic bump and grind rhythm, Scott describes how she has been driven from the flat down the hall by the constant attentions of a landlady who's convinced she's a Communist spy.

Accompanied only by the strumming of an acoustic guitar, Scott closes the side with the short but undeniably beautiful 'Cowbells Shakin' ', which sees another immigrant desperate for work, complaining to his girlfriend that her head-waiter brother is holding out on giving him a job.

After this compelling and varied selection, Side Two moves away from Scott's highly personal character-sketches and suffers badly as a consequence. The title track is undoubtedly the strongest of the seven remaining songs, but features a rather weak chorus that does not deserve the constant repetition it is afforded.

The final Engel/Semel composition, 'The War Is Over (Epilogue)', was obviously meant to be the big statement, but again fails to deliver a melody to match the intentions of a potentially triumphant chorus: 'Outside they sing/The war is over/Raise your blinds/The war is over/Tell your deepest dark goodbye'.

All that remains is the 'cornball shlock' – entirely forgettable covers of the Classic IV's 'Stormy', Henry Mancini's 'The Hills of Yesterday' and Michel Legrand's 'What Are You Doing The Rest of Your Life'. Scott manages to breathe a little life into the closing big ballad 'It's Over', but the only performance with any real verve is on the country standard 'Reuben James', a sign of the direction Scott's career was to move in inexorably before too long.

It is interesting to speculate on how the album might be viewed today were it not for those throwaway cover versions. Like its pre-decessor, ' 'Til The Band Comes In' is largely overlooked, which is unfortunate given the quality of several of the Engel/Semel originals, most notably 'Little Things' and 'Thanks For Chicago Mr James'. Where Scott managed to get into the heads of his semi-fictitious char-acters, the record succeeded. By allowing others to put ideas into his mind, notably by diluting the impact of his own songs with mean-ingless covers, he consigned it to the bargain bins.

Although Scott threw himself into a series of promotional inter-views, and even appeared on Derek Nimmo's prime-time television chat-show, the LP failed to chart. By now Scott appeared to be get-ting used to the idea. As he told the *NME*'s Gordon Coxhill: 'People listened to the first track which was an instrumental and thought: "Oh, here he goes again . . . gloomy Sunday." The sort of material I have been writing just isn't a saleable product. I wasn't disappointed because I knew it wouldn't sell.'

The ever-loyal Keith Altham described it as a beautiful album that was distinctly more accessible than his recent works. Yet his was virtually a lone voice; few others appeared to be listening. And there were moves afoot at Philips which meant it would be increasingly difficult for Scott to record his own material and avoid a relentless charge towards MOR muzak. It would be another, largely lean, seven years before Scott recorded any further self-penned tracks.

As the new year came in, the record label changed its name to Phonogram in an attempt to establish a new identity in the changing pop field, although the Philips name was retained for MOR acts such as Peters and Lee. It seemed that Scott was now being placed in the same category. Following the commercial failure of yet another LP, Phonogram naturally felt that all their previous doubts about Scott's material had been vindicated and the time had come for him to toe the line – which meant recording what they wanted him to record.

Scott had talked of travelling around Russia collecting ideas for his next project but clearly, given the circumstances, that was unlike-ly to happen and increasingly he complained to Semel that he was being preached to. And in the midst of all this upheaval, there were more bizarre matters to deal with. Wally Stott, the company's key arranger, at least as far as Scott was concerned, underwent a major change of his own. One that, had he still been in a position to write it, was eminently suited as material for a wryly-observed Scott Walker vignette.

Stott, who had only recently married for the second time, and had children by his first wife, went abroad for a couple of weeks, ostensibly to Scandinavia for a holiday. According to former Philips publicist Paddy Fleming, a shock was in store for Johnny Franz when he met Stott at the Lotus House a fortnight later to discuss forthcoming recording sessions.

'Johnny walked in and the head waiter announced: "Madam has arrived, sir." Johnny was understandably puzzled and said he had arranged to have lunch with Wally Stott. The waiter went off again but came back insisting: "Madam says lunch is definitely with you, Mr Franz." When Johnny walked around the corner to sort out the misunderstanding this woman, wearing high-heeled shoes, a dress and a blonde wig, stood up and said: "Hello Johnny, it's Wally." Johnny nearly fell over. He was absolutely shattered and later rang me from his office to say: "Come over, Paddy. I've something extraordinary to tell you." '

Franz's widow Moira, who today lives in a large house in Surrey surrounded by photographs of her late husband, says he received a lengthy letter from Stott explaining the reasons for his sex change, which nevertheless came as a real bombshell to the arranger's colleagues at Stanhope Place. Their reaction was perhaps best summed up by Harry Secombe's immortal remark: 'I've heard of leaving your heart in San Francisco, but this is ridiculous!'

Stott announced that from now on he would be known as Angela Morley, and it is a measure of the respect Morley commanded that when she considered giving up recording sessions, Franz organised a lengthy petition which prompted her to reconsider. Remarkably, the arranger's wife remained a close platonic friend.

By now Scott had tired of life in Amsterdam. Mette was keen to spend more of her time close to her family in Denmark, so the two set up one home in Copenhagen while Scott rented a large flat in the Regent's Park area as his base in London.

Phonogram was still insisting on having the final say on his next recorded work, and Franz believed he had found the song that would relaunch Scott into the big-time. 'I Still See You' was earmarked as the theme to *The Go-Between*, starring Julie Christie and Alan Bates, two of the biggest film stars of the day. With music by Michel Legrand and lyrics by Hal Shaper, many, including Franz, felt it was a sure-fire hit and a queue of artists were eager to record it.

Shaper, whose list of credits includes over a hundred Hollywood movie themes, would live to regret his decision to let Franz have his way. 'I had two vastly different experiences with Scott Walker,' he recalls. 'The first was in December 1967 when I took him across to Paris to record "The Rope And The Colt". It was not only a very complex song but also a very good one. I admired Scott's voice and thought I would give him a break because it was a move away from pop. He did an excellent job and was as professional as anyone could wish for, as well as being great company.

'The second time was in connection with *The Go-Between*. John Franz was absolutely potty over "I Still See You" and begged me to let Scott record it. Remembering how Scott had been in Paris, I was happy to let him do so even though five other major artists (including Shirley Bassey) had expressed an interest in recording it. It could have been a big break for him and opened up many doors. Once you start singing movie themes it's an entirely different ballgame. That doyen of arrangers, Peter Knight, had created a quite stunning orchestration and I was in the Philips studio to see my own song recorded.'

But Scott, it seemed, was not going to take Phonogram's demands lying down. He arrived drunk and clutching a satchel which contained a couple of bottles of vodka and what he announced was his own interpretation of the song. To Shaper's disgust, Scott had also brought a girl (presumably Mette) into the studio with him and as the three-hour session proceeded he swiftly drained the contents of the bottles and insisted on trying out his own musical ideas.

'I was aghast,' says Shaper. 'You don't mess with a writer of the calibre of Michel Legrand. The man's a musical genius. But Scott proceeded to sing something that was so psychedelically stupid that I had to get up and stop everything. John Franz went white. He was extremely upset but seemed to have no control over Scott.' After much haggling, the singer finally capitulated and agreed to sing the song the way it had been written – with the exception of one line which he persisted with.

Shaper: 'The original line was: "I see the fields/So green and fair/ The silent ghosts/Are everywhere", which fitted perfectly into the film, but Scott insisted on singing: "I see the fields/In still green air/ The silent ghosts/To dance their hair". Can you tell me what on earth that means? I still occasionally hear that bloody record on the radio and that line never fails to set my teeth on edge.

'All my admiration for Scott as a vocal artist evaporated. The entire episode remains painfully engraved on my psyche today. He was totally unable to grasp the correct lyrics, even though they were written in front of him. We finally ran out of studio time. John Franz and I had to decide what to do. In the end it was agreed that because of the time factor the single would have to go out as it stood. In retrospect, I feel that Scott should have been sacked and the single scrubbed. It was the last time I worked with him and I haven't seen him from that day to this.'

When he had first met Scott in 1965, Franz was hugely impressed by the singer's professionalism in the studio. Industrious and inventive and possessed with abundant enthusiasm which must have been infectious, Engel never threw the type of prima-donna tantrum so characteristic of some of the record company's temperamental recording stars. Six years down the line, something had gone terribly wrong. Faced with an unsympathetic régime at Phonogram, which clearly possessed little faith in his songwriting abilities, Scott was now merely going through the motions. Deeply unhappy, he again sought refuge in alcohol.

Paddy Fleming confirms: 'Scott seemed less and less inclined to do things. Johnny couldn't understand why he hid himself away in flats with the curtains drawn all day. He wondered whether he might be on drugs because his personality seemed to change and his enthusiasm for work appeared to vanish.'

The flawed single, Scott's first since 'Lights of Cincinnati' two years earlier, was released on 1 October. *NME* described it as a 'beautiful, haunting and poignant ballad with a delightful pizzicato score' and Scott sang the song on the 200th edition of ATV's *Golden Shot*. The film itself was a big success, winning the 1971 Cannes Grand Prix Award, but no one was too surprised when the single sank without trace. 'I Still See You', and its B-side 'My Way Home', were however included on yet another compilation, 'This Is Scott Walker', that October as Phonogram attempted to recoup some of their investment.

Scott lamely commented: 'I recorded the song because I dug the film. It's a beautiful song and I've always admired Legrand.' Adding insult to injury, he complained that he was only given an hour to record his vocal when he really needed six.

Some years later, Engel revealed that he had turned down an offer for a concert at London's Royal Albert Hall at around this time. 'It was to be a concert of my songs,' he said. 'But I had been away for a while and I had forgotten most of them. I just wasn't ready for something like that.'

No doubt wondering what to do next with his increasingly reckless charge, Semel decided the only course of action was to get him back on stage. A full-scale tour was out of the question, both financially and because of Scott's notorious reluctance to go on the road, but Semel finally persuaded him to take on a short residency at the Frontier Club in Batley, West Yorkshire.

From the outside the Frontier resembles little more than a glorified youth club, but it is in fact one of the top cabaret venues in the north. A year earlier, Scott had repeatedly told journalists that he was broke, so it was perhaps no surprise when he accepted the 'superb money' on offer for the week of dates. He would return there several times over the following years, whenever his bank balance demanded it.

In November 1975 he gave the *NME*'s Pete Erskine an alternative explanation: 'The original reason for playing there was that the lyrical content of some of the earlier solo stuff was considered pretty risky, so I simultaneously narrowed down the odds by doing this tiny place semi-anonymously from time to time.'

He came closer to the truth when he added: 'You see, I never had the guts for the big concert stuff. I'd rather rationalise the frequency of my solo appearances to this one club every year for more money than some of the others combined.'

By all accounts the shows went well. Dressed in black trousers, a pale blue shirt and a light brown corduroy jacket, Scott grimaced as he took to the stage and was greeted by half a dozen screams, but these immediately subsided as he launched into 'Amsterdam' and then sat on a stool to deliver Paul McCartney's 'The Long and Winding Road'.

The audience sat back in respectful silence while he introduced 'Make It Easy On Yourself' as 'a tune you'll probably know', following it with 'Stormy' from ' 'Til The Band Comes In'. Then it was back to the stool for 'Joanna' and 'Lights of Cincinnati' before the lights faded and came up again as the band went into 'Jacky', with Scott waving his mike in the air and giving it all he had. Finally, as he left the stage, the audience took to its feet and cheered. They were duly rewarded when he returned to thank them for coming, and most of all for listening, and sat back on his stool for 'If You Go Away' and 'Lady Came From Baltimore'.

Afterwards Scott seemed pleased with his 40 minutes' work, commenting: 'I didn't feel so good on the first night, but I was fine after that.'

The wolf had been kept away from the door once again, which was just as well, for he returned home to discover he was soon to have another mouth to feed. Mette was pregnant with their first child.

14 Copenhagen

'If I leave children in this world, then I'm leavin' part of myself here too.'

Scott Walker, 1968

METTE TEGLBJAERG WAS BORN three years after Scott, on 28 July 1946 in Lyngby, a quiet middle-class suburb some eight miles north of Denmark's bustling capital Copenhagen. Her father Rasmus (after whom Scott had named his St Bernard puppy) taught science at a local school. He has now retired but her mother Dorte still teaches English at an adult-education centre in Lyngby.

The two academics met at a party in a restaurant following their graduation from school and were married soon after. Their first child Annedorte preceded Mette by two years and they were blessed with a third daughter eight years later. 'Mette was a lively, jolly girl,' recalls Dorte. Although she went to a nearby school, neither Rasmus nor Dorte taught their strikingly beautiful second child, and Dorte is frank enough to admit: 'She was very well-behaved but not academically brilliant.'

After school, Mette trained as a children's nurse for a couple of years but as news of swinging London filtered across the North Sea to Denmark, she decided it was time to spread her wings.

The idea of joining her older sister Annedorte in London was confirmed shortly after in 1966, when she and her friends went to Copenhagen's Carousel Club for a concert by The Walker Brothers, whose combination of good looks and soaring ballads was already taking the rest of Europe by storm. As for Scott, the combination of her perfect figure and sultry but mysterious Scandinavian beauty was irresistible.

The singer had firm views on how his women should look and behave, declaring back in 1965: 'I like a girl to look like a girl when she dresses, but femininity is a state of mind, not a mode of attire. I don't expect her to come to see me every evening with her hair done. I like sensitive people, but most of all I like girls who try to understand or at least listen with some sympathy.

'She'd have to like the same things as I like and like living where I live. I'm pretty untidy so she'd have to be a good picker-up because I can't stand living in my own mess. I wouldn't want the girl I marry to be involved in my business interests. She'd be kept well away from the clubs and one-nighters. The whole Disney scene is not for my wife. I want a woman to come home to who is not involved in the same kind of hysteria that I get wrapped up in – someone who can untangle me a little. I need quite a bit of unravelling.'

While Mette might not have been blessed with the most academic of brains, her quiet but determined personality mesmerised Scott. Despite her stunning looks, she appears to have been a homely girl with little time for the more glamorous aspects of life on the arm of a top pop star. She certainly was not among the screaming brigade of women who made Scott's every public appearance a nightmare. More than anything, she was a good listener, one of the few people Scott could really open his heart to. In short, Mette was the dream girl he had earlier described and she would be his constant companion and confidante for the next nine years.

Perhaps it was the effect of thousands of girls throwing themselves at him, but by 1968 Scott revealed that he had gone off the idea of marriage, though not of having children, a responsibility he clearly relished. He told *Rave* magazine: 'I want a woman to have my children, but without having to marry her. An arrangement that would be legal, with full consent. I know how to handle children, how to educate them. They represent security to me. It's a kind of spiritual thing I believe in, to have something left of mine when I die. I could do more for children than the average person. I know how a child should be raised – in material security, free from pressures, completely relaxed with no mental hang-ups. These are all the things I wasn't!'

Doubtless Mette agreed with the sentiment of the latter part of Scott's perspective on a happy family life, but it is no surprise that she was not prepared to remain an unmarried mother. Within sixteen months of their daughter Lee's birth on 30 August 1972, the couple were married in a typically private ceremony at a chapel in Las Vegas, during one of Scott's rare trips home to visit his mother.

Bearing in mind Scott's stubborn streak, it is testimony to Mette's own strength of will that she was able to turn round his seemingly steadfast opinions on matrimony, although Scott later told Gary, ostensibly as a joke, that the Vegas wedding venue was: 'In case I have to get a divorce, it'll be real easy.'

Neither John nor Gary attended the ceremony, nor did Mette's parents, but the newlyweds and their baby daughter returned to Copenhagen shortly afterwards for a celebration party with Scott's in-laws.

With his personal life on an even keel, the singer's thoughts turned back to how he would support his new family. After ' 'Til The Band Comes In', Scott had told Tony Norman he would wait and see how it did before deciding on his next musical step: 'If this album is well-received, then I will try again. But first I've gotta see how many people are still interested in what I'm doin'.'

It is clear that Scott took the responsibility of fatherhood very seriously and he no longer felt he had the luxury of working just when it suited him. He might have been prepared to starve for his art, but he was not going to inflict that fate on his daughter.

In effect, he agreed to sell out to the whims of his record company bosses rather than risk being dumped from the label with no source of income for his family. They had a comfortable flat in Regent's Park and Scott quite understandably decided it was not worth rocking the boat.

In 1977, the *NME*'s Phil McNeill noted with sadness that Scott had allowed himself to be manipulated towards schmaltz. The singer was quick to defend himself: 'At that time I had a new manager and he told me to get a big pad. So I had this place and suddenly I had all the records I wanted to buy and became very complacent. And I thought: "If they don't want me to write anything, fuck it." So I just sat back and copped money for whatever they wanted me to do. If they wanted me to do movie themes, man, I would pick the best movie themes that I thought were possible and I would do them – Sinatra-type stuff. I'll imitate anybody. It was down to that. Whatever needed to be done.'

Not long after Lee's birth, Scott agreed to go back into the studio to record 'The Moviegoer', a selection of themes from some of his favourite films.

The songs were lovingly arranged and recorded by Johnny Franz and engineer Peter Olliff, with lush orchestral arrangements by Robert Cornford, but the MOR songs, by the likes of Henry Mancini, Neil Diamond and, once again, Michel Legrand, brought out equally run-of-the-mill performances from a singer who had seemingly resigned himself to mediocrity. The sleeve showed a stetson-clad Scott looking suitably disinterested next to a large cinema ticket marked 'rear stalls'. In all honesty, most people would not have wanted to be much closer to the action contained within.

The collection opens with 'This Way Mary', a lilting ballad completely at odds with the persecuted life and violent death suffered by Mary, Queen of Scots, the film from which it was taken. Other forgettable moments, such as 'That Night' and 'The Summer Knows', were culled from obscure cinematic offerings *The Fox* and *Summer of '42*. Neil Diamond's 'Glory Road', from *WUSA*, and *The Godfather* theme 'Speak Softly Love' fare a little better, but the highlight is undoubtedly the Ennio Morricone/Joan Baez composition 'The Ballad of Sacco and Vanzetti (Here's To You)'. With a spaghetti-western feel vaguely reminiscent of the celebrated 'The Seventh Seal' from 'Scott 4', it tells the story of two Italian/American anarchists found guilty of robbery and murder and executed in Massachusetts in 1927.

There is little to commend on Side Two. 'The Ballad of Joe Hill', from the film of the same name, briefly lifts proceedings and 'Easy Come, Easy Go', from *They Shoot Horses, Don't They?*, is at least kept simple with Scott crooning over a piano part that could have been taken from Michelle Pfeiffer's hit movie *The Fabulous Baker Boys*, nearly twenty years later. For the record, the other contributions are 'A Face In The Crowd' (from *Le Mans*), 'Loss Of Love' (from *Sunflower*), 'Come Saturday Morning' (from *Pookie*) and 'All His Children' (from *Never Give An Inch*, advice that Scott could well have heeded himself).

All things considered, 'The Moviegoer' is a record that can be recommended only to the most die-hard Scott Walker fan, and with no suitable single to support it, it is no surprise that they were the only ones to buy it when it appeared in the shops that October.

Scott claimed to have recorded the album while recuperating from an illness he had picked up in Scandinavia. Though, bearing in mind that there was no public announcement either of his marriage or the birth of his child, it is possible that this was his way of keeping recent events in his treasured personal life under wraps.

With yet another flop to his name, Scott again agreed to bring in some money by making a short series of cabaret appearances at Manchester's Fagin's Club in early 1973. But he made it clear that these once a year excursions were not in any way a labour of love: 'The way I live, the money goes pretty fast and I have to do some more gigs. It's just for the money. I work then relax until the money is gone but the truth is I never could face working to a live audience.'

Nevertheless, long-time fan Robin Edwards witnessed three Fagin's shows, and Scott seems to have hidden his distaste for this enforced activity rather well. 'He was dressed casually in denim jeans, a blue button-down shirt and trainers,' remembers Edwards. 'Just before the start of his performance on the first night, a girl from the audience got up on stage to present Scott with a bottle of Johnnie Walker whisky which he proceeded to open and swig from, much to the amusement of the audience. He seemed happy and relaxed and sang a Brel selection, including "Mathilde" and "Jacky", some songs from "The Moviegoer" and, most surprisingly, all The Walker Brothers hits.

'He even shared a joke or two with the audience, saying at one point: "I was talking to a guy the other day and he said that my solo version of 'Make It Easy On Yourself' wasn't as good as the record I did with The Walker Mothers" (he placed the emphasis on Mothers and got a big laugh). "I said: 'Hell, man, that had a hundred violins on it!' " '

Without the violins and backed only by a three-piece band, Scott was still in great form throughout. With the audience by now accustomed to the vow of silence Scott expected, one could have heard a pin drop as he returned for an encore of 'Black Sheep Boy', accompanied only by his own acoustic guitar.

No doubt relieved that he had once again conquered those self-created demons conjured by taking to the stage, Scott, according to Edwards, 'was beaming all over his face' as the performance drew to a close.

No sooner had the new year of 1973 come in than Scott was sent back into the studio to record another bland set of interpretations, and that May came the inevitable end of his eight-year association with Philips, with the release of 'Any Day Now'.

If anything, worse than its predecessor, the album was indeed the 'sad, end-of-contract story' described in the May 1992 edition of *Vox* magazine, which added that: 'It furthered his inexplicable move away from songwriting.'

Four years later, a puzzled Phil McNeill questioned how 'the man who made some of the world's most powerful records should have subsided into feeble bleats? How the lion became a lamb?'

In faltering, half-completed sentences, Scott explained as best he could: 'You sing this nice Jim Webb song or whatever the fuck it was [Webb wrote 'If Ships Were Made To Sail' and 'All My Love's Laughter' on 'Any Day Now'] because I was trying to find out what the hell they wanted me to do, which was dumb of me. I should have kept pursuin' what I was pursuin'.'

The record sleeve described how Scott Walker's music was his life and proclaimed: 'On this his latest LP are many great examples of vocal artistry that prove dedication is worthwhile.' The sleeve-notes were uncredited, which is understandable as the listener will search in vain for evidence of those examples of memorable vocal artistry. It was readily apparent that Scott certainly did not consider this to be 'his music'.

Among the low points in this sea of MOR sterility are Bill Withers' 'Ain't No Sunshine' and David Gates's 'If'. It is hard to imagine a more lamentable version of the latter than that by lollipop-licking TV cop Telly Savalas, who enjoyed a No. 1 hit with it a couple of years later, but Scott managed it.

Out of desperation, Philips put out the dreary Black/Barry composition 'The Me I Never Knew' as a single backed with the equally awful 'This Way Mary' from 'The Moviegoer'. No one bought it and both sides decided that the time had come to call it a day.

With the end of Scott's association with Philips came the demise of his working relationship with Franz and Olliff, who had stayed loyal to him throughout his recording career. The latter feels that the changes in Scott's personal life definitely had an effect on his work: 'The change in his lifestyle did affect his writing. From that point it seemed to lose direction. You can have the best people around you but ultimately you have to make a certain number of decisions yourself and he just seemed to have lost interest.'

There was no animosity about the parting of ways, but it was obvious Scott needed new faces to bounce ideas off. Ady Semel wasted no time in fixing him up with a new recording deal on CBS, and Scott quickly found the mentor he was looking for in the shape of an up-and-coming producer/arranger named Del Newman.

Newman had learnt his trade at EMI's Abbey Road studios, but got his first big break arranging hits for Cat Stevens. Now living in West Wales, he admits to never having heard a Walker Brothers hit prior to his first meeting with Scott, but when the two were introduced at CBS's London offices they hit it off immediately. Newman says: 'If he hadn't have liked me instinctively I'd never have got the gig.

'There are two types of producer. The first has an idea and tries to fit the artist into it, whereas I would find out what they wanted to do and how they wanted to do it. I always sought to give the artist freedom to do his own thing and I think Scott needed that space. I liked him because he was upfront and he knew exactly what he wanted to do.'

Scott had already dabbled in country music on each of his previous three LPs, and he decided that was the direction he would move in. His new bosses must have groaned since even today, country music is notoriously difficult to sell in Europe. In Scott's native America it was a different story, but by the mid-seventies his public profile there was roughly on a par with that of The Wombles, the furry denizens of Wimbledon Common, who enjoyed a spate of British hits around this time.

Newman, however, was happy to go along with the idea. 'His penchant for country was so obvious,' he says. 'As an American from the farm belt he had that voice and a good ear.' Bearing in mind that Scott left the Mid-West when he was just seven, the singer rather fancifully maintained: 'It's a return to my roots, because I was raised in Texas and I do know a lot about country music. It's very authentic and everyone worked very hard on it.' In fact, both Newman and seasoned session musician B. J. Cole, who added the LP's distinctive pedal steel guitar, agree that they did not achieve a true Nashville sound at all.

'Both the records I made with him would have been different albums had they actually been made in Nashville,' says Newman. 'People may think that it's up to the producer and artist to ensure that, but it doesn't work that way.'

Cole, a veteran of sessions with country superstar Johnny Nash, not to mention Elton John, Marc Bolan and Procol Harum, comments: 'It's very much an English version of country. A true Nashville drummer would have kept it much more simple, with the emphasis on the backbeat. The British drummers filled in the sound by going all over the kit and using lots of toms. And the bass-players played everything far too flowery with complicated runs.

'In country music that is the worst thing you can do, because the music mustn't get in the way of the songs. There was a lot of snobbery among British musicians at the time. They looked down on American players who kept everything simple and missed the point entirely. They assumed that because they didn't play much, they couldn't play much.'

But Cole adds: 'That's not to say I didn't like it, but technically it wasn't correct. I don't think it's surprising that Scott chose the style because they are very much songs for singers where the voice can actually tell a story. For a singer with American connections, it must have been a great source of inspiration.'

The new Engel-Newman partnership, bolstered by the presence of engineer Richard Dodd, threw itself headlong into the recording sessions at Nova Studios in Bryanston Street, near Marble Arch. Yet, even though it was years since he had enjoyed any sort of chart success, Scott's life was still made difficult by his die-hard fans, not to mention London's ever-vigilant traffic wardens.

Newman: 'Scott used to drive into Marble Arch in the Volkswagen Beetle he owned at the time. He'd get countless tickets but he had foreign plates so he used to enjoy the ritual of tearing them up. There were always queues of women outside the studio. He'd come in panting and dishevelled having been chased and shout: "Shut all the doors!" '

But it appeared that Scott was at last learning to see the lighter side of his followers' fanaticism. 'He was a lovable eccentric,' Newman fondly remembers. 'He came into the studio once after being chased, announced that he'd be back in a second, and went out the back door, right around the block and back in again. He was chuckling as he came in, as though it had all become a game to him.'

For Scott, the studio game now included an obligatory drop of the hard stuff. 'His favourite was bourbon – Old Grandad. He'd bring a bottle to the studio and by the end of the session it would be empty. The next day I'd feel obliged to bring a bottle myself. I'm not a drinker so I used to stagger back to my flat in Ladbroke Gardens next to Portobello Market.'

Contrary to Hal Shaper's experience, the heavy drinking seemed to have little effect on the singer's abilities, or on his celebrated good looks. To Newman, it was if, like Dorian Gray, Scott had sold his soul to the devil: 'He looked ten years younger than he actually was. I don't know how he did it. He didn't have a blemish. The control he had was phenomenal and he had a fantastic ear which wouldn't seem to go with someone who could down half a bottle of bourbon. Yet it didn't seem to dull his senses at all.'

Cole, too, was in awe, but for different reasons: 'Technically he's the best singer I have ever worked with. His vocal quality sent shivers up your spine. He had the best proper vocal of his time. There are

people who have quirky voices that work for them, but Scott Walker
has a proper voice. He's one of those people who can sing to order.
He only has to open his mouth and it sounds good. It might not
sound authentic but it will sound good. To me he was the male
version of Dusty Springfield. He was that good.'

The sessions were over quickly, in about four weeks, more
through necessity than choice. Newman: 'If you sell lots of records
then you get lots of studio time because you call the shots. So we
were working without the kind of power that allowed you to sit
back.

'It wasn't rushed, although I personally would have liked a lot
more time. But Scott hated to wait. He wanted to get it down on tape
and get out of the studio. Everyone smoked in those days, you're
breathing recycled air and of course there were no windows.'

The session band, hand-picked by Newman and Engel, laid down
the backing tracks live while Scott sang a rough vocal, returning later
to record the final takes in private with only the producer and engineer as witnesses.

Cole: 'Everything was done live in those days. We were all given
a chord chart and just got on with it. I didn't read music too well
then but afterwards I realised that the string players were usually
winging it as well. We weren't around for the final vocal takes but I
always tried to insist on a rough vocal to work with because in
country music the steel guitar in particular keys up to the words. If
there's no lyric there's nothing to feed on so you end up with guitar
all over it which isn't the job it should be doing.'

'Stretch' was released in November of 1973, its title a nickname
Walker had picked up through the years. Even though it was again a
collection of other people's material, Scott seemed more enthusiastic
than he had been about anything he had done in the past three years.

In a CBS press release that accompanied copies of the LP sent out
to music journalists, he explained: 'At Philips I'd been working with
the same team of people for eight years, and the new combination in
itself made a considerable difference. Del Newman is a totally different personality to Johnny Franz. I'd never heard any of his
arrangements but we got along and picked the songs that were going
well. I don't have any of my records at home because I find it difficult
to listen to myself. But this is the first album where I can listen to
most of it and say I really did my best on that. That's what's so good
about it.'

The press release questioned whether the lack of original songs meant his interest in writing had diminished. Scott's answer was effectively yes: 'Well, in those days I was writing about very personal experiences, and when you're younger you let it all out. When you get older you become careful, and I'm now very careful about the statements I make. I want my work to be to the point and as musical as possible, but it's very hard to get that combination.'

Scott's performances are certainly stronger on 'Stretch' but he would later cast doubt on just how committed he had been to the record. Mike Newbury's 'Sunshine' kicks it off in a true country vein echoed in Tom T. Hall's 'That's How I Got To Memphis' and the J. Owen-penned 'Where Love Has Died'.

But otherwise 'Stretch' is essentially another collection of ballads in the style Engel had been persisting with for years. Randy Newman, who Scott rated among the top three songwriters of all time, contributed two of the best – 'Just One Smile' and the plaintive 'I'll Be Home' with Scott putting in a heartfelt performance over a simple piano arrangement.

As *Melody Maker* reviewer Michael Watts pointed out, Scott still suffered from an inability to decide whether he wanted to be an artist or a balladeer in the true showbiz style: 'He occasionally verges on showy emotionalism such as in Goffin and King's "No Easy Way Down" and particularly Jimmy Webb's "Where Does The Brown Begin" which sounds stagey despite a great arrangement by Del Newman.'

The highlight of the album is provided by Spooner Oldham and Dan Penn's 'A Woman Left Lonely', a song made famous by Janis Joplin on her acclaimed 1971 LP 'Pearl'. Scott's soulful rendition is punctuated by a fine Jim Ryan guitar solo and the song puts across its tearjerking message without descending into schmaltz.

Watts concluded that is was an elegant, pleasantly melancholy album, unlikely to usher in a new era for Scott. His assessment proved absolutely correct.

Within a few weeks of the release and its subsequent chart failure, Scott was already at war with the record company's A&R department. In a *Melody Maker* interview with Watts, it emerged that enough material had already been recorded for a second, more overtly country LP, which CBS was blocking after the poor sales of 'Stretch'.

Accompanied by Ady Semel, Scott turned up for the interview at

Mayfair's Hilton hotel with a bush hat tipped over his eyes. As they chatted over a pot of Earl Grey tea, it transpired that Scott was not quite as happy with the record as the CBS press machine had made out. He complained that he had in fact signed to the label under the belief that he would be doing his own songs and not be 'just an interpretive talent'.

But the A&R department, he claimed, 'rode shotgun on my ass', gathering half the material for the LP themselves. The result, according to Watts, was inhibitory. Scott continued: 'Now they're comin' on to me and sayin': "Well, where's your own material? We must hear it some time." And I tell them, "I'm not gonna audition my songs for you." If I can come to some sort of agreement with them then I'll be happy, if I can't I'd rather go somewhere else.'

The seeds of Engel's departure from CBS in the summer of 1974 had already been sown, but for now he was intent on getting that second LP released.

Most of the songs had been written by country and western shooting star composer Joe Shaver. This, wrote Watts, sounded truly adventurous, but CBS's view was that country did not sell in Britain, and the album was on hold in the vain hope of securing an American deal.

An irritated Engel expanded: 'Most of the stuff was brand new, and that's very hard to get. I had it all when it was new. This was the thing that pissed me off. In my opinion it has what I had on my first two or three solo albums – it has the conviction that I lost, and I think by the time I get my writing into the framework I'll have achieved the circle again.'

It was not to be. The second CBS album 'We Had It All' was finally released the following August, but included no original songs. It was, indeed, a more overtly country record with four Shaver tracks appearing alongside standards such as 'Whatever Happened To Saturday Night' and Alex Harvey's 'Delta Dawn'.

Despite Scott's earlier enthusiasm, CBS's reluctance to put out the record was vindicated when it sank without trace. Even Del Newman admits of the two LPs: 'They just weren't commerical. Because of the financial involvement, lawyers and accountants were gradually taking over the music business and I think Scott reacted to that. If someone had given him his head then I'm sure he would have come up with some very commercial things.'

Fans have long speculated whether yet another potentially great

Scott Walker

Scott Walker LP was sunk by the demands of short-sighted record company executives. The four Shaver songs – 'Low Down Freedom', 'Black Rose', 'Ride Me Down Easy' and 'Old Five And Dimers Like Me' – are certainly the strongest on the record. Perhaps Scott did record a whole LP's-worth, only to see them watered down with safer, more recognisable fodder such as 'Saturday Night'. But this seems unlikely and more the stuff of music industry legend. Maurice Oberstein, who signed Engel to CBS, insists that every song he recorded for the label was released. 'We put out everything he delivered. It was getting delivery that was the problem with Scott,' he says.

And yet 'We Had It All' was at least a positive step in a new direction, something Scott had repeatedly insisted he wanted to do but rarely fulfilling the promise. At last he had moved away from his past. His very next move would be to embrace it wholeheartedly.

15 Always Coming Back To You

'A Walkers reunion? What a dreadful thought. My God –
regression. The Walkers are dead and buried and better for it.'

Scott Walker, 1969

F EVER AN ILLUSTRATION OF SYNCHRONICITY WAS NEEDED, the surprise
reformation of The Walker Brothers in the summer of 1975
provides it. Six months earlier, after the bitter break-up of his
second marriage and the years of scraping to make ends meet,
interspersed with wild spending sprees whenever a royalty cheque
came in, John Maus finally realised his life was going nowhere. Lying
on a Californian beach, the second-most famous Walker Brother decided he had had enough of surf and sun and idly wondered whether
the time was right to make it all happen again. Not long afterwards,
he was en route from Los Angeles International Airport to London's
Heathrow, determined to seek out Walker Brother number one.

Scott, meanwhile, was going through his own marital problems
and spending more and more time away from his wife and child in
Copenhagen. Without a permanent home in London, he was temporarily living in a room at White's Hotel on the Edgware Road.

The period leading up to The Walker Brothers' reunion was exceedingly traumatic for both men. Scott and Mette had begun to
grow apart within a couple of years of their marriage. Engel's frequent trips to England to fulfil recording or cabaret engagements
placed an increasing strain on the relationship, which was exacerbated by the girls who continued to congregate outside his dressing-
room door or pursue him along the London streets. 'He tried to keep
the marriage goin' but it wasn't workin',' says Gary. 'I'm sure it was
Mette's fault. She was a very jealous type. Girls would come backstage asking for Scott's autograph and stuff and it used to cause
terrible scenes.'

So what had appeared an idyllic partnership was weakened and
eventually broken by the demands of Scott's professional career. The
divorce was amicable and Scott continued to visit Lee regularly and
ensure that he played a major role in her upbringing. 'A few years

177

later I remember him sayin' that he was dreadin' goin' over to Copenhagen to see Lee,' says Gary. 'I asked: "Why? Because you'll be seein'
Mette?" He said: "No, because I've gotta take Lee on those rollercoaster
rides at Tivoli Gardens." He just hates those big dipper things, y'see!'

John had suffered a parallel personal crisis. Frankie Lee, who
formerly worked as DJ Simon Dee's personal secretary and introduced Maus to his second wife, Julie Parker-Cann, says the former
Walker Brother was barely surviving from one royalty cheque to
another by the early seventies.

Frankie, now a successful Hollywood agent, recalls: 'He got
around $5,000 a time, which in those days would see you through
six months, but the more we hung out with him the more we realised
how careless he was with money. Eventually, they became so in ar-
rears with their rent that they ended up coming to live with us. We
lent him money, his sister Judy lent him money, all his friends, everybody. He had tapped all the sources.

'We soon realised that John wasn't in great shape. As soon as he
got up, the first thing he did was smoke a cigarette and reach for the
Scotch bottle. It was his insulin. He just couldn't live without it. No
matter how poor they were he always had money for Scotch. In those
days you didn't dare tell someone they were an alcoholic, but he
obviously was. If Alcoholics Anonymous had been around I would
have dragged him straight there, but no one then knew how to deal
with drugs and alcohol.'

John, who did not eat very much, was painfully thin. Always a
late-night person, he would not retire to bed until six or seven in the
morning. He and Julie would stay with Frankie and her husband for
six months or so, then the arrival of a royalty cheque would send
them racing off to the South of France, where John could hang out
with Bill Wyman, a real life Rolling Stone . . . something he himself
had always yearned to be.

'Julie was as bad as John,' recounts Frankie. 'Once, when they
were down to absolute zero, he was forced to go out and find work
as a labourer. He worked damn hard to earn two hundred dollars
and Julie went out and bought a leather belt with half of it.

'Julie became pregnant and had their son Jamie in late 1975. John
panicked because he was now a father and had no money. That just
made things worse between them. John and Julie split before Jamie
was born and I was left to get Julie into a birth programme at UCLA.
In those days you had to pay about five thousand dollars to get into

a decent hospital and she just didn't have the money. She later found religion and returned to England with Jamie to spread the word.'

According to Frankie, John's current wife Brandy has never allowed him to have any contact with Jamie. Today, Maus, who apparently has no contact with his own parents, is still estranged from his son.

John appears to have recorded a couple of songs at Wyman's 'Honky Tonk' French château which eventually emerged in demo form on the American Greene Mountain label in 1973. October of that year saw him back in Britain, where he formed a cabaret act called The New Walker Brothers with a singer named Jimmy Wilson who had appeared on the hit television show *Opportunity Knocks*. Wilson's voice may have been a passable imitation of Scott's, but he actually looked more like Jack Wild's Artful Dodger in the hit musical *Oliver!*.

The New Walker Brothers worked the large cabaret circuit, including Allinsons in Liverpool, Talk of the Midlands in Nottingham, and Barbarella's. Their set, which included 'The Sun Ain't Gonna Shine Anymore' and 'Stay With Me Baby' whipped up fervent audience reaction and enthusiastic reviews which undoubtedly made John more amenable to suggestions of reforming the original group. The New Walker Brothers played their last gig in Brighton in May 1974 and Wilson's death in a farming accident some years later gave rise to bizarre rumours (which still persist) that Scott Walker was dead. The dubious nature of this cabaret venture perhaps explains why John was so reluctant to discuss his post-Walkers activities when the band reformed in 1975.

Back in London, John soon tracked down his old sparring partner. Scott returned to the hotel one day and: 'Who should be standin' at the bar but John. We got rappin' for the first time in years, tossed a few ideas around and both went away interested in gettin' back together again.'

Scott later commented: 'When we split we left a void and I don't think it has been successfully filled. I think the time is ripe for us.' With a hint of clairvoyance, he added: 'If it doesn't happen now . . .?'

A few months earlier, Gary Leeds, who had recently returned from his own lengthy sabbatical in the United States, persuaded United Artists to release his comeback single, a cover of The Easybeats' 'Hello How Are You', produced by The Hollies' Allan Clarke. It failed to make any impact, although Gary claims: 'The demand was there, but they just didn't print enough copies.'

While promoting the record in London, he made a spur of the moment decision to give Scott a call, and who should be with him but John: 'I met Scott and John at the hotel. They had already talked about reforming so when I called we decided to do it and just see what happened.'

As the undisputed star of the trio, it might, to outsiders, have seemed an odd move for Scott. But after following his 'brothers' out of the charts with six consecutive flop LPs, he needed a career boost just as much as the other two. With John and Gary both managerless, Scott's multi-talented Svengali, Ady Semel, took on all three.

Semel was well aware that one of Scott's biggest fans was ambitious record company boss Dick Leahy, who was currently looking for acts for his newly-formed GTO label. Leahy was a fresh-faced newcomer when he got a job with Philips in 1965 as assistant head of the company's new Fontana label.

Leahy recalls: 'I knew Scott in those days, but not well. At that time artists nearly always recorded in the label's own studios so they were always around the building. Philips was a small place so everybody got together in the canteen. I used to hear the work he was doing with Johnny Franz and Peter Olliff and when I went in in the morning they would play me what had been recorded the previous night.'

Leahy left Philips in 1970 to become general manager of Bell Records, transforming it in just four years from an unknown label into a pop phenomenon whose roster included Gary Glitter, The Bay City Rollers, Dawn, The Partridge Family and David Cassidy. While the artists may not be best remembered for their street credibility, there was no doubting Leahy's ability to spot a chart-topping act.

In June 1974 he had decided the time was right to launch his own label and begin earning some money for himself. He left Bell on a Friday and by the following Monday had set up shop in tiny offices on Regent Street. Leahy's first problem was a name for his new venture, as both the ideas he had considered were already in use.

Leahy finally picked GTO from the initial letters of the Gem-Toby Organisation, a company owned by two of his new partners. Although they often joked about it, the label's name had nothing to do with the owners' favourite tipple: 'Gin and tonic with an olive.'

Within a few months, the GTO staff had grown from four to ten and the label moved to more suitable two-storey accommodation in

Barlow Place, behind the Barclays Bank building in Bond Street. More significantly, it signed its first artists, Fox. The male/female vocal group went on to enjoy an eighteen-month run of Top Twenty successes with 'Only You Can', 'Imagine Me Imagine You' and 'S-S-S-Single Bed'. Leahy's second signing was the newly reformed Walker Brothers, who were quickly followed by Heatwave, Donna Summer and Billy Ocean.

Leahy: 'They had already made the decision to get together when I got a call from Ady Semel who asked if I fancied it. He said he was phoning because he had heard I was a big fan of theirs. I said: "Of course! Why not?" and agreed to meet up with all four of them at Barlow Place.

'Everything had to be cash with Ady Semel. Normally we would just give a cheque, but he said that for some reason to do with his international businesses he would like it in cash. I checked with my lawyer and accountant and they said there was no problem as long as the money was documented as going to them.

'I suspected they all had their own tax problems but at the end of the day when an artist has signed a contract and says they want to deal in cash there is no reason why you shouldn't. The deal was that they would produce an album. I think the figure was ten thousand pounds against the delivery of the recording. I seem to remember, in making the first album, we invested around forty thousand pounds all in, including recording costs, promotion, etc. I told them, "You've that much money to play with, go and do it." '

The GTO staff soon grew accustomed to the sight of Scott, that distinctive bush hat tipped over his eyes, waiting in reception for Dick Leahy with his head virtually touching his chest. 'We all thought he didn't want to talk to us,' says former GTO head of Promotions, Mike Peyton. 'But, of course, the opposite was true, he was a very shy person.'

As time passed, Scott came to know and like Leahy, and the pair would occasionally play tennis together. 'I don't know how he did it because he never trained but always looked good,' says Leahy. 'We played at the Van der Bilt at Shepherd's Bush before it went up-market. The Prince of Wales uses it now.'

Despite his outward reticence, Engel must have warmed to the relaxed and informal atmosphere at GTO, which made a refreshing change from the oppressive régime at CBS. After a few months at his new label, he began a relationship with Leahy's personal assistant,

Denise Simpson, an attractive girl in her early twenties with shoul-der-length brown hair. 'She was neurotic in a nice way,' smiles Leahy. 'I can understand Scott and her getting on because I imagine they could look at the darker side of life together.'

After closing the GTO deal, Semel put each of his new charges on a retainer of £400 a month and installed them in a large flat in the New King's Road, no doubt to save on hotel bills. The flat was above a trendy restaurant with a large gay clientèle. It was also di-rectly over the District underground line and on the first morning the rumbling of the trains caused Gary, who had had a phobia about earthquakes ever since he was a child in California, to leap out of bed in a panic.

Leeds remembers: 'This restaurant was a bistro-type place. It was great because we could record on the top floor and they would bring all the food up from the restaurant. John rigged up a ladder through the skylight so we could lie on duvets on the roof improving our suntans. I had a tent inside the flat, just like Lawrence of Arabia with all the cushions around it.

'Marc Bolan's place was just round the back. We were eating roast suckling pig in the restaurant one night when he came over. He had a real overpowering personality and said: "Hi, I'm Marc Bolan, the King of the Boogie." Then he started singing this song he was working on. I thought: "This is gonna be terrible because of the way Scott is." You know, he won't say boo or hello to anybody. But the whole thing struck Scott as real funny. Bolan wanted us on his TV show. We kept saying no, we're not ready, but a month later we went around to his place for a jam and he was real shocked that we could play and that we were actually a working band before we made it big. We played all this blues stuff. If only we had put some of it down on tape.

'Bolan was a real night and day type. You know, the way you saw him and the way he really was. He was really funny. I told him I was still upset with David Bowie – David Jones, right – because I saw him in Tin Pan Alley and gave him twenty pounds once and he never paid me back. And he said: "Cor, you were lucky, I gave him about two thousand, and he never paid me back either."'

With their own financial problems held temporarily at bay, the most pressing problem for the Walker Brothers Mark Two was find-ing suitable material to record.

Considering Scott's recent track record in this area, Dick Leahy took a remarkably liberal attitude over what he expected from the group: 'I didn't insist that they work with anyone or that they take any particular approach. I just said, let's give it a go. I wasn't particularly expecting original material. We discussed that and they said they had a few ideas so I just left it to them.'

In fact, the trio were already struggling to find the right songs with which to relaunch their careers. Scott recalled hopping into a car with Gary nearly every morning on huge record-buying sprees. 'I guess we must have bought three, four, even five hundred LPs,' he said. 'And y'know what? . . . I only wanted to keep about four out of the lot for my collection.'

Former GTO A&R man Paul Kinder, now with Virgin, says: 'The album consisted of songs that Scott wanted to sing. They were all covers because I think Scott was aware of his own commercial limitations as a writer.'

For a man who had constantly said he was interested only in looking to the future, Scott's choice of personnel for the LP was as inconsistent as his decision to reform the group. His first choice for producer was his old mentor Johnny Franz who, he assured Dick Leahy, was 'still the best fixer of a key there was'. But when Franz, who was still head of A&R at Philips, was forced to decline the offer, Scott took on the production role himself, with engineer Geoff Calver assisting.

'The only thing Scott couldn't do was the engineering aspect, he didn't know the mechanics,' says Gary. When the LP was finally delivered, not everyone at the record company would agree with that assessment.

The musicians on the album, which was assembled at London's Air Studios, Marquee Studios and Kingsway Recorders, were also a throwback to the previous decade. Guitarist Alan Parker and drummer Barry Morgan were among them. Dick Leahy notes: 'These were all people Scott knew from his work in the sixties. Great musicians love a great voice and they don't get too many opportunities to play with a really good singer so they jumped at the chance.'

By the mid-seventies, it was standard studio practice to record each individual instrument by itself. Across London, Freddie Mercury's Queen were taking the technique to its extreme on 'Bohemian Rhapsody', a six-minute epic which would top the charts that Christmas and remain there for over two months. Scott was having none of it. He would record in the time-honoured fashion he had observed with both Franz and Del Newman. Only the lead guitar and final vocals were added later and, as usual, visitors to the studio were discouraged.

'I only popped in once and there was only Scott there,' said Leahy. 'He always wanted to get everything right. He was very particular. I went in to hear the new guitar solo that Parker had done. John wasn't a bad guitar player but Alan Parker did it because that was what Scott wanted.'

Engel's decision was probably shaped by the fact that John's drink problem continued unabated and his behaviour was causing considerable problems in the studio. Scott later confided to *Melody Maker* journalist Steve Lake: 'We had a lot of situations. He was going through this gruelling divorce with his second wife and it was absolutely hell in the studio, man. He'd start a thing and he'd come back in and he was like cock-eyed, man. So we'd have to keep cancellin' sessions. It happened again and again so finally I said: "John you're gonna have to kick it or that's it." '

While John turned to drink in an attempt to ease his problems, Scott poured his heart into the work at hand. From the outset it was clear that the title track 'No Regrets' was outstanding. With Scott's own marriage heading for the rocks, the irony of the subject matter cannot have been lost on the singer.

Even so, it took the commercial ear of Dick Leahy to spot the full potential of Tom Rush's litany to a lost love, in which the Canadian songwriter pleaded with a clinging partner to admit their affair was over. Leahy told Scott to go back into the studio and think of the six-minute song as a possible single. Originally it featured Scott's voice alone, but he agreed to Leahy's suggestion of filling out the choruses with backing vocals by John and session singer Suzanne Lynch.

'Until Queen had their huge hit with "Bohemian Rhapsody", no one had thought of songs that were that long as singles,' recalls Leahy. 'I knew immediately that what Scott had done with "No Regrets" was wonderful.' The single was released in November to promising reviews and a good deal of regional radioplay. But for reasons best known to itself, Radio 1 ignored it.

Leahy: 'I suppose it wasn't exactly what they wanted to hear from The Walker Brothers, but people were buying it. We seemed to be on the edge of the Top 50 for week after week but the only way to get Scott Walker's voice through to the public was through national radioplay and we were really struggling.

'Then Warner Brothers released the Tom Rush version and Radio 1 immediately added it to their playlist. I went apeshit. I was so angry I wanted to shout at anyone I could get hold of. Derek Chinnery, the head of Radio 1, phoned me and asked for a meeting. Here was a record on a British label that they weren't playing, even though the public obviously liked it. Warners only put the Tom Rush version out because of us, and here was a British radio station supporting them. It seemed totally unjust.

'Chinnery's initial answer was that his producers decided the playlist and he couldn't interfere at all. We had an hour's meeting and he didn't waver an inch from his position. The next week he left the Tom Rush record on the playlist but it didn't get played once. Ours wasn't put on the list but it got played on every show. I thought that was a very clever executive decision. And the record took off, immediately, in one week.'

By February, The Walkers' 'No Regrets' had climbed to No. 5 and television offers began to flood in. 'The first thing we did was *The Vera Lynn Show* at the BBC's Shepherd's Bush studios,' Gary recalls. 'When we finished miming the song we got a standing ovation from the audience which really shook us up. They just kept clappin'. Scott got quite emotional about it – he couldn't quite believe it, I guess. We'd never had this type of reaction from an adult audience before.'

A short promotional film, shot in Copenhagen, shows the group driving through the streets of the capital and checking into their hotel before taking to the stage to perform 'No Regrets'. Live appearances on *Top Of The Pops*, Mike Mansfield's *Supersonic* teen-show, Germany's *Musik Laden* (formerly *Beat Club*) and Dutch television quickly followed.

On *Supersonic*, the band elected to prove a point and play live rather than miming. Scott appears unusually relaxed and shoots John a broad smile as the guitarist completes a note-perfect solo to his own obvious satisfaction and relief. Standing there side by side, wielding guitars and clearly enjoying a sound rapport, Scott and John look very much how they must have appeared at Gazzari's a dozen years earlier.

The *Supersonic* clip was subsequently screened on Twiggy's American television show, but The Walker Brothers still could not break into the lucrative market of their birthplace.

Leahy was not overly concerned. Within eighteen months of signing its first act, GTO was the number one chart company with 10 hit singles out of 22 releases. With their confidence high, The Walkers embarked on a tour of television and radio stations to promote the forthcoming album 'No Regrets'. 'Scott was glad to be back because the three of us together meant the pressure on him was eased,' says Gary.

Mike Peyton acted as minder on The Walkers' 'meet the people' trip: 'The media were fascinated that these guys who had been so successful during the sixties were back together again,' he remembers. 'We never struggled to get interviews, the problem was more trying to gee up Scott and persuade him to do them. He refused some of the interviews I initially tried to set up because he didn't trust me. When I'd suggest Radio 2, he'd say: "Well, no, that's not where my area is," and I'd tell him: "Scott, there's a lot of people who have transferred from Radio 1 to Radio 2 who know your work from the sixties and would be interested to hear you're back in the marketplace again." '

GTO was willing to put The Walkers up in first-class hotels, but drew the line at shelling out for a private plane. Peyton had unfortunately lost his driving licence and as there was no question of either Scott or John getting behind the wheel and Gary did not fancy taking sole responsibility for the 1,000-mile trek, the quartet were forced to travel everywhere by train or public transport, beginning in Scotland and working their way down through Edinburgh, Newcastle, Leeds, Sheffield and Manchester.

As the four-man tour made its way across the bleak February landscape of northern Britain, The Walkers' surrealistic odyssey must have been reminiscent of the railway carriage scene from *A Hard Day's Night*. This vision is confirmed by Gary: 'We spent hours gamblin' on the train, playing all these dice games that Scott knew. He always seemed to win all the money.'

Peyton: 'Scott was very nervous about his interviews which is one of the reasons he wanted the support of John and Gary. He always went straight to the hotel. I would do all the signing-in while he went up to his room and would not be disturbed until say, quarter-to-seven. I'd tell him we were off to some place to eat in the evening, but nine times out of ten he ended up staying in his room. Occasionally, he'd join us down in the dining room but it would always be in a secluded section so he wouldn't be confronted by the public.'

Although Scott had his idiosyncrasies, it was John who again proved the biggest headache. 'I actually lost him for a couple of days,' says Peyton. 'He did a disappearing act in Scotland and I had to put everything on hold until he turned up in Newcastle.'

According to Gary, John went off to see friends who no doubt kept a well-stocked liquor cabinet. Until then, Peyton had been able to keep a close eye on events: 'I was careful of where we went and what we did because I was aware of John's drink problem as he was prone to knocking off a bottle of Scotch at the GTO offices. We had to be up at 8 a.m. each day so I didn't want them out to one or two o'clock in the morning. When they said goodnight I didn't know where they went, but the itinerary was so tight their opportunities were limited.'

When John failed to show in Edinburgh, the remaining pair went ahead with the interviews, but afterwards Scott declared that unless John turned up he would take no further part in promotion. Peyton recalls spending an extremely nervous six hours on the train from Edinburgh to Newcastle, unaware that John was already on his way by plane.

'We were due to do Metro Radio, BBC Radio Newcastle and some TV show. We arrived in town about three hours before we were due on air at about 7 p.m. Scott announced: "If he's not here by 6.30, blow it." ' He must have relented, as John eventually appeared just ten minutes before transmission time, giving no account of his movements over the last 48 hours.

Fortunately for Peyton's sanity, there were no further mishaps and when John was around for interviews he proved extremely forthcoming. 'Scott always thought very carefully about the questions he was asked,' says Peyton. 'Sometimes he would ignore them but after the first couple of days, when he realised it was not going to be too difficult, he was a doddle. My abiding memory of our train journeys is that while the rest of us would have an occasional sandwich or a cup of tea, Scott would consume all these pills, bloody rows of them. I never asked what they were, but he took them on a regular basis.'

Paul Kinder confirms that Scott's increasing preoccupation with health and fitness led him to stuff handfuls of vitamin pills down his throat. In the studio, the A&R man would look on in bemusement as the singer produced various bottles of pills from his jacket pockets, almost like a conjuror pulling rabbits from a hat. 'Scott took so many pills that his bag rattled when he walked into the office,' says Kinder.

As far as Peyton is concerned, the fortnight he and Scott spent on the road together was the turning point in their relationship. 'He realised I wasn't bullshitting and that what we were doing would prove beneficial to his career. The fact he'd taken the time and the trouble to go around meeting people would hopefully mean that they'd be looking forward to buying the album when it finally appeared.'

But when the 'No Regrets' album did arrive, it was a big disappointment. Only the title track came anywhere close to matching the strength of past glories such as 'Make It Easy On Yourself' or 'The Sun Ain't Gonna Shine Anymore'. Only now did it become clear how sorely missed was Franz's contribution.

Paul Kinder: 'What that record needed was a proper musical and technical producer, but Scott wanted to do it all himself. Possibly because he'd been fucked around so much in the sixties, Scott had to control everything, from song selection right down to the photo shoots. The vocals, songs and sessionwork are fine, but the actual dynamics and range of the record are just not there. There are no highs and lows and the songs are pretty linear – that's what happens when you have an engineer acting as co-producer.'

The album sleeve tells its own story, with Scott putting a hand towards the camera to block out his face. Oddly for such a private person, he chose to take his shirt off and appear bare-chested for the shoot. Beside him, John and Gary flash cheesy grins, cheap gold jewellery and Californian tans from beneath faded denim jackets. Perhaps it was an ironic attempt to rid themselves of the gloomy image portrayed by the sleeves of their early Philips LPs, but with Scott swigging from a can of Newcastle Brown Ale, the trio look alarmingly like three beer boys gearing up for a Friday night stag-party.

By the mid-seventies, LPs had taken over from singles as the big money-earner for pop artists. But countless one-hit wonders underlined the need to hit the market with a second hit single in order to guarantee real sales success: a follow-up punch, to drive the LP into the public consciousness, was vital.

'No Regrets' was sadly bereft of a follow-up, and stalled at No. 49, its best moment reserved for the one song that echoed the singers' shattered personal lives. As Scott and John sang the lines of the title track, their estranged wives could well have believed a personal message was being sent out across the airwaves: 'I know you're leavin'/It's too long overdue/For far too long I've had nothing new to show to you . . ./There's no regrets/No tears goodbye/I don't want you back/We'd only cry again/Say goodbye again . . .'

Pedal steel guitarist B. J. Cole confirms that the musicians who contributed were well aware that 'No Regrets' was the only song of real quality that they produced: 'It was by far the most satisfying track. It stood out from the rest of the material then, and it still does today.'

The B-side, 'Remember Me' was credited to one A. Dayam. This Indian-sounding writer was none other than John Maus. He frequently used the name in an attempt to out-fox the British taxman, who was constantly on the backs of all three Walker Brothers.

Scott and John proceed to take lead vocals on alternate tracks, with John dragging his way through Donna Weiss's insipid 'Hold An Old Friend's Hand' and the laboured honky-tonk piano workout 'Walkin' In The Sun'. John's voice had never been strong enough to carry a lyric unaided, and on the reggaefied version of Curtis Mayfield's 'He'll Break Your Heart' Scott resorted to swamping the words under a mountain of echo which renders it almost unlistenable. John's best contribution is Micky Newbury's 'Lovers' but the string-laden ballad was not single material.

For his part, Scott chose to embrace gospel for the second time, with a degree of success, on 'Boulder to Birmingham' but reverted to safe territory on Janis Ian's dreary 'Lover's Lullaby' and Chris Kristofferson's 'Got To Have You'.

The record did at least close on a stronger note, with Scott blasting out the distinctly more commercial 'Burn Our Bridges', but Leahy had already decided to get the group back into the studio in search of another 'No Regrets'.

Freddie Winrose reveals that at around this time Scott brought John and Gary to him in a vain attempt to boost their vocal capabilities. Yet while the ageing vocal coach could point them in the right direction, he could not work miracles. 'It wasn't a success,' says Winrose. 'I gained the impression that John thought he was a better singer than Scott and that it would be difficult to teach him anything. As for Gary, it was a complete waste of time. He seemed more interested in my model aeroplane collection.

'After I had given them their singing lessons they ended up owing me two hundred and fifty pounds. I contacted the manager and asked for my money and it eventually arrived in a cheque. Then John rang me up and pleaded with me to return the money. When Scott found out he was deeply embarrassed by the whole thing.'

Scott Walker

No sooner had The Walkers returned from promoting their first comeback LP than the group was once again in front of a recording console with Geoff Calver at the controls. Just prior to recording, Scott and John travelled to Nashville, presumably with the intention of unearthing new material. All they brought back was a demo version of 'People Get Ready' (which appeared on the 1966 'Portrait' album) and their fresh reworking of the Curtis Mayfield classic never found its way on to vinyl.

Maus and Engel, both of whom embraced country music at various points in their careers, discovered Nashville did not match their expectations. On their return, Gary asked John for his impressions of the country music capital. 'It's a place you want to go when you want to die,' replied John cryptically. 'Didn't you like it?' asked Gary. 'No,' said John. 'I hated it.'

'Lines', recorded at Air Studios during the scorching summer, was released in September 1976. Once again, the title track was picked out as a single and given the full Walker Brothers treatment. Scott declared that Jerry Fuller's metaphor-laden song about cocaine abuse, the white lines of the title, was 'our best-ever single'. That was an overstatement, but it was certainly better than any of the album fillers on 'No Regrets'.

Opening with Scott crooning over delicate piano chords, 'Lines' bursts into a lush chorus with the singer delivering a warning message about the loneliness of drug addiction. In retrospect, it was never going to join the likes of Abba's 'Dancing Queen' at the top of the charts, but it is yet another powerful Scott Walker performance that has been sadly overlooked since, and certainly merited inclusion on Fontana's best-selling 1992 collection.

The single failed to chart, as did its parent album, largely because, after the disappointment of the 'No Regrets' LP, both media and public appeared to have lost interest. The Walkers neatly summed up the situation when they complained to the press: 'Nobody's playin' it.'

Although 'Lines' emerged as a more balanced record than its predecessor, there was nothing for the GTO sales team to latch on to. Mike Peyton: 'We listened to it over and over again and it didn't lift us. That was the reaction from the media as well.' There had already been arguments over the LP's stomach-churning yellow sleeve which extended the theme of the title by featuring line-drawings of each of The Walker Brothers.

Paul Kinder: 'It was Scott who wanted this sketched cover depicting the three of them and it was quite simply appalling. The record was just as bad – the performances were bland, the songs inferior and it just did not work.

The musicians who played on it were just going through the motions. There was nothing in the way of rehearsals. They would turn up, read the sheet music, play the stuff and go home – and it shows. "Lines" lacks heart and soul.'

'Lines' does at least include one of John's finest recorded moments on Tom Snow's 'Taking It All In Stride', but otherwise Kinder's bleak assessment is not far off the mark. Scott struggles through Tom Janis's truly awful 'Inside of You' – rarely has a lyricist delivered a more ham-fisted attempt at capturing the beauty of the act of love-making – and Randy Newman's 'Have You Seen My Baby' is best summed up by John's strangled cry during the fadeout.

Scott does his best with the Boz Scaggs-penned 'We're All Alone' which was released as a second single. After the shenanigans of the Tom Rush/Walker Brothers battle over 'No Regrets', it is ironic that 'We're All Alone' was a hit for Rita Coolidge just six months after The Walkers' version flopped. If truth be known, the song was far more suited to her voice than Scott's, as Dick Leahy readily admits: 'Even at the time, I felt our version wasn't that special. Rita Coolidge does a far better reading of the song. It didn't really extend Scott and he's a singer who needs to be extended by songs.'

'First Day' from the LP is also credited to John's alter-ego, A. Dayam, making it the first self-penned song to appear on record by the reformed Walker Brothers. One listen tells you why no one had pushed for more original material at this stage. The sum total of Gary's contribution to the GTO records was his salt-shaker on 'Remember Me' from "No Regrets". Although his face was prominently featured on both LP sleeves, Scott later admitted that, just as in the sixties, Gary did not actually play on either album. 'He's never played on any of the records. But his role is an important one in the band. He seems to bind it together in some way. He's a man who's an excellent buffer, y'know.'

Public reaction to 'Lines' is neatly summed up by an incident which occurred when John Maus attended a 21st birthday party in the West Country in late 1976. John, who made a grand entrance, presented the delighted birthday boy with a lavishly-wrapped gift that was obviously an LP. Perhaps anticipating the latest chart-top-per, the recipient eagerly tore off the paper, only for his excited smile to become rather fixed when he saw it concealed a copy of the latest Walker Brothers offering. The record was discreetly hidden behind his other gifts and even the party DJ declined to play it.

Dick Leahy was well aware that neither LP had been up to scratch: 'I just don't think they were really prepared for having any sort of success. "No Regrets" took them completely by surprise. After that, the LP and the follow-up were merely mildly pleasant records but they showed that The Walker Brothers were going nowhere. There seemed no point telling them to go back into the studio because they had no real belief in themselves as a unit.'

Though there seemed no hope of ever recouping the thousands of pounds he had already spent, Leahy kept the group on GTO's roster more as a personal indulgence than anything else. He would have to wait well over a year for fresh material, but his patience was finally rewarded when Scott finally rediscovered the confidence to write again. In the minds of many, Leahy's mistake was not getting rid of the excess baggage – John and Gary.

16 The Electrician

'Everyone is creative in his own individual sphere. I figure that
I'm a late bloomer, I really believe that.'

Scott Walker, 1976

OVER THE 30 YEARS of his rollercoaster career, Scott Walker
has missed out on hundreds of thousands of pounds because of his fear of the stage, but never more so than in
the late 1970s. No sooner had the 'No Regrets' single
been a hit, than concert promoters began besieging his record company and management with requests for The Walker Brothers to go
on tour.

'He turned down fortunes, which in a strange way I kind of admired,' says Leahy. 'The group was offered twenty thousand pounds
for one gig in one of the top London clubs that used to host Tom
Jones and Shirley Bassey, those kind of people. It didn't happen simply because there was no way Scott would go out and do the old
Walker Brothers hits.'

John Maus had always been the Walker Brother most at ease
with the idea of live performance, and he was understandably exas-
perated with Scott's refusal to cash in on the interest in their reunion.
But Gary Leeds admits that, apart from Scott's misgivings, there
were other reasons why a full-blown UK tour never happened.

'We weren't really in any shape to play live and we were worried
about John's drinking. We just didn't want to take the chance of
going out if it wasn't right.'

Just as before, Scott and John tore into each other over their
difference of opinion, with the latter openly taunting Engel about his
stage-fright. 'It got to the stage where John was sayin': "You're
scared to go out," ' says Gary. Scott calmly pointed out that he had
gone out on stage before by himself. In the end, they came to a
compromise when Scott agreed to yet more cabaret dates.

Not long after the release of 'Lines', Engel revealed to *Melody
Maker*'s Steve Lake that a tour was being considered: 'We'll go out
with two drummers, two guitars, two keyboards, bass, percussion

. . . oh, and there'll be a string section waitin' everywhere we go. That's what people hear on the records and that's what we need.'

The cabaret dates were arranged by former showbusiness agent David Apps, who had recently taken over as the group's manager. Ady Semel had gradually become more and more disillusioned with the music business, which is hardly surprising, given the amount of success he had enjoyed with Scott. Always something of an enigma himself, Semel disappeared without trace and is thought to have returned to his native Israel.

'I could be cynical and say Ady disappeared as soon as the money dried up,' says Dick Leahy. 'Money was his basic interest. He was a businessman rather than a music man. David was an English spieler, a typical amalgam of kosher and brash, but very experienced as an agent. He had worked with Tom Jones, Gilbert O'Sullivan and, I seem to recall, The Bay City Rollers.'

After handling Rollermania, Apps perhaps thought he could re-kindle the Walkermania that had accompanied the group's original rise to fame. He had met The Walkers during the sixties, when he had been a junior in the offices of their agent, Harold Davison.

'They contacted me in 1976 and said they weren't happy about Ady Semel,' he says. 'My gut reaction was that like everyone else he wanted Scott to wear a tuxedo and do those nice numbers. That wasn't where they wanted to go.'

Cabaret was certainly not the direction John Maus wanted to go in, but that was exactly where the group was headed. Gary recalls that the first show was in Birmingham: 'It was the three of us plus a big band which David Apps had set up. We didn't do "The Sun Ain't Gonna Shine Anymore" or "Joanna" or any of that stuff, Scott just didn't want to do 'em. We did a couple of Bruce Springsteen tunes, and some stuff from "No Regrets" and "Lines", as well as "Here Comes The Night".

'That first night was the first time I had played drums for twelve years, but the gigs went OK. Scott and I took the opportunity to get in some health treatment. We stayed in good hotels, swam in the pool and played tennis every day, while John slept in his room. Then our backing band started complainin' because they were in digs while we were in these top hotels. Scott insisted that they were booked into hotels as well, but when we saw the bill we couldn't believe it.'

The tour progressed around the various northern clubs obscure enough for Scott not to feel the glare of the spotlight too fiercely.

They spent a week at a time in Newcastle and Fagin's in Manchester before everything came to a screeching halt because of problems with John.

Gary: 'He still had a lotta personal problems and was a little wiped out. He admitted himself that things were a little flat and we decided to take a break so that he could straighten himself out.'

It marked the beginning of a recuperative period that would see all three Walker Brothers writing their own material. According to Paul Kinder: 'They disappeared for the whole of 1977.' Mike Peyton adds: 'John got over his alcohol problems and went back to America while Gary carried on living in the London flat and Scott got heavily into art. He just pulled the hat over his eyes again and went for a wander, just to find himself.'

Scott admitted at the time that he felt dwarfed by the achievements of contemporary songwriters such as Joni Mitchell and his favourite, Randy Newman. He told Steve Lake that they served more often than not to depress rather than inspire him, and in his mind his own talents shrivelled every time he placed one of their albums on a record deck. But, he added more positively: 'I'm slowly beginnin' to realise that that attitude is dumb. It's an inspiration to learn that Henry Miller didn't write *Tropic Of Cancer* until he was thirty-three. Of all the great writers in the world, he's probably my favourite. I'm thirty-three and I'm ready.'

By the time John returned from the States, Scott had already decided that, even if subsequent events proved a disaster, the only way to make any artistic progress lay in a return to writing his own material. By all accounts, he was under increasing pressure to ditch The Walker Brothers and return to a solo career.

Dick Leahy is honest enough to admit: 'I was getting increasingly disenchanted with Gary and John because they didn't seem to be doing anything. They were just playing at it whereas Scott did have some ideas he wanted to do. I would rather have had something that he wanted to do than just going through the motions of The Walker Brothers.'

Scott later complained to Phil McNeill: 'So now I've signed with a company – I came here with the group – where a guy behind a desk is sayin' to me: "When am I gonna get a solo album?" Now somebody wants me to do a solo album of original material and I'm really strugglin' hard to complete it. It's a long haul back, man, to that dark and dark and dark . . . it really is . . . Because it's . . . it's a real dark cavern.'

While Scott's description of his state of mind was typically obtuse, it perfectly described the torment that the return to writing represented, a fact confirmed by Gary, albeit in more down to earth language: 'The "Nite Flights" songs were written in our flat. It was real hard to do. It took months and months. Nobody knew what anyone else was doin'. We wrote in different rooms with notebooks and a guitar. John was spendin' most of his time livin' with a girlfriend outta town, but he would come over and we'd go through things.'

The protracted creative process was extended by Scott and Gary's habit of spending occasional nights drinking into the small hours at London's trendy Tramp's nightclub. Its clientèle included celebrities infinitely more hip than a couple of faded icons from the sixties, but that suited Scott perfectly as it meant he could mingle with the crowd without fear of being recognised. And when the ageing nightclubbers awoke late the next morning, or more likely the next afternoon, they would frequently spend the rest of the day at a cinema, watching the latest obscure film which Scott had heard about.

Gary recalls how Scott one day demonstrated his social conscience by rushing to help a drunken Indian man who had been hit by a car as he attempted to cross the busy Old Brompton Road: 'Scott rushed past me, ran right over and was holdin' this guy's head and everythin'. I was really shocked by it for some reason. I had to go fetch an ambulance but I said to Scott afterwards, "That's pretty good, y'know." No one else would have helped the guy.'

In between the Good Samaritan acts and the nights and days of leisure, The Walkers somehow managed to write some songs. 'Everyone was supposed to write four each, but I only managed two,' says Gary ruefully. Things were not helped by the noise of the restaurant from down below, but on nights when he was not out with Gary, Scott worked on undisturbed for hours after the last diners had left for their homes.

The four songs Scott came up with, for what proved to be the final Walker Brothers album, included 'Shutout', 'Fat Mama Kick' and 'Nite Flights', but his elevated status within the music business over the next decade would be the result of just one highly innovative track, 'The Electrician'.

By that summer of 1977, Scott was 34 years of age. With the burgeoning punk rock movement spewing out spikey-haired youths in bondage trousers on to London's fashion barometer, the King's

Road, Scott must have resembled a character from one of Jacques Brel's songs as he wandered along it in his faded denims, bush hat and Jesus sandals. Little did the world know that he was fashioning songs so far removed from those he had previously recorded that they amounted to a punk revolution of his very own.

It is said that 'The Electrician' was the inspiration for Midge Ure when he was writing Ultravox's worldwide hit 'Vienna'. Style and innovation leaders David Bowie and Brian Eno would later express an interest in working with Scott as a direct result of hearing this one track.

It was the first time in a decade that Scott had attempted to write a truly political song, and he directed his venom towards the country of his birth. Engel blasted the United States administration for dabbling in the affairs of South America, not least by sending in torture specialists (mechanics, as they were more usually known), to extract confessions from those it saw as a potential threat to the stability of the region.

'If you listen to the words, they speak for themselves,' Scott told German DJ Alan Bangs in 1984. An ambient synthesised growl heralds the entrance of 'The Electrician' as Scott twice mumbles the song's opening line: 'Baby it's slow/When lights go low/There's no help no Baby it's slow/When lights go low/There's no help no . . .'

The song roars into life with just four more lines delivered in a choked voice particularly suited to the subject matter: 'He's drilling through the spiritus sanctus tonight/Through the dark hip falls screaming oh you mambos kill me and kill me and kill me/If I jerk the handle/You'll die in your dreams/If I jerk the handle/You'll thrill me and thrill me and thrill me . . .'

With that, the track abruptly flies off at a tangent with a bank of strings and Spanish guitar playing the sweetest of melodies, completely at odds with the concept of violent interrogation. Unless, that is, Scott meant to portray the sadistic pleasure gleaned by the perpetrator, or perhaps the merciful release of the victim's death.

'The Electrician' is a truly remarkable track on several levels. The atmospheric production is straight out of the ambient music book that Scott's future admirer Brian Eno had already taken to one extreme with David Bowie, and with which he would experiment in later years with the likes of Irish supergroup U2 and David Byrne of Talking Heads. The lush orchestral arrangement of the closing section was a virtual throwback to the Wall of Sound that graced The

Walker Brothers' best-known hits, and over this strange collection of styles Scott spans the story of torturer and victim as though they were two lovers taking part in some sado-masochistic sex act.

As Phil McNeill pointed out in a glowing review of Scott's contribution to the 'Nite Flights' LP, the remaining three tracks are less explicit: 'But all conjure up similar feelings of night-time, unreality, nightmare.'

'Something attacked the earth last night/There were faces bobbing in the heat/In the shutout . . .' ('Shutout')

With honking saxophones blaring out a monstrous riff and stream-of-consciousness lyrics dedicated to one Bernard-Henri Levy, 'Fat Mama Kick' is only marginally less memorable than 'The Electrician', but equally eerie: 'Armed angels walk the city lights/Wait inside their master corpses/peeled raw betrayed . . .'

Wrote McNeill: 'These tracks are completely unexpected, not so much because they're innately strange but because they're entirely untainted by MOR. Hip or otherwise, this is front-line 1978 rock and roll.' He added presciently: 'Engel has always had similar interests to David Bowie, his European consciousness and Jacques Brel fixation predated Bowie's by several years. If there is any influence at play here, it is latter-day Bowie/Iggy Pop. Maybe Bowie should produce Engel's next album.' It is a matter of conjecture whether Bowie ever saw or was told about this recommendation, but the seeds of an idea had been sown.

Sadly, John and Gary's songwriting efforts were in a different, and inferior league. The better of Gary's two compositions, 'Death Of Romance', features a half-decent hookline, but is let down by Gary's thin voice. The song was at one time destined to lend its title to the resulting LP. Leeds reckoned it was appropriate, possibly because he had already seen the writing on the wall and realised that The Walkers, one of the most romantic groups of all time, were about to play their final card.

John's quartet of songs can at best be described as amiable, at worst as banal disco rock. Both John and Gary's offerings were, to quote McNeill, 'instantly disposable', which was exactly the fate Dick Leahy would have liked for them. Yet out of loyalty, his deep-seated insecurity, or perhaps an inability to come up with songs to match those he had already penned, Scott successfully resisted pressure for him to release 'Nite Flights' as a solo LP.

'We had to include John and Gary's songs,' moans Leahy. 'All I wanted were Scott's. I loved them because they were genuine Scott Walker. I remember telling him there was no point in him doing The Walker Brothers. There was no Walker Brothers, it was a sham. I'd rather he did what he really wanted to do and fail than just do something else for the sake of it. That was never going to work. I have always thought of that record as a Scott Walker EP, but there were certain restrictions in a small company. At times when you'd love to do something, maybe you can't afford it.'

Paul Kinder: 'Scott just wouldn't rid himself of The Walker Brothers shackles. Without John and Gary, "Nite Flights" could have been an extraordinary Scott Walker album. John and Gary's stuff was unlistenable. They were appalling songs, poorly executed. Scott's, on the other hand, were remarkable and are rightly revered today. The song structures were unusual and comparable with the stuff on Bowie's "Low" and "Heroes" albums. They sit very nicely against those.'

The 'Nite Flights' songs were completed in the spring of 1978 at Scorpio Sound beneath the Capital Radio building at Euston. The sessions were produced by Dave Macrae, a musician admired by Scott and one-time keyboard player with Pacific Eardrum, one of his favourite bands. As well as writing the songs, the three key players, and particularly Scott, took a greater role in the music than on any previous Walker Brothers LP.

Gary still left the main drumming duties to session musician Peter Van Hooke, but did contribute some percussion. John provided backing vocals on all four of Scott's tracks and handled the lead unaided, much to their detriment. Scott shared keyboards with Macrae, as well as returning to his first musical love affair with the bass guitar.

A suitably surreal cover was devised by Hipgnosis, the renowned sleeve-design company run by Storm Thorgeson, most famous for its work with Pink Floyd.

'The Electrician', backed by Gary's 'Den Haague' was released as a single. There was a flicker of interest from Scott when the disc received good reviews, but it failed to break into the Top 40.

The song and its style of presentation were way ahead of their time. The aggressive sounds of The Sex Pistols, The Clash and The Jam were blowing sixties and seventies has-beens out of the chart waters. Had 'The Electrician' been released three years later, when style-gurus such as Steve Strange and even the prototype Duran

Duran were making synthesiser-led waves with their fellow new romantics, who knows what might have happened?

'The commerical failure of the album was more our problem than Scott's,' Kinder generously offers. 'We just didn't know what to do with it. You have to remember that in 1978 people just didn't talk about The Walker Brothers. Punk was very much the thing . . . By that time I was really into it, but then this was Scott's punk record.'

Dick Leahy agrees: 'We can probably be criticised. There may have been a chance of doing something better with those songs. Ironically, I had sold GTO to CBS in 1977 and they definitely had a negative feeling about Scott, presumably because of their previous experience with him.'

A couple of promotional television appearances were set up in Europe, and Kinder vainly tried to get The Walkers on to the BBC's *The Old Grey Whistle Test*. 'But producer Mike Appleton wasn't that engrossed by them,' Kinder recalls. 'He didn't see them as a Whistle Test act.'

If 'Lines' had marked the beginning of the end for the reformed Walker Brothers, then the commercial failure of 'Nite Flights' effectively sealed their fate, although they battled on together for a few more weeks following its release that July. Scott, at least, appears to have decided that this was the end of the group and that GTO's days were numbered. A few months earlier, he had sought to spur John and Gary to write their own material with the words: 'This is it guys. If you wanna put out your own stuff now's your chance.'

GTO was indeed collapsing around them. The small, homely record label had been swallowed by the giant CBS with the sole aim of poaching Dick Leahy as the managing director of its UK arm. Leahy, however, quickly realised that he did not relish being dictated to by CBS bigwigs back in the United States.

Mike Peyton: 'We were riding high on the success of a Donna Summer No. 1 ('I Feel Love'). CBS got their money back within the first six months when Heatwave's 'Boogie Nights' broke in America, but Dick realised he just didn't like the politics of the company.

'GTO had not been like working for a record company. There were no set rules. We'd start work at ten in the morning and we might not finish until ten at night. Then we'd all go and see a band or go across the road to the pub.

'Barlow Place was a second home for the artists. They would wander into the office, sit down, have a drink and help package the records – it was like one big happy family. You'd have The Walkers around and in would walk Billy Ocean or a couple of members of Heatwave. Before you knew it, a couple of drinks cabinets would have been opened. CBS wasn't run like that.'

Before the final disintegration of both band and record company, David Apps persuaded The Walkers to go out for one last cabaret tour. It was a sad end to yet another sorry era in Scott's career. Once again, they concentrated on week-long stints in Manchester, Tyneside, Humberside and Birmingham.

Robin Edwards caught two shows at The Night Out in Birmingham not long after the release of 'Nite Flights'. His account of the Monday and Friday night performances makes grim reading: 'They were billed as "Live from the USA" which struck me as odd because, apart from John, they were permanently based in Britain. On the Monday the performance was messy and Scott was clearly unhappy. Halfway through, he spoke into the microphone and said something like: "I'm sorry that the performance is a little weak, because we arrived late and haven't had time to rehearse with the sound system." He clearly didn't want to be there and never smiled once.

'Reaction from the audience was mixed. A lot of people were taking no notice of what went on on stage. It was a traditional type of cabaret place: a semi-circle of tables on which people were eating, lots of drinking going on and a very smoky atmosphere. What surprised me was that there was no solo material of any description, nothing at all from "Nite Flights", only earlier Walkers stuff. They did "Make It Easy On Yourself", "The Sun Ain't Gonna Shine Anymore" and "In My Room".'

Friday's show was a little more polished, though Scott was again unsmiling. The Walkers had clearly had a little more time to rehearse, but about halfway through the set Scott and John went walkabout – they just disappeared. Gary then did "Fanfare For The Common Man" on his drums. He did it for about eight minutes and he was really very good, but still the others did not reappear.

'When Gary finally called it a day he picked up a microphone and wandered around the stage, looking rather lost. He was asking the audience questions like: "Anyone here having a birthday tonight?" then, "I hope you're having a good time." The audience started a slow handclap, which was pretty sad. Scott walked back on stage and patted Gary on the back. A lady behind us shouted: "Sing 'Joanna', Scott!" He totally ignored her. John rejoined them onstage, they did a couple more numbers, did a bow and went off.

'I had "Nite Flights" in my hand and was hoping for an autograph before they went. My wife shouted over at Scott and he raised his hand and frowned, as if to say "shut up". Then he came over and tried to sign the album, except that the pen refused to work. He ended up leaving a very faint signature and John came over and did the same. We were hoping to meet them backstage but they just didn't want to know.

'Gary and Scott seemed friendly enough to one another but I sensed a bit of tension between Scott and John. I think John looked to Scott for inspiration at various points but he was just going through the motions.'

John later stated that following the Birmingham debacle, Scott developed a 'total phobia' about live appearances, a claim backed up by the fact that Scott has not set foot on a stage since that unhappy night in the summer of 1978. The Walker Brothers were all washed up, and they knew it. Just as in 1967, they were an anachronism. Eleven years earlier they had been blown away by psychedelia, now it was by the new wave of young bands, some of whom could hardly play their instruments but who injected an urgency and sense of danger into their music that three coiffeured Californians in their mid-thirties could not hope to match.

It is interesting to speculate on what would happen were The Walker Brothers to reform today. With interest in nostalgia at an all-time high, they could probably attract bigger audiences than they drew in their heyday. But Scott would surely not be interested – the idea of playing to 15,000 eager fans at Wembley Arena or Birmingham's National Exhibition Centre would make his blood run cold.

Mass demonstrations had accompanied The Walkers' first split. This time, there was not even a public announcement of their demise. To coin Johnny Rotten's phrase, rather than burn out they simply faded away, without so much as a whimper. Or at least, not a public whimper. In private, it was a different story, with Scott and John having an almighty row and allegedly not communicating again for five years.

Commenting on the reunion, Scott told *NME* in March 1984: 'It started off as a situation that we thought might be amusing. But everybody just got sick of each other again. When we're not workin' together it's fine. Nowadays I keep in touch with the guys every week.'

The final break-up of The Walker Brothers again left Scott facing an uncertain future. His finest achievements now a decade behind him, he faced the stark choice of roaming the trackless wastes of the northern cabaret circuit or drifting out of the music business altogether.

Then a report in *Melody Maker* on 17 March 1979, brought Scott Walker's name once more into the public spotlight and made one superstar's millions of fans aware of his name: 'David Bowie, in New York, finishing work on his next album "Lodger" with Tony Visconti, recently approached Scott Walker indirectly with a view to producing his next album.

'Bowie was impressed by the European feeling of the last Walker Brothers' album which owed its critical acceptance to Scott's work. It is understood that while Walker appreciated Bowie's interest, he turned down his help. He is working on his own on his solo album and is anxious to avoid contact with other musicians at the moment.'

The ever-tolerant Dick Leahy, who was still prepared to retain Scott on the GTO roster as a solo artist, confirms the story: 'Purely as a result of hearing "The Electrician", Bowie, who I had worked with briefly years before, tried to get hold of Scott. They had met at Philips but, of course, in those days Scott was the big star and Bowie the unknown. He phoned me up and said he loved that song and "No Regrets" and he would love to see Scott doing more work like that. But Scott just wasn't interested.

'He didn't have a telephone at the time so he told me to tell Bowie he didn't want to do it. It was typical Scott. His only reason was that he wanted to pursue his own ideas. Scott's problem has always been that he so much wants to say what he has to say, but has never been able to write in a form that's acceptable to the public. It's difficult to say how it would have worked but to get support from a big star would have been very useful to him.

'At the time, he insisted he didn't want to work with other people even though everyone felt he would have benefited from a sympathetic producer. Not someone to dictate or dominate him, just someone to drag it out of him and help him put it in a form that people would listen to. I certainly thought Brian Eno could have helped him, but Scott wouldn't even get together for a chat and by this stage I was tearing my hair out. It was the first time I had ever faced a problem like that.'

Leahy finally lost his patience and laid his cards on the table in a meeting with Scott at Barlow Place. 'I told him: "I don't know what else I can do for you." I also remember very clearly telling him: "Much as I love what you do, you have to remember that at the end of the day I am in the commercial record business which means I have to sell records." He was very cool about it. He just shrugged and said: "That's life, Leahy." He always called me by my surname. There was no formalised end of contract. I just didn't take my option up and I haven't seen him since that meeting.'

But just before GTO went down with all hands, including John and Gary, Scott was tossed an unexpected lifeline by Virgin Records, which promised a fresh beginning for an artist whose career had seemingly foundered.

Simon Draper, Virgin's managing director at the time, whose signings had included Japan and Culture Club, had had his curiosity aroused by Brian Eno's enthusiastic appraisal of 'The Electrician', from 'Nite Flights', in *Melody Maker* in 1978. Eno raved about the single to such an extent that Draper rushed out and bought it. What he heard made him resolve to sign Scott Walker to the label. His chance arose at the end of 1979, by which time Scott's four-year association with GTO Records, which had promised so much yet delivered so little, was clearly at an end.

After The Walkers' final disintegration, Gary Leeds married Barbara Goodman, a long-time fan who he had first met when she had taken part in the demonstration march protesting at The Walkers' original split back in 1967. Gary left the music business once more and set up an East End business which made sculptures out of sand. Some cynics may have felt that his new line of work was not so far removed from what The Walker Brothers had been striving to achieve since they reformed.

Gary's delicate models of the Tower of London, Big Ben, and other famous London landmarks were a bigger hit with tourists than anything the group had produced during their second three-year period together. But just as the group's musical career had blown away in the wind, so too did Gary's business venture, which eventually fell victim to the recession of 1990.

John, who was said to have lost a considerable sum of money when 'Nite Flights' bombed, settled in Brighton and married Brandy, his third wife, by whom he has a daughter. His days of wild-living and free-spending now a receding memory, Maus worked for some years as an antiques restorer, his pop career seemingly beyond repair. Scott was alone again, naturally.

17 On Your Own Again

'I don't listen to the old songs, I don't have the records. People don't believe that, but I say you can come and listen to my apartment, like Gene Hackman.'

Scott Walker, 1984

AS THE 1980s DAWNED, Virgin had every reason to believe that its gamble of signing Scott Walker would pay off handsomely. Phonogram, by allowing the singer's first five solo albums to drift out of stock ('Scott 4' was available for a mere nine months), had unwittingly helped to create a myth ripe for polishing. Moreover, while the Walker Brothers' corpse was still warm, echoes of Engel's most searing songs could be detected in the work of musicians as diverse as Joy Division, Magazine, Simple Minds and David Bowie. It marked the beginning of a resurrection to rank alongside that of Lazarus. As one pop writer wryly observed, it became almost obligatory for any artist who aspired to sounding tortured, desperate and personal to waffle on about how these Scott Walker songs inspired them.

Not surprisingly, this new wave of Walker admirers chose to ignore the terminally unhip 1970s reunion and instead looked back to Scott's halcyon days at Philips for inspiration. Significantly, Phonogram's 1981 'Scott Walker Sings Jacques Brel' compilation bore the same sleeve as Scott's first solo album. In the eyes of these second-generation fans, Scott had not aged. Like James Dean, his image remained frozen in time: a heroically tormented standard-bearer for the new romantics.

How ironic that the short-sightedness of Scott's old record company should trigger a growing cult which, in turn, would eventually boost Engel's own sagging finances. By the early 1980s Scott was probably only marginally better off than he had been on arriving in London in 1965. He was forced to sell his entire record collection after ploughing much of his savings into the largely abortive GTO albums, while the deletion of his earlier work had slowed the flow of royalties to a trickle.

Yet even this parlous financial state failed to rekindle Scott's creative fires. He later said that attempts to write songs at around this time foundered because 'the neighbours were too loud or the working conditions were too bad'. On one occasion, Scott was virtually dumped on the pavement when his landlord suddenly decided to sell up.

Years later, Bob Nolan, catalogue manager at PolyGram, Phonogram's parent company, conceded that the company had been slow in exploiting its Scott Walker archives. The artist himself, who had advocated the re-release of his Jacques Brel songs as far back as 1973, may have been forgiven for responding with a derisive snort. To stay on catalogue, albums had to sell at least 500 a year; to get back on catalogue, Phonogram needed to be convinced that they could sell at least 5,000 just to recoup costs. No one, it seemed, was willing to take the plunge.

The Virgin deal which Scott signed in February 1980 became something of a legend in itself within the industry. Little did the record company suspect that it would have to wait four years for some payback on its investment. Up until the 1980s, however, the artist's output had been prolific. Apart from the GTO years of 1977 and 1979, new Scott Walker material of some description had been released every year from 1965.

Heartened by this knowledge, Virgin confidently expected its new signing to swiftly cash in on his renewed popularity although Engel later complained that he had received 'hassle' for failing to produce an album within a couple of months. According to Simon Draper: 'David Apps came to see me and we agreed on a deal. Looking back, striking up a deal wasn't so difficult; it was actually trying to get Scott to make a record which proved a problem. In those days we rarely did deals of less than eight albums with options after each one and Scott would have received an advance in the region of £20,000.'

When Draper met Engel at Apps's Kensington office the singer appeared ill at ease and agitated. As Draper and Apps finalised details of the deal, Scott prowled around the room like a caged animal. He then informed the startled Virgin executive that he wished to start recording in May as his creative juices flowed when flowers bloomed and trees were in leaf. Draper, while slightly bemused, was more than happy to concur, and wasted no time in booking studio time for May.

'Scott, it has to be said, tended to talk complete gobbledegook. In the beginning I just thought he was being terribly cool; it was only after we signed him that I started to think he was rather strange. We had the studio reserved for May but he cancelled the booking, so we had a meeting with him to find out why. The explanation he came up with was totally bizarre. It was to do with the state of the world or the state of his head or something.'

But there was a further surprise in store for Virgin's managing director. Scott, restlessly pacing around the office of A&R man Arnold Frolows, suddenly complained that Virgin were 'getting' at him. 'They're shoutin' at me beneath my flat,' he said accusingly. 'Makin' noise and disturbin' me. I'm findin' it hard to work and it's all down to Virgin.' Draper sat there open-mouthed.

'At this point I remember thinking: "My God, this guy is completely paranoid." It was only later that I discovered what Scott had been getting at. Virgin funded something called the Help Organisation, which started out by giving advice to unmarried mothers and evolved into a counselling organisation with properly qualified psychiatrists. They had an office directly below Scott's flat off High Street Kensington, where they held encounter groups at which people were encouraged to shout, so what I had taken to be paranoid ramblings turned out to be completely true!'

Al Clark, head of Virgin's press department at the time, who later got to know Scott probably better than anyone else at the record company, recalls: 'It was a bizarre encounter principally because there were five or six people in the room at the time and everyone seemed to be talking at cross purposes. Scott spent a lot of time describing the kind of state that would lead to him making a record while we were looking for dates, times and places.'

Ed Bicknell, who took over as Engel's manager in 1983, viewed the Virgin deal as ridiculous. 'It was legally unenforceable and would be illegal now. It was for an enormous number of records, the advance was really low and the royalties were negligible, but it probably reflected Scott's commercial standing at the time. In fairness to Virgin, they were very supportive, particularly Simon Draper, a full partner in the company, and Jeremy Lascelles, head of A&R.'

While Virgin continued to play a waiting game into 1981, one of Engel's most high-profile and vociferous supporters grasped the initiative. Julian Cope, the critically respected leader of The Teardrop Explodes who loudly proclaimed Scott as his greatest influence, unveiled plans to bring out a Walker retrospective called 'Fire Escape In The Sky: The Godlike Genius Of Scott Walker', an overblown title which had its subject cringing with embarrassment. By a remarkable coincidence, Phonogram suddenly awoke from its slumbers and announced that a collection of Engel's Jacques Brel interpretations was being prepared for the autumn.

Cope, an avid record collector, had been a Scott Walker fan for several years, and Walker Brothers tapes as well as Scott's solo material were constantly played on The Teardrop Explodes tour bus. The band's manager, Bill Drummond, became an instant convert and, according to Cally, Cope's one-time manager, decided to release a Scott Walker compilation consisting of material culled from the first five solo albums on his own Zoo label. 'It was the first time Scott Walker had come above ground,' he says.

Cally (Martin Callomon) had been playing drums for an art school band in St Albans in 1976 when he discovered the old Scott Walker albums through a long-time enthusiast called Phil Smee, who designed book and record sleeves and today runs the Bam Caruso label which specialises in recycling semi-forgotten 1960s artefacts.

During the high summer of punk, the pair would scour London's second-hand record shops, ferreting out Scott Walker albums wherever they could. Traditional rock, pop and fashion values were being overturned and such was the prevailing attitude of the times that most records issued before 1976 were totally derided. Consequently, record shops were virtually giving away huge stockpiles of sixties material. 'We used to pick up these Scott Walker records for about £1.50 – and in mint condition,' says Cally. 'People used to laugh at us.'

Around this time, Richard Cook, who interviewed Engel for NME in 1984, bought a copy of 'Scott' for just 90 pence. Instantly gripped by Walker fever, Cook scoured London until he had everything his new idol had ever breathed on. Cope and his fellow Walker disciples had simply rediscovered a route which Scott had pioneered a decade earlier and were flying in the face of fashion. During these lean years, the Scott Walker flame was kept alive by an eccentric widow named Maisy van Courtland who claimed to be in touch with Betty Engel and intermittently published a 'Scott Newsletter' from her South London home.

'Fire Escape In The Sky', its title taken from 'Big Louise' on 'Scott 3', was licensed through Phonogram, who held the bulk of Engel's back catalogue, and distributed through Rough Trade. Cope apparently wanted to release a far longer album, but the record which

The classic image of Scott Walker on stage *(Simon Dee)*

Above: Scott on the Simon Dee show *Dee Time*, September 1967 *(Dezo Hoffman)*
Below, left: Backstage at the Bradford Gaumont, October 1968 – Scott's last big
solo tour *(Richard G. Leach)*
Below, right: 1973 – Scott, glass in hand, poses moodily for the CBS publicity
department. His expression shows something of his foreboding about the times ahe

November 1975 – Scott
just before the release of
the Walkers' reunion
single 'No Regrets'

Scott and John
performing on German
TV in 1976, clearly
enjoying themselves

Scott in 1984, around
the time of the release of
Climate of Hunter

Above, left: Scott, pictured in 1984
(*Bob Carlos Clark/Virgin Records*)
Above, right: Scott Walker's last
British TV appearance to date –
in an advertisement for Britvic 55
(*Abbott Mead Vickers/Britvic*)

Left: Scott Walker in 1992 – the most
recent photograph to be published in
Britain (*Syndication International*)

eventually emerged contained just a dozen Walker originals including 'Such A Small Love', 'Always Coming Back To You' and 'Montague Terrace (In Blue)'.

The sleeve was grey with a green border and the record's cultish appeal was fuelled by a bizarre space on the back cover which served to heighten the air of mystery surrounding its subject. According to Cally, a planned photo of Scott had failed to materialise. 'People thought this was a fantastically arty concept, but Martin Atkins, who designed the sleeve, regarded it as a cock-up. He was furious that the cover was rushed through without a picture.'

However, both Cope and his associate Mick Houghton, who today runs a London PR agency, maintain that the sleeve came out precisely as intended. 'It was all meant to be very low-key, even down to the title which was in very small letters,' says Houghton. 'I'd like to be able to refer back to my cuttings of the period but most of them are missing. In 1981 an unidentified murder victim was found in Cardiff clutching a ticket for a Teardrop Explodes concert in his hand. The Cardiff constabulary came up here to check out some dates and took away all my cuttings relating to the 'Fire Escape In The Sky' period. I still haven't had them back.'

Cally recalls how the flurry of interest which greeted the Cope/Drummond compilation forced Phonogram's hand. 'The album got so much press that Phonogram decided to issue their own "Scott Walker Sings Jacques Brel" compilation. It came out with a totally misleading cover lifted from the first solo album and effectively killed the Zoo compilation, which still must have sold around 10,000 copies.

'It was quickly deleted because Zoo did not pay Phonogram any royalties and they got pissed off. People were thoroughly confused by these two albums coming out almost together. It was widely thought that the Zoo compilation was an album of Julian Cope cover versions.'

Phonogram's 'Scott Walker Sings Jacques Brel' compilation also suffered and is dismissed by Cally as a 'totally pointless exercise. What that record needed was the endorsement of somebody like Julian to make it sell. For example, when Paul Weller wrote the sleevenotes for an album by The Action, all these Jam fans rushed out to buy it. It sold around 11,000 copies for Demon, which was pretty phenomenal.'

As for Cope, he clearly holds Scott in the same kind of awe as

Engel regarded Brel. Curiously, Cope's feelings towards his own artistic touchstone mirror Engel's attitude towards the Belgian songwriter: while enthralled at his work he stopped short of actually wanting to meet his idol. Indeed, when one of the music papers endeavoured to set up such a meeting shortly after the release of 'Climate of Hunter', Cope demurred, apparently fearing that such an exercise would be both contrived and uncomfortable.

Despite a constant stream of Walker retrospectives in various publications, Scott remained in total seclusion; his return to the recording studio seemingly as far away as ever. 'I wasn't ready,' he later explained. 'Unless I'm ready to go at any time for anything it would take a bear to drag me out.' Scott's daily routine was 'probably like that of every person out of work in Great Britain ... I was lucky to have so much time on my hands, time to read, to watch movies, to do things I like to do.'

The task of compiling sleevenotes for the Brel compilation fell to veteran NME journalist Fred Dellar who made a determined, if fruitless, attempt to contact the reclusive star. 'It proved a mysterious process,' recounts Dellar. 'A record company executive having to contact a nameless girl who, in turn, would contact Scott at his hideaway. And though the message was passed down the line, no answer ever came back through the same channel.'

Dellar's failed quest was duly embroidered into the growing fabric of Walker legend, which was given fresh impetus by Chris Bohn's engrossing NME article of 11 July lamenting Scott's continuing absence from the recording scene. Describing 'The Electrician' as Scott's most devastating twilight song, Bohn added: 'To date, it's the last Scott Walker song on record and it's the one that got me into the murk of his mind in the first place.

'It still moves and frightens me – more so for being equally relevant today as it was three years ago. It left me hungering for more, but, typically, the contrary Scott Walker has been silent ever since.' In 1981, almost like it had been in 1965, the pop world was both tantalised and intrigued by the enigma of Scott Walker.

Engel's low profile sparked a series of progressively outlandish rumours. One report had him fleeing to live in Toronto, Canada, while another solemnly stated he had taken up residence on an island in the Outer Hebrides. Then American crooner Andy Williams was reputed to have offered to buy Scott's back catalogue for $2 million and launch him as a star in Las Vegas. In August, an article entitled

'Scott Walker Through The Past Darkly', in the Australian magazine *Juke*, suggested the time had come to 'reach into the closet and drag the Scott Walker legend out of mothballs'.

Then, in an imaginative variation on Kirsty McColl's 1981 hit 'There's A Guy Works Down The Chip Shop Swears He's Elvis', came reports that Scott was running a fish and chip shop in the village of Betley, near Stoke-on-Trent (and serenading customers with bursts of Walker Brothers' songs over the fryer, no doubt). Almost overnight, Scott had been transformed from a seemingly washed-up sixties has-been into one of pop's living legends, to rank alongside such luminaries as Pink Floyd founder Syd Barrett, Beach Boys eccentric Brian Wilson and Love's enigmatic leader Arthur Lee. Renewed cult status took Scott totally by surprise.

'I wasn't aware of it until then,' he told Richard Cook three years later. 'And I didn't know what to think. You know, when it's just one guy doin' it . . . I can't think about that too much. Yeah, I guess I was embarrassed by it, since I didn't know anyone who's connected with it. I wasn't bombarded with it. I was sent Cope's compilation and I put it on and listened to this young guy singin' . . . thought, hey, that's not bad. But one play was enough.'

By the summer of 1982 Virgin was becoming twitchy. Two and a half years had elapsed since Scott had signed to the label and there was still no sign of an album. The singer kept coming up with obscure excuses, his manager was asking for more money and Simon Draper's patience was running out. 'I refused to provide any more money and we effectively suspended the contract because it was starting to look as if we were never going to get a record,' he says.

'Scott is an extraordinarily likeable man but he talks in strange abstractions and it is quite hard to follow his thought patterns,' confirms Jeremy Lascelles. 'He wanted to make music that was true to him and fought shy of anything that had even the faintest aroma of commerciality. We respected that totally and decided that we just had to leave him alone.'

Engel's public appearances from 1980 to 1982 were principally confined to the tea-room of the Kensington Hilton where he would occasionally meet up for a cuppa with Al Clark, who, as a freelance journalist, had interviewed the singer at Ady Semel's office back in 1973. 'Far from being a lugubrious and silent figure Scott was very buoyant and communicative and cracked lots of jokes,' says Clark, who is now a film producer in Sydney, Australia. 'This was the impression of him that I carried with me until we met up again in 1980.'

The two men discovered a mutual love of the cinema and would regularly meet either at the Kensington Hilton or a nearby pub. So began what Clark describes as 'a friendship uncomplicated by expediency'. The journalist felt his main function was to introduce Scott to influential people who could then help to navigate him through the next phase of his career. Indeed, it was Clark who introduced Engel to electronics wizard Brian Eno over tea at the Hilton, although nothing came of a mooted 1981 collaboration.

Engel, who occasionally joined Clark for a fish-pie lunch at a quiet Fulham Road restaurant, clearly welcomed having a companion who shared his main interest and never pressed him on his forthcoming album or who was going to produce it. Scott also became friendly with Arnold Frolows, who shared his taste for modern jazz and avant-garde cinema, and became his squash partner.

'I cannot remember Scott ever being recognised when we were down in the pub,' says Clark. 'But if you stay out of the limelight the public tend to invent their own image of you. Most people probably thought Scott Walker was locked away in some castle wearing a cape or something and scarcely could have expected him to suddenly materialise in their local.'

Asked to provide a summary of Engel's character, Clark ponders for some time before replying: 'Driven by curiosity rather than achievement. Contemptuous of mediocrity and suspicious of sanctification, but with an unerring sense of absurdity about the world that made him the best of company.'

Scott's modest means of transport was still an old orange Volkswagen with a stereo on which he would play endless Miles Davis tapes. His only foray into the studio at this time appears to have been to produce a mooted album of songs by John and Brandy Maus on the Blue Guitar label. Suffice to say, nothing ever emerged apart from a song entitled 'Dark Angel', backed by 'Remember Me', (the B-side of 'No Regrets') which was issued as a demo on the Spectra label in the United States. The record's only real achievement was to repair the five-year rift between Scott and John.

That year again saw Phonogram, undeterred by the disappointing sales of their Brel compilation, scrambling into the vaults to salvage more of Scott's material. Released simultaneously, 'Walker Brothers Hits' and 'The Best of Scott Walker', the latter featuring the pick of

Engel's solo material, served to keep the artist's work in the public eye, even if the subsequent royalty cheques made a return to the recording studio less imperative. In June, an insipid remake of 'No Regrets', by Ultravox's Midge Ure, hit the charts and undeservedly matched the success of the Walker Brothers' version six years earlier. Indeed, Ure's arrangement was almost identical.

While everyone else was falling over themselves to praise records he had made at Stanhope Place all those years before, Scott, who had now parted company from Apps, clearly had no desire to hitch a ride on the creaking 1960s revival bandwagon. 'I think a lot of it was absolutely awful,' he insisted. 'That's not false modesty, it's absolutely true. It's the old story of the guy who made it seein' flaws. Some of it was very good. But the time I wasted after those first records was shameful.'

Chris Welch, along with several other media critics, attributed Scott's torpor to a lack of direction and the absence of a strong managerial hand. 'He needed someone to give him confidence and guide him directly, but those kind of managers did not appear until later.

'Most of the successful bands usually end up with one manager that they can identify with, who understands what they are trying to do and who sticks with them through thick and thin – Ed Bicknell and Dire Straits is a good example.'

Although Welch did not know it at the time (and was considerably surprised to discover later), Scott actually signed with Bicknell's Damage Management in February 1983. 'I was tryin' to get some studio work on the quiet, but I didn't know who to go to,' he explained the following year. 'Then I found this management through Al Clark. I was pretty broke. They said: "Well, why don't you finish your contract?" I had a bad history – I'd lost three flats just as I was gainin' any kind of impetus – but they said at least start talkin' to Virgin again. I didn't know if that was the problem – they didn't realise I had to have money to complete it.'

Bicknell, who remains one of the top managers in the business, says he took on Scott in 1983 simply because he had been a huge fan for many years. While at university he bought Scott's first solo albums and rapidly discovered they were ideal records to play in a student bedroom preferably in the company of a member of the opposite sex. 'It was great music to fuck to,' he smirks.

'I happened to know Al Clark at Virgin and we once had this

conversation about the sort of music we liked. I told him that I thought Scott Walker was simply the best and that I would love to work with him. I never thought anything of it, then out of the blue my telephone rang one day and a voice said: "Hi, this is Scott Walker." I nearly dropped the phone. I went into a sort of gibber-speak, like you do when you try to tell someone you have all their records. But he was very gracious about it and in due course arrived at my office. I was petrified. I have worked with many, many people but only two have ever intimidated me. One was Buddy Rich, the other was Scott Walker.'

Over the course of the next three years, Bicknell strove manfully to kickstart Scott's career. Having arrived at an informal agreement with the erstwhile Walker Brother, Bicknell's initial brief was to find Scott work as a producer and not as a singer. Unfortunately, the manager's overtures to Virgin were ignored. The record company wanted Scott for his singing, not for his production abilities. Engel was also highly selective about the type of work he wanted to do, so Bicknell set about the rather seductive process of trying to persuade him to record again.

By the summer, Scott himself had decided that the time had come to put something down on vinyl. It really was now or never. 'It seemed like everythin' was crumblin' around me each time I tried to get started,' he told Richard Cook. 'But I knew I had to find it this time even if I never made another record. C'mon you old bastard, keep movin'!'

It was the timely arrival of a fairly hefty publisher's cheque which finally persuaded Scott to piece together his various 'bits and pieces' and complete the album for which Virgin had waited with mounting consternation. 'I had to finish it,' he said. 'I couldn't seem to get anywhere in my life until I had done this – completely leave or murder myself or anythin'.

'So I rented a cottage in the country. I looked in the paper and saw this workman's cottage near Tunbridge Wells, so I rented it for two months, on my own. I put all of "Climate Of Hunter" together down there. I told Virgin I'd have it ready in two months – I had to run a bluff on myself. I knew I had it,' Scott clenched a fist to emphasise the extent of his tortuous struggle. 'And I made it.'

When Scott returned from his rural retreat in September, he was faced with the ghastly prospect of floundering in the face of the latest studio technology. If a week was a long time in politics, five years was an eternity in the fast-moving music business.

Having been sent various tapes by Virgin, Scott eventually chose Peter Walsh as producer, best known for his work with another Virgin act, Simple Minds. Scott apparently concluded that his work was 'more total'. This having been decided, Virgin promptly rushed Engel into the studio to begin work on a comeback album which reportedly cost around £75,000.

Although Virgin stumped up the cash without a qualm, their A & R men were naturally a bit perturbed when Scott banned them from entering London's Sarm West studios, where the album was recorded. 'Climate Of Hunter' was therefore conceived in an air of complete mystery. Simon Draper recalls Scott's obsessive secrecy led him to hire a hall in Islington to test his vocals in complete solitude along with backing tracks he had recorded on a small tape recorder.

'Scott didn't tell any of the musicians the shape of the songs and he was loath to let people hear any of the melodies or the top lines. He was really paranoid. None of us were allowed to go into the studio as he didn't want anyone to hear his voice. Consequently, we didn't know what kind of album we were getting, but by this stage we were prepared to take anything that he came up with.'

The extent of Scott's paranoia is confirmed by Lascelles who remembers that when the singer photocopied his lyrics at Sarm West he hunched himself over the machine to shield his work from prying eyes. Only when the tracks on 'Climate Of Hunter' were about to be mixed was Lascelles invited to hear the fruits of Scott's labours and he was bowled over by the material.

'We were not expecting a commercial record, but some of those tracks sent a shiver down my spine. I thought it was wonderful. I remember playing it to various people at the office although, it has to be said, their opinions were divided. Some clearly expected something more commercial and were really taken aback. Having said that, even if it had been a pile of shit I was just relieved to get something out!'

Although the vocals, production and overall feel of the record were highly original, Draper realised with a sinking heart that it would not fit into any niche in the UK record market. Virgin therefore placed its faith on the fanaticism which Scott's earlier work inspired and hoped the album would sell on the strength of his name. Bicknell remembers Lascelles telling him that while musicians could produce avant-garde, experimental records in the 1970s, now that 'Climate Of Hunter' had emerged, this was no longer the case.

Some time later, Scott stated that 'Climate Of Hunter' was based on *Lieder*, an essentially Germanic form of song in which equal importance is placed on words and music with poet and composer completely in harmony. Some of the great composers of *Lieder* (which sets to music a poem invariably about love or fear of death) include Schubert, Schumann, Beethoven and Brahms – but particularly Schubert, who appears to have exerted an immense influence on Scott.

Despite his lengthy recording break, 'Climate' took off exactly where Scott had signed off with his four contributions to 'Nite Flights'. The singer's own description of the music as 'trance-like' is quite apt.

For no reason that can be gleaned from the lyrics, Scott chose to title the opening track 'Rawhide'. Anyone hoping to hear him start bellowing 'Move 'em on, head 'em up' while hitting himself over the head with a tin tray was in for a disappointment.

In fact, the words to the classic Dimitri Piomkin TV theme are a good deal more comprehensible than Scott's stream-of-consciousness thoughts. It seems unlikely that Scott, who pondered for hours over the meaning of his lyrics, should resort to the cut-up-and-paste technique pioneered by David Bowie and Brian Eno, but it is difficult to glean any real sense from lines like 'Cro-magnon herders/Will stand in the wind/Sweeping tales shining/And scaled to begin'.

'The words of the songs are how they come to me,' Engel told Terry Terrill of *Debut* magazine, adding somewhat paradoxically: 'They need to be singable. I listen to some of the lyrics around today and I just think some of 'em are really silly. I'd find it difficult to sing those songs.'

Much of 'Climate Of Hunter's' appeal lies in attempting to decipher just what the hell Scott is on about. As Terrill noted, many of the words work better as poetry than they do as lyrics. They certainly were not likely to catapult their writer on to daytime radio.

Nevertheless, 'Track Three', one of four on the album to be identified only by its number, was chosen as a single. Scott told Terrill that as a rule he did not make a point of listening to chart music but admitted: 'About two weeks before recording I listen to the radio and buy some of the chart LPs just really to use as a gauge of the newer technology.'

The likes of Nik Kershaw's eminently catchy 'Wouldn't It Be Good', which was dominating the airwaves at the time, evidently failed to rub off on Engel. Although 'Track Three' has one of the LP's few barely discernible choruses, its chances of breaking into the top 20 were clearly negligible.

It mattered not. 'Climate of Hunter' was a return to heaven for most Scott Walker fans. As so many people had pointed out, he was at his best when following the path he had chosen for himself and ignoring those who might tempt him to sacrifice his art for commerciality.

Others, however, notably the Radio 1 disc jockey Mike Read, were deeply perplexed by the abstract nature of the record. It was not what they had expected.

As should be, it is Scott's voice that dominates the LP, but with the meaning of what he is singing shrouded in mystery the listener is left to concentrate on its beauty as a pure instrument. Perhaps for that reason, 'Climate' is the one post-sixties Scott Walker LP that still sounds as relevant today as it did when it was recorded.

Yet 'Sleepwalkers Woman' is a virtual remake of one of his greatest past achievements, 'Boy Child' – the same opening notes, an almost identical half-spoken delivery. Track Five continues in the same vein before bursting into life with Peter Van Hooke's distinctively brittle drumming. In contrast, Track Six is almost funereal in pace, with an eerie insect-like guitar sound throughout adding to the mystery.

The record closes with a cover of the only song ever written by playwright Tennessee Williams. Scott had heard the song 'Blanket Roll Blues' in a Marlon Brando film on one of his many solitary visits to the cinema.

'The problem was he hadn't a clue what the film was,' recalls Ed Bicknell. 'So someone was sent out to find it. All Scott knew was that Brando had sung the song, so the poor guy had to go out and get a copy of every film he had ever made and sit through the lot until he found it. It took four days before we hit on the right one which I think was *Sweet Bird Of Youth* [actually *The Fugitive Kind*].'

Bicknell's star signing, Mark Knopfler of Dire Straits, was called in to play guitar. As he improvised some introductory licks on his trademark instrument, the chrome National Steel guitar that graced the cover of the hugely successful 'Brothers In Arms', Scott walked into the studio and began to sing.

Bicknell: 'Mark almost stopped dead in his tracks because he was so amazed by this voice. If you listen carefully you can hear him falter as the singing starts, but they played it through just that one time and Scott decided it was a wrap. Knopfler said it was the only voice he had ever heard that actually filled the studio.'

Brian Gascoigne, whom Scott appointed as arranger after hearing some of his orchestral work with Japan's David Sylvian, says: ' "Climate Of Hunter" is a strange record. It has long spells of static motion rather than the frantic chord changing of most pop records which I found extremely odd. Scott was extremely reluctant to let anyone know what was going to happen in the studio. When it came to laying down the backing tracks no one knew what the melody or lyrics were. Some of the musicians asked Scott to sing a guide vocal but he said he didn't want to.

'But that's just Scott's way. He is striving to create something completely different. He played me some classical music which he liked and then told me he wanted a still, glassy texture. "I want you to write one chord and hold it for sixteen bars," he said. This was a highly unusual orchestral texture – in other words, the harmony did not change for sixteen bars.

'On the few occasions I have worked with pop musicians I am always struck by how illiterate they are, whereas Scott is trying to operate on another level. He's constantly searching in his mind for a new vocabulary of songs and perhaps the reason he was so secretive was that he feared Virgin might sense the album's lack of commerciality and pull the plug on the whole thing.'

Somewhat predictably, Scott only did a modest amount of promotional work for the album, his old fear of flying restricting the amount of interviews he gave on the Continent to a bare minimum. Richard Cook, of the *New Musical Express*, conducted Scott's sole British interview in a West London hotel bar. The *NME* writer was rather overawed at the prospect of meeting his idol, but Scott, sitting at a table and sipping at a modest scotch and soda, seemed relatively relaxed even if his broken, unfinished sentences indicated that he had not been interviewed for several years.

Pressed for an update on his recent activities, Scott informed Cook that he liked sitting in pubs watching people throw darts. 'But where have you been all this time?' persisted the puzzled writer. 'In a trance,' replied Scott mischievously. 'I've been here drinking!'

Asked about the state of his voice, Engel, his luxuriant golden hair showing no greyness and only a pair of steel frames altering those one-time teen-idol features, claimed his vocals had improved with age. 'This is the best age to sing at – until you reach 50, when it starts to go down,' he asserted. 'Right now, you're at your peak. I was very worried about it but once I started it was easier than I've ever found before.'

His six-year sabbatical had not erased the fear of live performance, however. 'Performing is one of those things I don't like to do, like flying,' Scott said firmly. 'I'd do it if anything happened to my record. But I think they've got a long wait.'

The following week Scott materialised for a live interview on *The Tube*, Channel Four's anarchic Newcastle-based pop programme which was then at the peak of its popularity. Sitting on a sofa alongside interviewer Muriel Gray, his brow furrowed, tongue flickering, and eyes darting back and forth behind his spectacles, Scott looked only marginally more comfortable than a mod at a rockers' convention.

He appeared to have difficulty understanding Ms Gray's strong Scottish accent and the faintly menacing background presence of groups of tough-looking, beer-swilling Geordie lads evidently increased his discomfort. (Scott had wanted to be interviewed in his dressing room.)

Asked to elaborate on his return, Engel, who visibly bridled at the word 'comeback' ('I just look towards the next album'), replied: 'It was many, many things which would take about four *Tubes* to go into and it's not very interesting.'

Speaking in a voice as richly languid as his singing, Scott expressed relief that the type of hysteria his old group inspired was a receding memory and re-affirmed that he was 'not a get-up-and-sing type of singer'. The highlight came when Ms Gray laughingly quizzed him on the bald, numeric titles of various 'Climate of Hunter' tracks. 'Well,' grinned Scott, nervously snapping his fingers, 'the old creativity kinda ran out, I guess. I felt the songs were complete and that puttin' on titles would maybe lopside or overload 'em a little.' His ordeal over, Scott noticeably relaxed as he sat back to watch the 'Track 3' video.

Artily shot in black and white and crammed with violent and disturbing surrealism, Scott's first video, which depicts a chase through a hellish, rat-infested subterranean landscape interspersed with moody shots of the artist playing his guitar, was shot in the basement car park of a South London tower block. Bicknell recalls that filming was interrupted by the news that someone had been stabbed in a nearby pub and vast numbers of police cars set off in hot pursuit of the assailant.

'Every so often a police car would fly by with its sirens wailing,' he says. 'Unfortunately, our generators then blew up so we had to wait for six hours until they came back on. In that time Scott managed to get himself pretty drunk.'

Charles Negus-Fancey, who was destined to take over as Scott's manager four years later, felt *The Tube* interview was ridiculous. 'With respect to Muriel Gray, I don't think she quite understood who she was talking to. She was a bit ill-informed. When you read Scott's interviews abroad with people who are well informed about his music and career he gives much better interviews. Unfortunately, British interviewers tend not to be so interested in the music and consequently Scott withdraws.'

Negus-Fancey's view, while seemingly a little harsh, is supported by the interviewer herself. 'All my *Tube* interviews were crap,' says Muriel Gray. 'If Scott came across really badly then it was entirely my fault. Perhaps it would have been better if Jools Holland had interviewed him. If I interviewed Scott Walker now, I'm sure I would do a much better job.

'The reason I remember that particular interview is that the poor man was like a rabbit in a car's headlights. If I seemed to end up doing most of the talking for three minutes it was because Scott appeared to have lost the power of speech. So many of the people I interviewed on *The Tube* would make rather pathetic attempts at being cool, but he wasn't at all like that. I was looking into his eyes and they were absolutely terrified.

'Perhaps interviewing him in The Green Room wasn't a good idea. It always tended to be full of these horrible roadies with their great big beer bellies hanging out and the pub-like atmosphere must have been rather intimidating to someone who was very shy.'

A week later, Scott, accompanied by Michael Beck of Virgin Records, flew to Cologne to be interviewed on BFBS Germany's *Night Flight* radio programme. Disc jockey Alan Bangs spent a pleasant evening in Engel's company at a restaurant the night before the broadcast and they parted on the understanding that Scott would not arrive at the studio before the programme started, thereby precluding the possibility of discussing unwelcome topics twice. Having agreed on this, Engel and Bangs shook hands and the latter departed, eagerly anticipating the following night's broadcast.

Bangs, then, was understandably annoyed when Engel and Beck arrived at the studio three-quarters of an hour late, having spent the entire evening in another restaurant. Scott's time-keeping had clearly not improved, since he habitually kept the *NME*'s Keith Altham waiting for interviews in the mid-sixties. The disc jockey, who had already begun to play Scott's records in connection with other music, angrily signalled to Engel and his partner to sit down without removing his headphones or saying a word.

He then repeated two of Scott's songs which had already been broadcast at the beginning of the programme. Scott sat down in the dimly lit studio, closed his eyes, and seemed lost in thought. The trio sat in silence for fifteen minutes before Bangs asked his first question.

Scott, who seemed fearful that his song-writing ability would disappear if subjected to excessive analysis, was reluctant to talk about the circumstances under which his new material was composed ('I don't like talkin' about it because I don't understand it completely myself'), but revealed that he had spent much of the previous six years searching for inner peace. 'In that state things develop all by themselves,' he said. 'It was very important for these things to come by themselves and that I didn't have to force it, so I looked for the right environment, and suddenly there it was: time and receptiveness fit together, don't ask me why.'

But as far as Scott was concerned, the Ides of March brought only disappointment and anti-climax. 'Climate Of Hunter', while receiving lavish acclaim from the music press, remained essentially an unknown album due to its lack of commerciality and sheer inaccessibility. 'From a commercial point of view I was disappointed because I felt Scott was capable of making an absolute blockbuster of a record,' says Simon Draper. ' "Hunter" was just a little too bleak and extreme for public consumption.'

Despite rumours that the album was the worst-selling in Virgin's history (one estimate put sales as low as 1,500), 'Climate Of Hunter' actually sold around 10,000 copies and reached No. 60 in the British charts. Although the music papers proclaimed that Scott had achieved a comeback on his own terms and with complete artistic freedom, it must have seemed a hollow victory. Far from heralding his artistic rebirth, 'Climate Of Hunter' abjectly failed to instill in him sufficient confidence to make a full-blow return.

Yet is it possible that Scott deliberately impaled himself on the sword of public rejection? Rumour has it that Engel, angered at what he considered was pressure from Virgin, deliberately wrote the album in a wanton and haphazard manner and then sat back to gauge the reaction to something he regarded as nothing more than a throwaway. Subsequently confronted with the effusive and empty praise of reviewers, Scott is reputed to have shrugged and said: 'If that's what they think about something that's crap, why should I produce anything worthwhile?'

The notion of Scott gleefully thumbing his nose at the record industry while at the same time settling an old score with the music press is highly appealing, if exceedingly unlikely. It is, after all, conduct scarcely befitting such a great perfectionist and the story smacks of a leg-pull perhaps conceived by an ardent Walker admirer embarrassed by the album's disappointing sales.

Nevertheless, after the interminable delay which preceded the record and the expansive praise heaped upon it (' "Climate Of Hunter" invites the listener to scream into the face of destiny', *NME* solemnly declared), it is amusing to think that the Hunter's numerous devotees may just possibly have been following a false trail.

18 30 Century Man

'There's a lot of things I'd like to do still. Or I could be good at just doin' nothin'.'

Scott Walker, 1984

THE COMMERCIAL FAILURE of 'Climate Of Hunter' caused Scott to retreat back into his shell while Bicknell and Virgin haggled over what should happen next. Eventually the record company picked up the option to finance another album and Bicknell sought to persuade Scott to record an LP of cover versions written by some of the top songwriters of the day.

This was an exciting development. The dormant career of Sandie Shaw had been revived by her critically acclaimed collaboration with The Smiths and the possibility of Scott Walker making a similarly dramatic return to the Top Twenty was irresistible. Despite Engel's initial wariness, he agreed to consider the proposal and Bicknell duly contacted Chris Difford and Glen Tilbrook from Squeeze, Mark Knopfler, Boy George and Joan Armatrading.

'Without exception, they all wanted to write for him, but he eventually demurred. I don't know why. Scott wasn't given to explanations. Everything with Scott took place very slowly and by this time it was 1985. I got into the whole "Brothers In Arms" success with Dire Straits which took me through to 1986 and in all that time I did not speak to Scott or communicate with him at all. I didn't consider it that unusual but one day in 1986 he came into my office. He never made appointments, he just appeared.'

When Bicknell asked Scott what he had been up to, the singer replied that he had been concentrating on painting. 'Oils or watercolours?' enquired his curious manager. 'Oh no,' said Scott, shaking his head. 'Paintin' and decoratin'.' Engel had, for the time being at least, broken all links with the music industry as he had threatened so often to do. 'I can do anythin' if I have to,' he had said way back in 1968. 'Even go out and dig ditches if necessary. Or pick up my guitar and sing around bars somewhere.'

Following further discussions with Bicknell, Simon Draper decided that an LP would be produced by Brian Eno and Daniel Lanois who had recently completed work on U2's 'The Unforgettable Fire'. Five years earlier a projected Eno–Engel collaboration had come to nothing ('I thought rather than destroying his career too, I had to do one on my own,' Scott laughingly told Richard Cook); this time Engel actually got as far as recording. According to Bicknell, four or five backing tracks were laid down at former Roxy Music guitarist Phil Manzanera's studio in Chertsey, but the sessions collapsed after two weeks.

'What seemed to be happening was that the material was just too experimental. Scott had said something about inventing some new chords, but he would not relate any lyrical content to Eno and Lanois. So they were working on the music without knowing what any of the melody lines or lyrics were. Scott just rang up one day and said he wasn't going into the studio the next day.'

Draper remains puzzled by the collapse of the sessions. It was on his insistence that the record should be co-produced by Eno who was, after all, directly responsible for Virgin signing Scott in the first place. 'Eno and Lanois seemed a wonderful combination, yet Scott ended up firing Lanois. When we asked him why, Scott said he didn't like the way Lanois looked – too saturnine and gypsy-like, perhaps. Brian doesn't like to exercise too much control in the studio but prefers to act as a sort of catalyst. He didn't want to work with Scott on his own, so we were just left with these wonderful backing tracks with Robert Fripp on guitar. It was great stuff, but we never heard a single top line and by this time I had totally lost confidence in Scott.'

Brian Gascoigne, who also worked on this aborted album, believes Scott feared that Eno and Lanois were unwittingly trying to force him in an alternative direction and felt that both men tended to be blinded by technology. 'One day, Eno and Lanois were experimenting with various pieces of equipment and I can distinctly remember catching Scott's eye as we stood in the control room,' he says. 'Although Eno and Lanois certainly did not impose their international hit-making methods on Scott, he started getting rather uncomfortable.'

Following the departure of Eno and Lanois, Scott attempted to press ahead with the recording of the album, but diplomatic relations with Virgin were deteriorating and matters came to a head when the record company only agreed to finance a single three-hour orchestral overdub session. 'Scott said that three hours was insufficient and if he couldn't do it his way he'd rather not do it all,' says Gascoigne. 'When it comes to producing albums Scott insists on a time scale more comparable with musicians who enjoy unlimited recording budgets. His approach to rock music is not sex and drugs and rock 'n' roll. He sees no reason why pop music cannot contain the meat of classical music.'

Lascelles says he was 'stunned' by the quality of the Eno/Lanois backing tracks, so Scott's decision to shelve the album was a crushing disappointment. 'He felt very paranoid about having two producers in the studio. He seemed very freaked about the whole thing and more or less intimated that he did not want to make another record. We thought we were sitting on one of the great artists of his era and it seemed tragic that he wasn't wanting to make more music. It was such a criminal waste of talent.

'After the collaboration with Eno fell through, Scott asked me if he could become an A&R man at Virgin. I was extremely tempted, although I did not feel he had a real sense of the business side of the industry. In the end, it just did not quite make sense.

'I found it all a little sad. Why on earth should he want to work for us when he could be making music? Although I knew Scott for several years, I cannot pretend to have ever understood him.'

A determined attempt to refloat Engel's career had been scuppered by the artist's maverick nature. It was the last straw as far as Virgin was concerned and the company waived its contract option for six more albums after Draper rejected plans for a proposed follow-up to 'Climate Of Hunter' with Scott in the producer's chair. 'There was no point in making an identical record. It didn't seem fair to both parties,' said a Virgin spokesman. In his last act as Scott's manager, Bicknell vetoed a move to issue the freshly recorded backing tracks on EG Records, which Eno was signed to. 'I felt it was being done for pure greed,' he says.

In February 1986, John Maus, who was still living with Brandy in Brighton, was persuaded to join fellow 1960s artists Screaming Lord Sutch, Tommy Bruce, Ricky Valance, Billie Davis, and Heinz and Jet Harris on The Monster Rock and Roll Show which travelled extensively around seaside resorts until June.

The tour was badly organised, with most of the acts having little idea of when they would appear or how long their sets would be. John's set, which rather poignantly included a medley of Walker

Brothers hits, was well received in venues like the Skegness Empire Ballroom and the Lakeside Country Club near Camberley, although he was quite hurt that Scott failed to attend a single performance. Somehow it is hard to envisage Scott coming within a mile of such an obvious exercise in nostalgia. By all accounts, The Monster Rock and Roll Show was indeed pretty gruesome.

At the time, Maus talked animatedly of another Walker Brothers reunion ('We seem to reunite every ten years, don't we?') and persuaded an associate to put the idea to Scott, who did not reject it out of hand. Once again, John's hopes were dashed as the right offer never came along. (One source claims Engel and Maus each demanded £25,000 upfront.) Soon afterwards, he and Brandy disappeared back to San Diego.

In May 1986 the musical *Chess*, written by the award-winning lyricist Tim Rice with music by Bjorn Ulvaeus and Benny Andersson, formerly of Swedish supergroup Abba, opened in London amid intriguing rumours that Scott had been offered a major on-stage role. Sadly, this tale is apocryphal although Rice, a huge Walker fan, says he would have loved Scott to have participated.

The following summer, the Bam Caruso label released 'Walker Brothers In Japan', a live album recorded at the Osaka Festival Hall during the group's farewell tour in January 1968. The 21-track listing includes Scott performing 'The Lady Came From Baltimore' and 'In My Room' (the latter being issued as a single), John's renditions of 'Annabella' and the Beatles' 'Yesterday', and Gary attacking 'Twinkie Lee' and 'Dizzy Miss Lizzie' with gusto.

The Walkers pose in traditional Japanese kimonos on the attractive front cover and the inside sleeve contains details of virtually every Japanese single and EP release. Despite the packaging and the album's historic interest, sales proved disappointing. 'There was not enough of Scott on it to get people excited,' reckons Phil Smee. 'The sound quality was quite good but, personally, I didn't like all that screaming.'

A couple of months later, Keith Altham, sitting waiting for the main feature to begin in his local cinema, was mildly amused by the orange-juice commercial which preceded it. The film, shot in grainy black and white and set to the strains of Dusty Springfield's 1963 hit 'I Only Want To Be With You', was a pastiche on Carnaby Street in the 1960s and Altham watched with interest as several of the stars from that era flitted across the screen as extras.

There was Sandie Shaw resplendent in a white mini-skirt and

weren't those The Tremeloes cavorting around a phone box? And, hang on a minute, the chap wearing dark shades . . . 'Good God!' exclaimed Altham, loudly enough to make the lady sitting in front jump slightly. 'That's Scott Walker!'

It surely could not be, yet it was. Scott, billed simply as 'Man in Café', is momentarily glimpsed sitting at a table and peering quizzically out of a window as a girl in an open-top sports car flashes past. It was his last public appearance of the decade. The cast included Georgie Fame, Dusty Springfield, Sandie Shaw and Dave Dee, who had talked Engel into participating. The cinematic version also features former Animals vocalist Eric Burdon, seen clad in a raincoat and walking a ferocious-looking bulldog. Details of Scott's fee have never been revealed, but he presumably received rather more than a crate of orange juice. The Abbott Mead Vickers advertising agency entrusted Dee with the task of rounding up the various artists.

Dee and Engel had known one another ever since Dave Dee, Dozy, Beaky, Mick and Tich supported the Walker Brothers on tour in 1966. But Scott reacted cautiously when Dee asked him to appear in the advert. 'Are you sure they don't want me to sing?' he asked nervously. 'Come on!' replied the garrulous Dee. 'It's a non-speaking role and just half a day's work. Get paid and go out and have yourself a holiday!'

'It turned out to be a good laugh. On location, Scott and I ended up sharing a caravan with Eric Burdon, who Scott hadn't seen for years. We sat around chatting while we waited to do our respective parts. Scott's was filmed in a café just off the Wandsworth Bridge Road.'

Scott, who back in the 1960s had said he was 'selling his fans a real person', may have identified with Britvic's theme. 'At the time, there was a sixties revival and the theme of the advertisements was "unmistakably real," ' says a spokeswoman. 'The idea was to use real stars from the 1960s, in real settings, drinking real fruit juice, i.e.: Britvic 55.' The British public's last glimpse of Scott to date shows him to be in remarkably good physical shape for a man of 44. Consuming all those vitamin pills, exercising regularly and, of course, drinking copious amounts of Britvic 55 had clearly paid off.

Although few were to know it at the time, Scott next resurfaced in the autumn of 1987 when John Maus made one of his periodic attempts to resuscitate his career. On this occasion Scott produced three demos for John and Brandy for Rough Trade. Although the tracks were never released commercially, the sessions did at least introduce Scott to the label's founder Geoff Travis and raise the possibility of a potentially fruitful association.

Travis, a widely respected record company boss with a formidable track record, was desperate to sign Scott to his Blanco Y Negro label, believing that such a move would help get Engel's career back on the rails.

However, intransigence on the part of Warner Brothers, Blanco's parent company, and Scott's characteristic stubbornness combined to throw a spanner in the works. (Three years later a move to sign Scott to Rough Trade would be undermined by the bankruptcy of the label's distribution company.) Travis today looks back on his unsuccessful attempts to sign Scott with considerable frustration.

'Scott initially approached me and asked to do some production work for John and his wife Brandy. Tarquin Gotch, an A&R man at Warner Brothers, and Rough Trade put up the money. The three songs which John had written were respectable AOR but in the end I decided that they were just a bit too old-fashioned to be released, even though it was powerful rock and quite melodramatic.

'The great thing from my point of view was that the sessions enabled me to work with Scott, someone who I'd always admired. I was extremely conscious that this was ostensibly John's project but, if I'm honest, it was Scott's presence which made it memorable for me.

'The demos were recorded at Marcus Studios. Scott was very quiet and thoughtful and seemed to know what he wanted. He looked in great shape – almost like he appeared in the sixties – and he wore this baseball cap which I think was some attempt at a disguise. He told me he had gone back to art college and was living in Maida Vale. I really liked the guy but gained the impression that he was only doing the job as a favour for John, although I like to think we gave him an insight into how an independent label worked, which must have been a new experience.'

Not content at seeing Scott confined to a production role, Travis tentatively explored the possibility of getting him back behind a microphone. 'We must sign him to Blanco Y Negro,' he urged Warners. The Warners executives, however, apparently unaware of the singer's cult status, could not be convinced. As far as they were concerned, signing Scott Walker made about as much sense as re-launching Tiny Tim. He was, after all, simply a former member of a mid-60s group of Spector soundalikes. 'So many people in the industry do not appreciate what Scott has achieved,' says Travis.

'Scott insisted that he did not want to record demos and I think that made Warners rather nervous. Having said that, perhaps I should have gone into that office, screamed and shouted and banged my fists on the table and forced them to accept my point of view. In retrospect, I wish I had done that now.'

But while others agonised and fretted over his stagnant career, Scott took his creative talents elsewhere. Art had been his first love and he once said that he had 'left a little bit of myself back at Hollywood High' where he had first studied almost 30 years earlier. His sporadic attempts to attend art school in the mid-60s were always ruined by the curious stares of fellow students and another twenty years would elapse before Scott had both the time and the means to indulge in his abiding passion. In October 1987, a part-time lecturer on a foundation course in fine arts at a North London college noticed a middle-aged pupil whose face was maddeningly familiar . . .

'One of my students on the year-long course was an American called Noel Engel. He was tall, wiry and quiet and probably in his late forties. After the course was over he moved to another class to study for a two-year diploma which I don't think he completed. The work ranged from painting and drawing to conceptual portraits.

'During the year I taught him I had no idea who he was, even though I remembered the Walker Brothers from the 1960s. He did nothing to indicate he was Scott Walker – he didn't go round singing Walker Brothers songs or anything like that. A lot of the teaching was on a one-to-one basis, but as we only discussed the work I cannot remember an actual conversation with him. There must have been around twenty other students in the class and he was just a quiet American guy who looked vaguely familiar.'

The lecturer says that if a fellow member of staff had not drawn his attention to a certain landscape portrait at a college exhibition a couple of years later, he would still be none the wiser. 'He pointed at this painting and said: "Scott Walker did that." Only then did the penny drop and I remember wondering why I hadn't recognised him during the year I'd taught his class.'

In the spring of 1988 Scott took a significant step towards a return to the music scene by employing Charles Negus-Fancey as his manager following a couple of directionless years. A trained solicitor, Negus-Fancey specialised in film and music law, representing the

Grades, London Management, International Artistes, Famous Music and many artists, producers and songwriters until he joined the Robert Stigwood Group where he was managing director during the halcyon days of the mid-seventies which spawned hit musicals *Saturday Night Fever*, *Grease* and *Evita* as well as the rebirth of the Bee Gees.

Negus-Fancey subsequently joined forces with Allan Carr, co-producer of *Grease*, who set up a film company with EMI with the intention of making international films. Their first project, *Can't Stop The Music*, was a disappointment and Negus-Fancey then established himself as an artists' manager who represented the singer Gilbert O'Sullivan throughout his lengthy court battle with MAM and Gordon Mills.

'I was introduced to Scott by a mutual acquaintance. Scott is very reserved when you first meet him but as I came to know him better I realised that he is a remarkable person. Very intelligent and well-rounded. He is forward-looking and nostalgia doesn't interest him at all. Any anecdotes about the past he may tell simply concern their relevance to today.'

Coincidentally, Negus-Fancey was also managing Mort Shuman, the man who introduced Jacques Brel to the English language, at that time. Shuman ('a colossus of a man'), who died of cancer in November 1991 at the age of 52, vaguely recalled briefly meeting Engel in the late 1960s, but their paths never crossed in London in the late 1980s and, despite press reports to the contrary, the possibility of a joint concert appearance featuring the works of Brel was never mooted.

'Scott approached me in order to get a record deal to make a new album but this was to be the album that he wanted to make and it would only come out when he was well and truly ready. It would not be what someone else directed or fitted into any marketing hole that they perceived for a Scott Walker album.'

The following year it was said that Scott was ready to record a new set of songs, most likely in collaboration with David Sylvian, the former lead singer of pretty boy art-rockers Japan. The project was said to be 'at the concept stage' but Sylvian's fascination with Scott Walker stretched back to the singer's largely barren spell at Virgin. B. J. Cole, the pedal-steel guitarist who worked with both Engel and Sylvian as a sessionman, recalls a conversation with Declan Colgan, who ran Virgin's independent labels, shortly after the release of 'Climate Of Hunter'.

'He said: "David Sylvian has been befriended by Scott Walker. Sylvian is very influenced by him and has become him." Apparently, they came into Virgin together and Declan said Scott made Sylvian look like a lager lout. Scott is less affected than David who is reclusive because it's a sort of fashion-stance.'

As the decade drew to a close, 'Make It Easy On Yourself' was bizarrely resurrected for a government advertisement urging British citizens to pay the newly implemented, and almost universally despised, poll tax (one wonders which advertising genius came up with that one). Scott's epic lament for a lost love was artlessly reinterpreted to carry the implicit threat: 'Do yourself a favour and pay up or we'll see you in court, folks.' Considering the outcome of the poll-tax debacle – widespread non-payment and scenes of public disorder leading to the eventual downfall of premier Margaret Thatcher – Brel's 'Funeral Tango' might have been more appropriate.

The beginning of 1990 saw Negus-Fancey actively pursuing a new recording deal. At one point it seemed possible that Scott would sign for Rough Trade where he would be guaranteed total artistic freedom. Geoff Travis, who had come so close to signing him three years earlier, was encouraged by reports that Scott wanted 'one last serious shot at getting an album out'.

'He said it was going to be commercial and that he would promote it by doing interviews, TV work and live performances. The Jesus and Mary Chain, who were signed to Blanco Y Negro at the time, were going to produce a track for Scott. But Rough Trade's distribution company went bankrupt and we were not in a position to make a record. The last thing I wanted was to offer Scott a deal giving him the freedom he wanted and then having to go to him halfway through and say: "I'm sorry, but the money has run out." If that had happened I never would have got it off my conscience.'

By the summer, the re-appraisal of Scott's solo career, as well as that of The Walker Brothers, was extremely fashionable and Phonogram responded to increasing demand by releasing 'Boy Child', the best Scott Walker compilation to date, as well as 'After The Lights Go Out', featuring some of the group's finest moments on vinyl. On the sleeve notes, singer Marc Almond, whose admiration of Scott led to him releasing his own album of Jacques Brel covers in 1989, described Engel's voice as having 'become a simile for all crooning deep tones and liquid vibrato'.

Cally, who compiled the albums, met Engel in a Kensington hotel to discuss how the old Philips songs were recorded. 'If Scott had been the recluse of legend he would never have agreed to meet me,' he says. 'He is odd in as much as he refuses to play the pop-star game. But, to me, the pop-star game is far odder.' At the time Cally assured Chris Heath of the *Daily Telegraph* that Scott Walker was far from being a tortured, morose recluse. 'Tortured?' he laughed. 'Not even slightly. People think that because the songs are very introspective and some are very sad, and because he is interested in explaining the depths of the inner psyche. But they are not autobiographical. If they were, he'd be dead.'

Both compilations proved successful, with 'Boy Child' selling 8,000 copies and 'After The Lights Go Out' considerably more. A couple of months later, Cally, in his capacity as A&R man for Warners, attempted to sign Scott to the label after hearing he was willing to record again but had no desire to 'produce hit singles to order'.

'We had a meeting and Scott said he was interested in working with a big orchestra again, using arrangements and delivering a song properly. He also cited the Jesus and Mary Chain as an example of a band he could produce material for. I went back to Warners and told them: "Look, Scott has still got a great voice, he's a great songwriter and I really think this could work."

'I also pointed out that the Pet Shop Boys had put Dusty Springfield back into the charts and, more cynically I suppose, I reckoned that Scott could easily be booked on to TV shows like *Wogan*. Unfortunately, I ran into the same brick wall as Geoff Travis. Rob Dickins, the Warners chairman, doesn't believe Scott can sing.'

At around the same time as the disillusioned Cally left his job at Warners ('They thought I was peculiar because I wanted to sign Scott Walker'), Negus-Fancey was refuting suggestions that Scott had stockpiled vast amounts of new material. 'He believes it is against the creative spirit to write songs and not record them,' he said. 'Time doesn't move on for Scott. He'd rather make no records than the wrong record. It's all so important to him.'

The following December, Mike Peyton, former head of promotions at GTO and now running his own PR company, was loading Christmas hampers into a van parked on a yellow line outside Fortnum and Mason in Piccadilly. 'It must have been a good year business-wise,' he smiles. It was 5.30 p.m. and almost dark as Peyton and his assistant dodged crowds of pre-Christmas shoppers as, hampers in hands, they scurried back and forth across the pavement while keeping one eye open for traffic wardens.

Glancing nervously down the street, Peyton suddenly caught sight of a tallish figure weaving through the pavement hordes and coming in his direction. This was no traffic warden, however. The man, who wore a long black coat and red scarf, walked with his head slightly bowed and, as he passed, Peyton stepped out in front of him, his arm outstretched. 'Scott Walker,' he said quietly. The man halted and turned his head. 'Michael Peyton,' drawled a mellow American voice.

'I said: "How the devil are you and what are you up to?" Scott said that he was very much into the art world and was painting and was very happy. Unfortunately, we didn't have time to chat because I was afraid that a traffic warden would come along any minute. "Nice to see you," I said and we shook hands. I gave him my business card and said that if he ever wanted a chat to give me a ring.' Suffice to say, Peyton is still waiting.

When Scott finally signed a deal with Phonogram's Fontana label the following spring, his career had effectively turned full circle. Twenty-six years after startling Johnny Franz by wandering into the Philips offices with John and Gary, Engel had returned to the company which held the bulk of his back catalogue. The fact Marc Almond had just taken Brel's 'Jacky' into the Top 20 was a sound portent.

'When Scott walked into my office and said he was interested in making a comeback, my jaw just hit the floor – I simply couldn't believe it,' Fontana A&R man David Bates told David Wigg of the *Daily Express*. 'He is currently writing new songs and seems very excited about the prospect of making an album. He hasn't aged a bit – he still looks slim and young looking. It was like seeing him back in the sixties, except with shorter hair.'

The deal struck up with legendary PolyGram chairman Maurice 'Obie' Oberstein, who had signed Engel to CBS in 1973, was simply to make an album with no exchange of money at all. Charles Negus-Fancey, referring to the progressively longer gaps between each new Scott Walker album, probably has his tongue in his cheek when he describes the deal as capable of seeing out the rest of Engel's recording career.

'Our brief to Fontana was to make an album that we wanted to make, under the terms we wanted, without anyone ever hearing anything in advance. In other words, to make it in collaboration with the record company but not under their direction. We would be paid on our royalties and the press would simply be told that Fontana were signing Scott Walker to deliver an album. Dave Bates, David Clipsham, the managing director, and Obie were all enthusiastic and it was the perfect home. It makes perfect sense to them because they hold Scott's back catalogue and they all happen to be great admirers of his.'

Oberstein, one of the record industry's most colourful characters, who once signed a deal with eccentric Some Bizarre boss Stevo while sitting on a stone lion in Trafalgar Square at midnight, alluded to a 'master plan' whereby a definitive Walker Brothers compilation would pave the way for a new album of Scott Walker material, whenever that might be. While Oberstein recognised that extracting records from Scott was about as painful as pulling teeth, he vowed that the company would stand by its man.

'It isn't costing us anything. He is in a financial position where he doesn't need to get a retainer. We only pay him when he produces a record. Scott is a nice man, thoughtful, but easy to talk to. He simply lacks the desire, or at least the will, to make himself a public figure. Somewhere along the line he decided he didn't want to be a star and unfortunately we are in a business where you have to get out there and hustle, whether you're Dire Straits, Bon Jovi or whoever. You have to get out on the road in front of people and Scott just doesn't seem capable or willing to do that.

'Rather than looking for the next big thing, which has always been his problem, he should be making records every year with whatever material comes his way. If he would only make records like Sinatra or Tony Bennett, or even Johnny Mathis, just find some songs, hire an arranger and put them out. He could sing anything, even Lloyd Webber. Why should we have an album by Michael Crawford when a voice like Scott's is not being used?'

Early in 1992, The Walkers found themselves back in the headlines when Fontana released 'No Regrets: The Best Of Scott Walker And The Walker Brothers' and watched it climb into the upper reaches of the charts. Despite the presence of 'Boy Child', 'Montague Terrace (In Blue)' and all the big Walker hits, the compilation suffered from the inclusion of 'Walking In The Rain', the below-par 'Deadlier Than The Male' and 'We're All Alone' from 'Lines' (the title track from that 1976 album is far stronger, if less commercial).

The total omission of 'Scott 3' material plus that of 'The Seventh Seal' and 'The Old Man's Back Again' from 'Scott 4', was inexplicable, although Fontana partially atoned for this by re-releasing Scott's first four solo albums following the success of 'No Regrets'.

Intrigued by this unexpected wave of interest in a long-extinct sixties group, the *Sunday People* newspaper carried an extensive article on the Walkers under the entirely predictable headline: 'Great Scott! We're Top Of The Pops Again'. Reporter Danny Buckland caught up with Gary in East London and succeeded in tracing John to his San Diego home. Scott however, remained tantalisingly elusive.

'Fame really bothered him,' Leeds told Buckland. 'It destroyed Scott Walker. He could have gone on for years makin' records written especially for him. He could have been a modern-day Sinatra and a multi-millionaire, but he turned his back on it. He was drivin' a VW Beetle the last I heard. Fame drove him into the cave he lives in now. He is no mad hermit or anything, just a deeply private person. But I dread to think what would happen if adulation strikes again on the same scale.'

'I had no idea the record was being released,' said John. 'I got a phone call from Scott's mother Mimi sayin' we had a record in the charts. I thought she had got it wrong and didn't believe her. Then Scott phoned out of the blue. I was elated. It is terrific to be back in the charts. I was surprised that the record was out but I am not that shocked it has done well. Modern music is mainly computerised sounds, there is no depth and feeling like our music.'

Although John and Gary were both remarkably forthcoming, the dogged Buckland was after bigger game: the Walkers' enigmatic leader. However, all his enquiries drew a blank and the *People* resorted to inviting readers to ring a 'Walker Hotline' if they knew of Scott's whereabouts.

The following Sunday the paper triumphantly carried a blurred snatch-photo purporting to show a heavily disguised Scott making his getaway on a mountain bike. 'This Wheely Is Scott!' trumpeted the headline. For a mercifully brief period, Engel must have felt he had been transported back to 1966 with fans and press baying at his heels. Once again, he followed a fugitive's path.

19 No Regrets

'I'm lookin' to open people's eyes. I'll fail, but in the process I'll get self-satisfaction . . . and I won't fail completely. At least a minority, a strong minority, will listen and that's the important thing.'

Scott Walker, 1967

CHARLES NEGUS-FANCEY SITS in a spacious office in a quiet Bayswater backstreet on a thundery, oppressive afternoon in July 1993. A youthful-looking fortysomething with an easy manner and well-modulated tones befitting the solicitor he once was, Negus-Fancey currently represents several artists including Willy Russell, the playwright and composer, as well as 1960s chanteuse Sandie Shaw, her one-time songwriter Chris Andrews and, of course, Scott Walker, whose 1974 *Melody Maker* portrait hangs on the wall behind him. There are no chanting 'screamagers' milling around on the pavement outside or hordes of photographers encamped on the doorstep and Scott's current manager is the complete antithesis of Maurice King.

Negus-Fancey is used to being asked when the new Scott Walker album will appear. It is a query he answers virtually every week. According to a report in the *Daily Express*, the album was originally due to be released in October 1992, but Scott apparently decided that a little more work on the lyrics was required.

'Scott's been working on this album for some years, I guess, but that's a realistic attitude when you're only going to make the album that you want to make. So really time is irrelevant. There is no deadline and no one is pressurising him because everyone has complete faith that it will be a brilliant album. Whether the public are going to like it is another matter altogether. This time we hope that apart from attracting critical acclaim it also gets across to the public.

'Scott writes his lyrics first and then he writes the music afterwards. It's all essentially complete now, although there is, perhaps, the odd melody that's not finalised. Scott has always been stretching barriers and seeking to go that little bit further and experiment with different sounds.'

Almost unbelievably, Scott actually put a record out in France in the spring of 1993. 'Man From Reno/Indecent Sacrifice' is part of the soundtrack for a French-language film called *Toxic Affair*, a comedy about 'romantic detoxification', directed by Philomene Esposito and starring Isabelle Adjani. The 'Man From Reno' video included shots of the casually attired singer writing out the song lyrics and wandering the Paris streets wearing his trademark shades.

The music was written by Yugoslavian Goran Bregovic, who had recently scored *Arizona Dream* (a movie boasting a four-song Iggy Pop involvement), but the lyrics were by Scott who recorded his vocals at London's Matrix Studios. The fact he wrote the lyrics over a weekend mocked a widespread belief that Scott was suffering a creative block stretching back almost a decade.

As he inserts the new compact disc into the office stereo, Negus-Fancey explains that there are no plans to release the single in Britain as it is entirely different to the material on Engel's forthcoming LP. A more obvious explanation is that both single and film failed to make a significant impact on the Continent. 'If anyone ever doubted whether Scott still has the voice, this little exercise shows that it is still as fantastic as ever,' smiles his manager.

Seconds later that majestic voice fills the room just as it did back in 1965 when Johnny Franz placed 'Love Her' on his office turntable at Philips.

Negus-Fancey may be understandably biased but he is quite correct. Three decades on, Scott's voice has lost none of its rich timbre or depth as he croons over a simple keyboard string sound. Just as the listener anticipates another dirge-like ballad, the song perks up with a jaunty guitar picking up the rhythm and Scott spitting out the lyric: 'Zodiac killer, needs that crack, he wants you back, he's waiting in the bars. Neighbours all say he's got no friends, his friends all say you've got him by the balls.'

Neither 'Reno' nor its B-side 'Indecent Sacrifice', which is vaguely reminiscent of Chris Isaak's 1990 hit 'Wicked Game', is a classic, but they provide tangible hope for those who fear they might never hear another note from their hero.

Retrieving the compact disc and returning to his desk, Negus-Fancey considers the inevitable yoke of public expectation that a Scott Walker return carries. 'It's difficult for Scott because he's so highly regarded in the music business. It's hard to step out and expose yourself again and be as well received the next time. Icons get knocked down, don't they? This must be one of the most highly anticipated albums that anyone can deliver.'

Negus-Fancey declines to divulge any details about Scott's personal circumstances, but confirms he has retained an interest in all kinds of culture. An avid cinemagoer with an encyclopaedic knowledge of films, Scott enjoys opera as well as all forms of music, art, literature and politics. 'He lives a very full life. He certainly does not spend his time sitting up in a tower somewhere like a lot of people seem to imagine. He goes to the supermarket, he cycles, he lives the same life as you or me.'

Mention of the *Sunday People*'s Great Scott Walker Hunt provokes a sharp reaction from his manager. 'That was absolutely farcical!' he snaps. 'I thought it was stupid and totally unacceptable. Scott's reaction was one of annoyance – that invasion of privacy is just what he hates. It didn't enrich anyone's life to know whether Scott Walker was living in Birmingham or in London or anywhere else. It had no significance whatsoever.

'I don't think anyone cares where he lives, apart from the odd maniac who wants to know where everyone lives, so that's not something you should feed. They photographed him going to the supermarket. He was really annoyed because it stopped him doing what he wanted to do. What really made him peeved was the fact everyone had missed the point. All that had happened was that the record company had repackaged some sixties songs. It's hardly newsworthy is it? It was not exactly going to change the world.'

Engel once said he would spend ten years making an album he could be proud of. 'If not, I'd rather make none at all.' His records may seem to appear with approximately the same frequency as Halley's Comet but, by 1994, the ten-year cycle will be complete as a decade has elapsed since the release of 'Climate Of Hunter'. The world waits for Scott Walker to sing again.

Today, little remains of Scott Walker's sixties London. Clubs like The Scotch of St James and the Cromwellian have themselves acquired legendary status in the enduring myth of the Swinging Sixties. The Lotus House restaurant, scene of so many drunken Walker evenings, has also disappeared, along with Dudley Court, where Scott made that desperate suicide attempt at the height of his fame back in 1966.

Down at Stanhope Place, Johnny Franz's old hit-making factory stands silent and empty behind an ugly, graffiti-strewn, cream-coloured wall stained with exhaust fumes from the heavy traffic thundering past on the Bayswater Road. Vacated by Phonogram in April 1977, the premises were purchased a few years later by Paul Weller's father, John, who ran the Solid Bond Studios there until 1990. Now the building where Scott's finest work was recorded has been transformed into a block of offices, most of which have still to be let.

Franz's death, in January 1977, can truly be said to have marked the end of an era. Three months later, while Scott toiled over material for 'Nite Flights' in the flat he shared with Gary in the New King's Road, Phonogram moved into new premises at 129 Park Street on the other side of Marble Arch. In July 1980, soon after Scott's eagerly anticipated move to Virgin, the record company moved to New Bond Street. Today Phonogram's offices are located in Chancellor's Road, Hammersmith.

It would be a falsehood to suggest that the entire pop world awaits Engel's next vinyl offering with bated breath. There are undoubtedly some who regard Scott Walker as much a relic as that old, deserted Philips building. Reviewing the 1992 'No Regrets' compilation, *Melody Maker*'s Steve Sutherland launched a fierce attack on the sacred Walker cow. 'It's the classic underachiever's tale,' he wrote. 'Our moody hero so hung up on what he perceives as his plight that, like so many self-obsessives, he misses the point entirely. Disengage his output from his chosen legend and we discover the brutal fact: Scott was so fucked up that when he thought he was crap, he was very, very great and when he thought he was expounding dramatic profundities, he sounded as daft as a brush.'

Warming to his theme, Sutherland argued that Scott's solo work paled into insignificance when compared with the three great Walker Brothers hits. 'The fact Scott himself considers them shallow beyond redemption just goes to show how utterly mistaken he was, and still is, about what constitutes his talent.' By requesting his audiences to remain silent during performances, Sutherland believed Engel had made 'a right prat of himself'.

Jacques Brel was dismissed as 'mysteriously overrated' and Scott's most famous solo works 'Boy Child' and 'Montague Terrace (In Blue)' denounced as 'overwrought and insufferably self-regarding'.

Twisting the knife still deeper, Sutherland opined that Scott was 'just one more nutter too deeply involved in his own self-pity to ever squeeze anything remotely resembling a decent tune through the intestines of his own self-regard'. Not since he had aroused the wrath of fourteen teenage *Disc & Music Echo* fans back in 1969 had Scott been subjected to such a stinging attack. Walker fans the length and breadth of Britain howled for Sutherland's blood.

It was, perhaps, no coincidence that *NME*, *Melody Maker*'s bitter rival, took the opposite view the following week when Stuart Maconie's affectionate and humourous Walker tribute included a possible snipe at Sutherland's howitzer. 'Yes, there are people in the world who do not love Scott Walker,' he wrote. 'But what must their hearts be like? This is the voice. More than anyone before or since, the voice of mystery, suffering, heartbreak, nostalgia, yearning and joy.'

Yet Sutherland's earthy, forthright opinions were somewhat refreshing following the reams of often empty praise heaped on Engel over the years. The writer undoubtedly had a point about Scott's attitude towards his audiences. His solemn pleas for silence could be construed as a gross insult to the very people who paid his wages, although such a view does not take the singer's almost neurotic quest for perfection into account. He poured an enormous amount of effort into his songwriting and desperately wanted to ensure that his lyrics were heard.

Where Sutherland's argument fell down was his summary dismissal of Scott's finest solo work which conveniently overlooked a host of classic compositions including 'The Amorous Humphrey Plugg', 'Such A Small Love', 'Big Louise' and 'The Old Man's Back Again'. Such bewitching combinations of poetic splendour and majestic tunes confound the *Melody Maker* writer's acerbic views.

By now it must be obvious that, contrary to Sutherland's assertions, self-regard is the very commodity which Scott has always lacked. It undermined his live performances, ultimately spilled over into his songwriting and even affected his professional relationships. Public pronouncements at various points in his career consistently suggest that Scott actually holds an extremely low opinion of himself.

Someone, somewhere along the line, should surely have imbued Scott with sufficient confidence to tackle his stage fright before it became such a phobia. Yet despite the unqualified support and encouragement of such influential figures as Jonathan King, Dick Leahy and Ed Bicknell, Engel's career ground inexorably to a halt. Innocent queries as to when the next album would appear in Scott's mind constituted harassment.

It is tempting to speculate on what path Engel would have followed had he possessed the tenacity or sheer bloodymindedness of the Irish troubadour Van Morrison, another musician not exactly renowned for his jocularity.

There are similarities between the two: both swapped fleeting success as lead singers of groups (in Morrison's case it was the Belfast R & B combo Them) for highly individual solo careers; both are singular men who detest the limelight and zealously protect their private lives; and both are driven by a relentless desire to produce something entirely original, if not commercial.

Yet while Morrison has nurtured and developed a variable career stretching back 30 years, Walker's unique appeal stems almost entirely from the memorable work he produced between 1965 and 1969. Apart from the 1976 hit 'No Regrets' (a song he did not write) he has not been a chart contender since the sixties, yet by some strange edict of the rock 'n' roll fates, the Scott Walker image remains compelling. Never have so many expectations been borne by someone whose actual recorded output over the last twenty years has amounted to so little. Both Engel's very reclusiveness and an absence of contemporary photos have inevitably heightened public interest. In the minds of fans, he remains the Scott Walker he was in the sixties.

Despite being one of the few leading sixties groups whose original members are all still alive, the Walker Brothers are conspicuous absentees from today's thriving supper-club circuit and endless 'Sixties Revival' packages. Not even the most ardent Walker buff seriously expects the erstwhile 'Blond Beatles' to rise again.

Of course, the group's mid-seventies reunion pre-empted the current wave of pop nostalgia and inspired the resurrection of a clutch of semi-forgotten bands. Anyone who witnessed the embarrassing reformations of groups like The Animals and The Monkees may feel that The Walkers have a lot to answer for.

If Scott lacks self-regard he is, on his own admission, inherently selfish and his reluctance to ditch John and Gary arose not so much out of a misguided sense of loyalty, but from the gnawing fear of live solo performances. Although life with his adopted relatives became intolerable, Scott's live act quickly withered and died without them, although the comparatively genteel demands of the cabaret circuit enabled a lobotomised version of The Walkers to prolong his stuttering career for a few more years.

Those who have kept the faith were heartened when 'Climate Of

Hunter' indicated that the artist had returned to mine a seam he had first struck in the late sixties, and still possessed both the desire and ability to break new ground. It is Scott's continuing quest to produce something entirely original, allied to a voice which has retained its magnificence, that has left fans thirsting for more. Like Beatles fans who still hunger for Paul, George and Ringo to play together again, Scott Walker fans yearn for the day the legendary singer returns to the stage.

Yet, with interest in his past work running as high as ever, a steady flow of royalties lessens the need for Scott to return to the one activity he has always dreaded. Paradoxically, each Scott Walker album which is sold across record-shop counters diminishes the possibility of a stage comeback.

At some point Scott appears to have formed the opinion that anything which smacked even remotely of commericialism was effectively a waste of time. Consequently, he has become an increasingly remote asteroid whose ever-widening orbit brings him into contact with an alien pop world every few years or so.

Are these interminable delays between each successive Scott Walker album really the result of a quest for perfection or, perhaps, the fear of having work subjected to public scrutiny? In one of his last interviews to date, Scott admitted that he had suffered an erosion of confidence in the six-year gap leading up to 'Climate Of Hunter'.

'You see, if you have to wait for such a long time things slip from your hands slowly but surely,' he said. 'You lose your self-assurance – composing, singing, somehow everythin' slips away, but you try, nevertheless, to keep up.'

If a deep-rooted fear of the accursed press has helped to restrict Scott's output to a single album over the last sixteen years, such timidity is difficult to rationalise. With, perhaps, the exception of 1969's 'Scott 4', Engel's sixties work was almost universally lauded by the critics of the time and, with the notable exception of Steve Sutherland, is rightly revered by pop writers today. The blunt truth is that Scott simply did not want to be a singer. Not really. All those excuses for the missed television and stage performances – the nervous breakdowns, faked car accidents and illnesses – indicate that he lacked the necessary will and desire.

There is a widespread misconception that those four mordant albums which Scott released following the break-up of The Walker Brothers were largely ignored by the record-buying public. As recently as 1990, Chris Heath of *The Daily Telegraph* wrote: 'The dark and often uncomfortable melodramas on his solo LPs were in stark contrast and sales were both disappointing and declining.' Embittered and frustrated by this series of failures, Scott resigned himself to covering sub-standard material.

Yet this scenario is a fallacy. Scott's first three albums were all significant successes. Each went top five, with 'Scott 2' actually attaining the top spot and paving the way for his short-lived television series. Admittedly, 'Scott 4' proved a commercial failure in late 1969, but it had been a pretty good run.

Not only did the richness of Scott's smooth brown voice and his remarkable songs of beauty and desolation rewrite the pop vocabulary, but he also introduced Jacques Brel to mainstream audiences long before artists such as David Bowie latched on. This ability to see beyond trends also enabled Scott to recognise the greatness of the work of writers such as Randy Newman.

'Scott 4', however, was an unmitigated sales disaster, and the first bitter taste of failure since he had been a struggling teenage crooner proved too much for Engel's fragile psyche. He committed artistic hara-kiri by giving up his writing, and subsequently spent years drifting without any real sense of direction. The chronic lack of self-confidence which made live performances such an ordeal spread to his composing and was the heavy price he paid for selling out. That Scott effectively gave up the ghost should not be regarded as particularly surprising. He had, after all, dropped numerous hints over the preceding four years.

'I don't think I could stand the taste of failure. I'd quit and go wandering off into obscurity for ever,' he told one pop reporter in 1966. Three years later, he mused: '[Sibelius] is quite unique in that he made a lot of money from his music when he was alive. Then, he knew when to stop, when his music was goin' off, he packed up. That must have been difficult.'

A modern-day Sibelius, or a second-rate Tom Jones? Opinions on this 'neurotic boy outsider' are still divided and the jury will remain out long after the release of his forthcoming album, whenever that may be. Reg Guest, Engel's one-time associate, wryly observes: 'I cannot recall a time when Scott hasn't supposedly been in the studio, working on his new album.'

Reports which suggest that the LP will again consist of abstract material are apparently borne out by rumours that Scott wishes to enlist some of the personnel who worked with him on 'Climate Of Hunter' and has been buying the work of Bill Laswell, the New York avant-garde artist. Fans hoping for a return of that magical combination of wistful tunes and thundering orchestrations are liable to be disappointed again. This album may well be his last.

Engel, we are told, lives only for the present and does not keep in contact with those he was close to at the height of his fame. Jonathan King, for example, has not seen him since the sixties, although both he and Dick Leahy still receive the occasional cryptic message via a third party. Paradoxically, at the end of the sixties Scott bemoaned the rise of underground music at the expense of good old-fashioned glamour.

The new album, which at one time looked set to be released in the autumn of 1992, has yet to appear and Fontana executives now find themselves in the same state of jittery anticipation that was generated by Scott's largely unproductive stay at Virgin a decade ago.

At the time of writing, the new LP is unofficially earmarked for a spring 1994 release, but, in the words of *NME*'s Stuart Maconie: 'Once you have joined the Walker congregation, you enter a shadow world of rumour, falsehood and broken promises. But we can only hope.'

Yet those searing songs of yesteryear bear eloquent testimony to the success of Scott's resolutely anti-fashion stance of the late sixties. Miraculously unravaged by the passage of time, songs like 'Boy Child' and 'Montague Terrace (In Blue)' have retained their ageless quality like exotic, brightly coloured insects preserved in amber.

Indeed, their creator seems to have anticipated his elevation to legendary status in the midst of his battles with unreceptive record companies all those years ago: 'My music is not instantaneous, but in years to come the small number of people who have bothered to listen ... should feel I have made some kinda effort which was worthwhile in retrospect.'

Perhaps Scott Walker has had the last laugh after all.

KEITH ALTHAM: 'Scott was really the great could-have-been, that should-have-been, that never-was. It would have been so easy for Scott to remain with that projected image of him as the prince of melancholy. If he had stayed with that and exploited it then he could have become a young Sinatra.

'Sinatra was a torch singer and in a simplistic way Scott was also a torch singer. That was how he was identified by the public most readily. He looked as if he was tortured – which he was, sounded as if he had some pain and problems – which he had, and that was the most commercial aspect people picked up on.

'When I did publicity for him he could be difficult, obstinate and a pain in the arse but, at the end of the day, I really liked the man.'

ED BICKNELL: 'He was one of the greatest singers I've ever worked with and if he were to walk into my office tomorrow, I'd offer to manage him like a shot.'

REG GUEST: 'Scott was wonderful to work with and I enjoyed every second. They were huge, complicated writing efforts for me – but I see now (and saw then) how solid our achievements were. Scott was badly mishandled. He is a major, major artist. If someone had the courage to do a Scott Walker concert, well rehearsed and with a big orchestra, it would sell out in hours. He's still the idol of so many. Just one success would revitalise Scott – he'd come to life with a colossal benefit to us all.'

JONATHAN KING: 'The most tragic thing about Scott was that he had every single ingredient needed to be one of the biggest stars of the nineties if he had decided to go down the Rod Stewart/Elton John path. But I've seen so many people become stars and watched it destroy them.

'Can you imagine? Scott still having to get up there and sing "Make It Easy On Yourself" and "My Ship Is Coming In" – My Ship Is Fucking Sinking, more like. If Scott had become a top cabaret singer doing Las Vegas he'd now be living in a huge house in Los Angeles, married to his fourth wife who would be about nineteen with blonde hair and very long legs. That wouldn't be the Scott who was my closest friend in the mid-60s.'

DICK LEAHY: 'There's no one reason why it all went wrong. The success of The Walker Brothers was based very much on *the* voice and a lot of it on the songs, but songs that Scott was actually not very happy singing. It has always been his problem that he became successful for the things he cared least about and had no success with the things he cared most about.

'The Walker Brothers were two people who just wanted to be

pop stars and Scott who didn't. Scott Walker wanted to be Scott Engel. Being in The Walker Brothers was his problem right from the start. I still don't consider anything he did with me as The Walker Brothers. Most of the later stuff was substandard. In retrospect, it would have been better to put out "No Regrets" as a Scott Walker record.

'There's no question that what happened during the time of The Walker Brothers fucked him up totally. I'm not saying he was crazy because he wasn't, but I'm sure he had some neuroses over what happened, over the money, the posturing, the whole mix of things.'

MAURICE OBERSTEIN: 'I remain disappointed that, in the creative sense, Scott has been reclusive. I don't like to quantify my disappointments but Scott Walker could, and should, have gone on to be a major world star. He has a wonderful voice and an immensely powerful personality on stage.'

PETER OLLIFF: 'I feel that Scott had such enormous talent that it is intensely frustrating that he did not evolve into one of the most successful artists within the industry. That's a great disappointment because I think he deserves that sort of position – although perhaps he didn't want that. He had all the ability to perform live but there was always that nagging fear which really stopped him from what he should have been doing.'

HAL SHAPER: 'I had a great admiration for Scott's voice but he squandered his talent. He could have been one of the greatest ballad singers ever.'

BRIAN SOMMERVILLE: 'Scott always talked about the way Sinatra did things. He had the same approach of wanting everything and everybody dead right. And he had the ear for it. While he was going through something he would be listening and if there was one slightly false note from anyone else, he would spot it straightaway.'

CHRIS WELCH: 'Scott perhaps should have been a little less cynical about the music business; everyone appreciated his voice and he had a lot of supporters. There was no need to run off and desert. Maybe the scene was against what he was trying to do, but I think he should have hung in there.'

Epilogue

'The Sun Ain't Gonna Shine Anymore'

On a dank, depressing, overcast morning in January 1992, Gary Leeds, clad in helmet and leathers, weaved his motorbike between lines of hooting traffic in Hammersmith's crowded King Street. Life since the final break-up of The Walker Brothers has not been easy for the man who once drove expensive sports cars, stayed in the best hotels, rubbed shoulders with the likes of Paul McCartney and joined an all-star cast for the famous televised rendition of the Beatles' 'All You Need Is Love' in 1967.

His Stratford-based business, which specialised in the creation of sand models, fell victim to the recession of 1990, forcing Gary, by now living with his wife and five-year-old son in a modest ground-floor flat on a sprawling East London estate, to take a job as a motor-cycle courier.

'We had a lot of money, but it just went on high livin',' he told *Sunday People* reporter Danny Buckland. 'I've no idea how much we made. If we made ten million pounds, then we only saw about one million. All our money went in management wrangles between people we hardly knew.'

On this particular morning, Gary happened to pull up alongside an Our Price record shop. He turned his head lazily towards the window and did an immediate double take. Staring back at him from the window was a giant poster of his 23-year-old self. Youthful images of Scott and John hovered eerily alongside.

The Walker Brothers were back in the charts and no one had bothered to tell their drummer. Released on Fontana at the beginning of the year, 'No Regrets' had stormed to No. 4 in the album chart in just six weeks and reached the top of the Radio Two chart on the very morning Gary meandered down that congested West London street. The record went on to generate sales of close to a million pounds.

'I didn't know anythin' about it. I was just drivin' past and there it was. I couldn't really have missed it – the thing was about as big as the side of a house. I was real shocked for a while. Then I guess I felt pleased that a lot of people were pickin' up on all that good stuff we did back in the sixties.'

Some weeks later, Gary was dispatched to the Phonogram offices to collect a package to take to a Bayswater address. He walked into the foyer wearing his crash helmet just as he had done in the days when he was mobbed by screaming teenage girls. Almost 30 years later, no one at the record company would have recognised him even if he had removed his visor.

When Gary glanced down at the address on the package he received another major shock. It was addressed to 'Scott Walker (c/o Charles Negus-Fancey)'. As it had come from Phonogram's royalties department, Gary assumed it was a cheque for the 'No Regrets' compilation. He delivered the parcel without disclosing his identity to Scott's manager. In that instant the gulf between the two one-time Walker Brothers must have seemed immeasurable.

'I guess Scott's manager would have been real shocked,' says Gary. 'I'm still waitin' for my royalties. Who knows? Maybe one day I'll get to deliver a cheque to myself!'

His hair may be greying and receding but Gary remains the fast-talking hustler whose dogged persistence opened so many doors for The Walkers all those years ago. 'I'm constantly writin' material and I have at least four Top Ten records ready and waitin',' he says. Although he has not seen John since 1978, and Scott since 1984, Gary refuses to discount the possibility of a Walker Brothers' reunion.

'Lookin' back at the sixties I guess it all happened too fast. If I could do it all over again I'd have different management and maybe our attitude could have been better. We could do it again now. If we hired the Albert Hall would anybody come and see us? I think that they would.'

Rancho Barnardo is an up-market satellite suburb some twenty miles from downtown San Diego and surrounded by rolling California hills, a million miles from the cold that John Maus found so intolerable in London.

John, his third wife Brandy, and their twelve-year-old daughter Nicolle live in a quiet backwater street. Unexpected visitors to the home are met by a prominent sign advertising the electronic security system that has been fitted and by the more immediately obvious high-pitched barks of the family's pet poodle which leaps onto a sofa and yelps through the living room window at the slightest disturbance outside. All the windows have venetian blinds to prevent prying eyes seeing inside. Clearly the John Maus of the 1990s guards his privacy almost as much as his enigmatic fellow frontman in The Walker Brothers.

Houses on the street are built in blocks of four, with each family occupying a two-storey home on one corner of the block. With their dour brown shutters the functional dwellings are unimpressive from the outside, belonging to comfortable rather than super-rich occupants.

Inside, it is very much the home of a middle-aged family man with the plush carpets and middle-class sofas that the rebellious young turks of the late 1960s might well have associated more with their parents than themselves. Nicolle's numerous toys litter the living-room floor and to the right there is a small open-plan kitchen.

The stairs are of the open wooden variety and, according to Brandy, John is upstairs in bed asleep trying to shake off the bronchitis that has laid him low for the past three days. There is ample evidence of this about the room where John has shed the wrappings of dozens of cough sweets he is taking for his ailment. 'The weather here in California is perfect for breeding pneumonia and bronchitis,' says Brandy. 'John can hardly speak with bronchitis but, of course, he refuses to go to the doctor because "there's absolutely nothing wrong with me!"

'We are very private people, myself, John and Scott. We are all still very close. We change our number as soon as it gets out. There are no plans for John to work with Scott again. But nothing has been ruled out, so perhaps they will do some songs together some time.

'Both Scott and John have agreed not to do a book. It's not the right time to do it. There might be a time but it's not likely to be soon. The music isn't over. John's not directly involved in music at the moment but he has a whole recording studio set up through there in the back room. He's certainly not finished with music.

'John and I are both night people. He does vaguely remember speaking to somebody, but if you get either of us at 8 a.m. in the morning we probably wouldn't even remember that we'd spoken to you later the same day.

'John's not in computers. We were amused to hear that that story was going around England and we were happy to let it stay that way. There was even one that John's father was a rocket engineer. That was very amusing. I can't say what John does do because that would be traceable.'

Brandy is a diminutive figure with shoulder-length brown hair with just a hint of orange in it. Her name perfectly describes the colour. Slight she may be but her forceful personality comes across clearly even to the stranger speaking to her for the first time. If she is the ogre some claim her to be she hides it very well.

She is perfectly polite and even offers a cup of tea or lemonade. The tea is lukewarm and confirms everything you have ever heard about Americans not being able to make tea. Is it any wonder John stuck to coffee when he first arrived in England?

John, who told Danny Buckland he was the inspector for a successful West Coast software company, added: 'It's not the best job in the world but I don't hate what I do. You have got to earn a living and this is a good job even though it's a million miles from The Walker Brothers.

'I'm concentrating on family life but I'm not out of music. I have an eight-track studio and I hope to have a record out later this year. People still recognise me, which is nice, but it is nothing like those days in London – that was frightening.

'It was a wonderful feeling to be adored but our private life went completely. We often got hurt by over-eager fans. We had our clothes ripped and I always seemed to have bruised ribs from the crushes. It was mass hysteria.

'I know Scott perhaps as well as anyone and he is a recluse, but he is not weird in any way. He is a very private person and wants to stay that way. I think he is a lot more together than most people who are very public showbiz personalities.'

Meanwhile, back in London, Scott Walker was unavailable for comment.

Afterword

The slightly weary tone of the Fontana record company press officer betrayed the fact that this was a query she had answered many times before. 'I'm sorry,' she said, 'but we cannot say exactly when the new Scott Walker album will appear.'

On the other side of London in Woodford Green, Essex, Lynne Goodall, who for the past dozen years has edited a quarterly newsletter about a singer whose last public appearance in Britain was in that 1987 orange-juice commercial, greets the news with stoic good humour. 'Anyone who follows Scott Walker requires a good deal of patience,' she says, 'but Scott is such a perfectionist that we are sure the wait will prove worthwhile.'

Her views mirror those of Dave Bates, the man who signed Walker to Fontana in the spring of 1991. 'Scott is still hard at work in the studio,' he says. 'Recording has been conducted in almost total secrecy so I haven't a clue what his new material sounds like. When this album finally appears it will be as much a surprise to me as to everyone else.'

Down in Brighton, 71-year-old Reg Guest, whose orchestrated arrangements graced so many of the singer's finest recordings in the late 1960s, ponders the possible implications of a Scott Walker comeback. 'I have never lost faith in Scott,' he declares. 'Some people tend to write him off but believe me, he has never lost his capacity to surprise.'

It is, perhaps, no surprise that rumoured deadlines for the release of Scott's long-awaited follow-up to 'Climate Of Hunter' have come and gone without any sign of an album. Production was apparently slowed when producer Peter Walsh had to take time off to participate in Peter Gabriel's world tour. An item in the November 1994 edition of *Vox* must have raised sceptical smiles from those beginning to tire of Scott's seemingly limitless supply of excuses. According to the monthly magazine, Walker had put his album on ice 'until the high pollution levels and pollen floating around London start to abate. The eccentric genius stunned his colleagues by announcing that his irritated nasal passages needed a break and he wouldn't return until later in the year.'

The claim was actually not as preposterous as it might at first seem. Brian Gascoigne, the orchestral arranger for the new album, confirms that Scott (a vehement anti-smoker) suffers badly from hay fever which naturally wreaks havoc with his voice. Nevertheless, the episode can be viewed as telling evidence for those who believe the singer is weighed down by the burden of his own legend. 'He would love to erase people's memory banks and start completely afresh,' confirms Gascoigne. 'It's difficult to envisage him taking his new material on the road, but should he decide to tour, he knows full well that audiences will be expecting some of the old Walker Brothers material.'

Meanwhile, Scott Walker continues to be a name to drop in the pages of the music press. Recent disciples include bands like Pulp and One Dove. In the spring of 1993 David Bowie, whose offer to produce Scott was spurned in the late 1970s, included a cover version of 'Nite Flights' on his 'Black Tie, White Noise' album. In a television documentary, Bowie confirmed that he had been a Walker fan for several years. 'I used to go out with someone who had been a girlfriend of Scott Walker,' he smilingly recalled. 'When we were together she would insist on playing his music, but never any of mine. I have retained a great love of his voice.'

Asked to comment on the new material, Gascoigne says: 'It's got some extraordinarily strange noises on it which will probably prompt a good deal of discussion as to how they were achieved. Richard Evans took over as producer while Peter Walsh was on the Peter Gabriel world tour. It's hard to tell how enthusiastic Scott is about the new songs because he's trying to put so much passion into the tracks. It's hard to tell whether he's happy. If he's satisfied with something he'll simply move on. He's got a unique way of working. The studio process is so draining for him that he likes to work in short bursts and then step back and look at what he's done which of course is terribly inconvenient for freelance musicians. The voice is wonderful; as good as ever. It must be the best male white voice on the face of the planet although he's very shy about using it and usually just sings in front of Peter Walsh. On one occasion I asked him, "When's the tour Scott?" He said, "Well, you never know." I think he's torn between retreating from the world and going out to promote his new material by staging a presentation gig. He's proud of the new stuff but one part of him says why can't they just buy the album and leave him alone.'

One man who refused to leave Scott alone during his self-imposed silence was Jean Daniel Beauvallet, editor of the French music magazine *Les Inrockuptibles*. A Walker fan of long-standing, Beauvallet inundated the singer's manager Charles Negus-Fancey with calls and letters begging for the interview that had eluded rock journalists for a decade. His persistence paid off in November 1993 when Negus-Fancey rang out of the blue and invited Beauvallet and reporter Gilles Tordjman over to London. Tordjman had recently compiled the sleeve notes for a French LP of Walker material. Both men had briefly met the singer while he was filming the promotional video for 'The Man From Reno' in Paris earlier that year.

'The interview was originally due to take place at Charles's office, but then it was changed to a house somewhere off the Portobello Road which I believe was owned by a friend of Scott's,' says Beauvallet. 'We arrived some 20 minutes before Scott who eventually turned up in a cab. He spoke with Charles for a bit downstairs before coming up to meet us. He was wearing a New York baseball cap and looked in great shape. He could sense our nervousness and went out of his way to make us feel more relaxed. We chatted for a while about Paris before launching into a two-hour interview.'

The first thing they wanted to know was exactly how he spent his time during the 1980s. Scott explained that the 'yuppie years', as he called them, were simply not his decade. He described how people had come to perceive him as a kind of Orson Welles figure. Although it had become the done thing throughout the record industry to invite him to dinner and heap praise on him, no one wanted to finance his records. He occupied himself painting, reading, travelling and studying conceptual art. He saw little point in writing songs just to imagine how they might sound when recorded. Musically he felt more isolated than ever before although he did express a liking for quirky Icelandic singer Bjork, as well as more established mavericks including Tom Waits and Neil Young. He remained puzzled about why so many young artists cited him as an influence, declaring he had always believed his solo work was not destined for mass consumption. But he told his Gallic interrogators that knowing he was helping young musicians to break new ground was some compensation.

Scott Walker

As dozens of frustrated interviewers had earlier discovered, persuading Scott to open up was no easy task. Throughout his career, Walker has demonstrated a marked reluctance to allow others to delve too deeply into his life. While this book was in preparation, it became obvious that he had quietly told friends and family he would prefer them not to speak. Among them was Scott's former wife Mette. She finally overcame her reluctance to speak having read the first hardback edition and been surprised by some of the revelations of Scott's former colleagues.

'The idea that I caused the break-up of the Walker Brothers is ridiculous,' she said, in a lengthy telephone interview with the authors. 'The suggestion that I wouldn't let Scott see John was ludicrous. At the time of the split, he was still married to Julie Parker-Cann and they lived quite close to us. We didn't see Gary quite so much. If Gary and John have any animosity towards me that is their problem. I thought Gary was a bit crazy. John was the flashy type – "Don't you think I look like a Greek god?" I would just fall about laughing. The guy was actually serious.'

Recalling life with Scott, she continued, 'Our daughter, Lee, and I would fly over from Copenhagen to spend weekends in London with him. We lived a very normal lifestyle. It wasn't the usual pop star scene with parties all night and nightclubs. We could go to the movies twice a day if we wanted but you just can't do that with kids.'

Unlike the Walker Brothers' split, their own separation was amicable: 'I sometimes felt I was looking after two kids instead of one. There was no third party involved and no big deal about it. In the beginning, when Lee was too little to put on a plane alone, Scott would come over and stay with us even though we were legally separated.'

They were actually married in December 1973, a year later than generally believed. 'We didn't want to make a fuss about it. I knew if we had it in Denmark my parents would want to have a traditional wedding. If it had been in Hollywood, Scott's mun would have wanted likewise. Scott is just not a public person. Just to get him into a suit, forget it!'

Mette revealed few fond memories of the group's erstwhile manager Maurice King. 'I preferred to stay out of the haggling between him and the boys. Sometimes I regret not having butted in a bit more. It turned out he had actually forged their signatures on various cheques. He hadn't paid taxes for them for about five years and we were suddenly landed with a huge bill from the Inland Revenue. This was more or less around the time The Walker Brothers split up. It was a bit of a blow. It never went to court. Before it went anywhere near that stage, he died. The thing about me having to go back to Denmark to face shoplifting charges was another big scam. It was a stunt set up by the publicity machine to get Scott's name in the papers. I didn't think it was very funny afterwards and my parents were very upset.'

Over the last three decades, Engel's career has swung crazily from the peaks he achieved with the Walker Brothers and his early solo work to the nadir of those wretched CBS albums. More recently his isolated stance has tested the patience of even the most loyal supporters, yet there is little doubt that the forthcoming album (possibly due for a spring 1995 release) will reaffirm the singer's penchant for the unexpected. His occasional bursts of activity over the years have helped keep the legend alive.

Just as the reformed Walker Brothers finally keeled over in 1978, the singer startled rock journalists with a quartet of highly innovative songs on 'Nite Flights'. Six years later, when it seemed the game was finally up, the brooding 'Climate Of Hunter' was lauded by critics despite failing to capture the imagination of fans. But with the periods between each record growing inexorably, Scott Walker's new album may indeed be his final statement. In all probability it will in turn puzzle, delight and intrigue, perhaps even infuriate. If so, it will provide a fitting epitaph to one of the strangest careers in popular music. And given Scott Walker's track record, who would dare rule out more to follow!

November 1994

Discography

WALKER BROTHERS

BRITISH SINGLES
Pretty Girls Everywhere/Doin' The Jerk – Philips BF1401 (1964)
Love Her/The Seventh Dawn – Philips BF1409 (1965)
Make It Easy On Yourself/But I Do – Philips BF1428 (1965)
My Ship Is Coming In/You're All Around Me – Philips BF1454 (1965)
The Sun Ain't Gonna Shine Anymore/After The Lights Go Out – Philips BF1473 (1966)
(Baby) You Don't Have To Tell Me/My Love Is Growing – Philips BF1514 (1966)
Another Tear Falls/Saddest Night In The World – Philips BF1514 (1966)
Deadlier Than The Male/Archangel – Philips BF1537 (1966)
Stay With Me Baby/Turn Out The Moon – Philips BF1548 (1967)
Walking In The Rain/Baby Make It The Last Time – Philips BF1576 (1967)
No Regrets/Remember Me – GTO GT42 (1975)
Lines/First Day – GTO GT67 (1976)
We're All Alone/Have You Seen My Baby – GTO GT78 (1976)
The Electrician/Den Haague – GTO GT230 (1978) Pic sleeve
First Love Never Dies/The Sun Ain't Gonna Shine Anymore – Phonogram IPS 001 (1982) Pic sleeve (re-issue)
The Sun Ain't Gonna Shine Anymore/In My Room – Bam Caruso OPRA 090 (1987)

THE WALKER BROTHERS/SCOTT WALKER

BRITISH SINGLES
The Sun Ain't Gonna Shine Anymore/Jacky – Fontana (UK) WALK R1 (INT) 866372-7 (1991) Pic sleeve (re-issue)

The Sun Ain't Gonna Shine Anymore/First Love Never Dies/Jacky/
Joanna – Fontana (UK) WALK R112 (INT) 866373-1 (1991) 12″
Single/Pic sleeve (re-issue)
The Sun Ain't Gonna Shine Anymore/Jacky – Fontana (UK) WALK
M1 (INT) 866372-4 (1991) Cassette single (re-issue)
No Regrets/Boy Child – Fontana (UK) WALKR-2 (INT) 866600-7
(1992) Pic sleeve (re-issue)

Tracks as above: Fontana (UK) WALKM-2 (INT) 866600-4 (1992)
Cassette single (re-issue)

MAXI-SINGLES

Love Her/The Sun Ain't Gonna Shine Anymore/Make It Easy On
Yourself – Philips 6051 017 (1971)
The Sun Ain't Gonna Shine Anymore/Make It Easy On Yourself/
Stay With Me Baby – Philips 6160 050 (1976)
Make It Easy On Yourself/The Sun Ain't Gonna Shine Anymore/My
Ship Is Coming In – Philips Classic Cuts series (1980)

EPs

I NEED YOU: Looking For Me/Young Man Cried/Everything's
Gonna Be Alright/I Need You – Philips BE12596 (1966)
SOLO SCOTT, SOLO JOHN: Sunny/Come Rain Or Come Shine/
The Gentle Rain/Mrs Murphy – Philips BE12597 (1966)
HITS OF THE WALKER BROTHERS: Another Tear Falls/Summer-
time/The Sun Ain't Gonna Shine Anymore/Make It Easy On
Yourself – Philips MCP-1002 (1967?) Cassette only – EP compilation
HITS OF THE WALKER BROTHERS & DUSTY SPRINGFIELD:
Two track by Walkers – Philips MCP-1004 (1967?) Cassette only
– EP compilation
THE WALKER BROTHERS EP: Shutout/The Electrician/Nite
Flights/Fat Mama Kick – GTO GT295 (1981)

LPs

TAKE IT EASY WITH THE WALKER BROTHERS: Make It Easy
On Yourself/There Goes My Baby/First Love Never Dies/Dancing
In The Street/Lonely Winds/The Girl I Lost In The Rain/Land of
1,000 Dances/You're All Around Me/Love Minus Zero/I Don't
Want To Hear It Anymore/Here Comes The Night/Tell The
Truth – Philips BL7691 (1965)

Scott Walker

PORTRAIT: In My Room/Saturday's Child/Just For A Thrill/Hurting Each Other/Old Folks/Summertime/People Get Ready/I Can See It Now/Where's The Girl/Living Above Your Head/Take It Like A Man/No Sad Songs For Me – Philips BL7732 (1966)

IMAGES: Everything Under The Sun/Once Upon A Summertime/Experience/Blueberry Hill/Orpheus/Stand By Me/I Wanna Know/I Will Wait For You/It Makes No Difference Now/I Can't Let It Happen To You/Genevieve/Just Say Goodbye – Philips BL7770 (1967)

NO REGRETS: No Regrets (Scott's solo version)/Hold An Old Friend's Hand/Boulder To Birmingham/Walking In The Sun/Lover's Lullaby/Got To Have You/He'll Break Your Heart/Everything That Touches You/Lovers/Burn Our Bridges – GTO GTLP 007 (1975)

LINES: Lines/Taking It All In Your Stride/Inside Of You/Have You Seen My Baby/We're All Alone/Many Rivers To Cross/First Day/Brand New Tennessee Waltz/Hard To Be Friends/ Dreaming As One – GTO GTLP 014 (1976)

NITE FLIGHTS: Shutout/Fat Mama Kick/Nite Flights/The Electrician/Death Of Romance/Den Haague/Rhythms of Vision/Disciples of Death/Fury And The Fire/Child of Flames – GTO GTLP 033 (1978)

THE WALKER BROTHERS LIVE IN JAPAN: Land of 1,000 Dances/I Need You/Everything Under The Sun/Tell Me How Do You Feel/Watch Your Step/Uptight/In My Room/The Lady Came From Baltimore/Living Above Your Head/Dizzie Miss Lizzie/Twinkie Lee/Hold On I'm Coming/Annabella/Yesterday/Reach Out I'll Be There/Make It Easy On Yourself/Saturday's Child/Walking In The Rain/The Sun Ain't Gonna Shine Anymore/Turn On Your Lovelight/Ooh Poo Pah Doo – Bam Caruso AIDA 076 Double Album (1987)

COMPILATION ALBUMS

THE WALKER BROTHERS STORY – Philips double album DBL002A/B (1967)

THE FABULOUS WALKER BROTHERS – Wing WL1188 – re-released on Fontana FL13078

THE IMMORTAL WALKER BROTHERS – Contour 6870 564 (re-released as The Walker Brothers: Make It Easy On Yourself – Contour CN2017)

THE WALKER BROTHERS: MAKE IT EASY ON YOURSELF –
Philips International 6336 214

THE WALKER BROTHERS: GREATEST HITS – Philips International double album: 6640 009

SPOTLIGHT ON THE WALKER BROTHERS – Philips International double album: 6640 013

POP LIONS: THE SUN AIN'T GONNA SHINE ANYMORE –
Fontana 6430 152

THE BEST OF THE WALKER BROTHERS – (Cassette only) Philips Sonic Series 7175 500

WALKER BROTHERS' HITS – Phonogram 6463 139 (1982)

THE WALKER BROTHERS: MUSIC FOR THE MILLIONS – Fontana 812-345-1

THE WALKER BROTHERS: AFTER THE LIGHTS GO OUT –
THE BEST OF 1965–1976 – Fontana 842831-1 (1990)

THE WALKER BROTHERS/SCOTT WALKER

COMPILATION ALBUM

NO REGRETS: THE BEST OF SCOTT WALKER AND THE
WALKER BROTHERS 1965–1976: No Regrets/Make It Easy On
Yourself/The Sun Ain't Gonna Shine Anymore/My Ship Is Coming
In/Joanna/Lights Of Cincinnati/Another Tear Falls/Boy Child/Montague Terrace (In Blue)/Jacky/Stay With Me Baby/If You Go Away/
First Love Never Dies/Love Her/Walking In The Rain/(Baby) You
Don't Have To Tell Me/Deadlier Than The Male/We're All Alone –
Fontana 510 831-1 (1992) Cassette 510 831-4 (tracks as above)

COMPACT DISCS

THE WALKER BROTHERS: GALA – German: Philips 830 212-2
(Phonogram) (1986)

THE WALKER BROTHERS: German: Star Club Records 832256-2
(Phonogram Inc) (1988)

DOUBLE BEST COLLECTION OF THE WALKER BROTHERS
AND THE RIGHTEOUS BROTHERS Dutch: Qualitel Records
Q-CD-255-2 (1988)

THE WALKER BROTHERS: GREATEST HITS German: Duchesse
Compact Disc SACEM 352025 (1988)

THE WALKER BROTHERS COLLECTION German: Impact
Records GEMA 836976-2 IMCD-900714 (1989)

THE WALKER BROTHERS: AFTER THE LIGHTS GO OUT –
The best of 1965–67 Fontana 842831-2 (1990)

THE WALKER BROTHERS: THE COLLECTION: MAKE IT
EASY ON YOURSELF France: Object Enterprises ORO 161
(1992)

THE WALKER BROTHERS/SCOTT WALKER: The Sun Ain't
Gonna Shine Anymore/First Love Never Dies/Jacky/Joanna – Fontana (UK) WALK C1 (INT) 866373-2 (1991) CD Single (re-issue)

NO REGRETS/THE BEST OF SCOTT WALKER AND THE
WALKER BROTHERS 1965–1976: No Regrets/Make It Easy On
Yourself/The Sun Ain't Gonna Shine Anymore/My Ship Is
Coming In/Joanna/Lights Of Cincinnati/Another Tear Falls/Boy
Child/Montague Terrace (In Blue)/Jacky/Stay With Me Baby/If
You Go Away/First Love Never Dies/Love Her/Walking In The
Rain/(Baby) You Don't Have To Tell Me/Deadlier Than The
Male/We're All Alone – Fontana 510 831-2 (1992)

No Regrets/Boy Child/Montague Terrace (In Blue) – Fontana (UK)
WALKC-2 (INT) 866 601-2 (1992) CD Single (re-issue)

SCOTT WALKER AND THE WALKER BROTHERS: A VERY
SPECIAL COLLECTION: No Regrets/Nite Flights/We're All
Alone/Boulder To Birmingham/Ride Me Down Easy/Lines/I'll Be
Home/Brand New Tennessee Waltz/Sundown/Many Rivers To
Cross/No Easy Way Down/Just One Smile/Delta Dawn/We Had
It All/We'll Burn Our Bridges/Shutout – Pickwick PWKS 4165

SCOTT WALKER

SINGLES

SCOTTY ENGEL: When Is A Boy A Man/Steady As A Rock (USA)
– RKO Unique 386 (1957)

SCOTT ENGEL: The Livin' End/Good For Nothin' (USA) – Orbit
506 (1958) Pic sleeve. (UK) – Vogue Pop 45 V9145 (June 1959)
– 78 rpm – V9145

Charley Bop/All I Do Is Dream Of You (USA) – Orbit 511 (1958)
Pic sleeve. (UK) – Vogue Pop 45 V9150 (1959) – 78 rpm – V9150

Bluebell/Paper Doll (USA) – Orbit 512 (1958) Pic sleeve. (UK) –
Vogue Pop 45 V9125 (1959) – 78 rpm – V9125

Golden Rule of Love/Sunday (USA) – Orbit 537 (1959) Pic sleeve

Comin' Home/I Don't Want To Know (USA) – Orbit 545 (1959) Pic
sleeve

Take This Love/Till You Return (USA) – Hi-Fi 586 (Dec 1959)
Anything Will Do/Mr Jones (USA) – Liberty 55312 (1961)
Anything Will Do/Forevermore (USA) – Liberty 55428 (1962)
Devil Surfer/Your Guess (USA) – Martay 2004 (June 1963)
Devil Surfer/Your Guess (USA) – Challenge 9206 (Oct 1963)

SANDY NELSON (with Scott on bass)

Let There Be Drums/? (USA) – Warner Bros 5283 (1962)

SCOTT ENGEL AND JOHN STEWART (recorded as The Moongooners)

Mongoon Stomp/Long Trip (USA) – Candix 335 (Feb 1962)
Willie And The Hand Jive/Moongoon Twist (USA) – Essar 1007
(1962). (USA) – Donna 1373 (Dec 1962)

CHOSEN FEW (Engel, Stewart and others)

Jump Down/Wish You Were Here (USA) – Marsh 201 (Oct 1962)

THE ROUTERS (with Scott on bass)

Let's Go/Mashy (USA) – Warner Bros 5283 (1962)

NEWPORTERS (Engel and Stewart)

Adventures In Paradise/Loose Board (USA) – Scotchdown 500 (Aug
1963)

SCOTT ENGEL and JOHN STEWART, recorded as the Dalton Brothers

I Only Came To Dance With You/Greens (USA) – Tower 2181. (UK)
– Capitol 15440, released 1966, recorded 1963

SCOTT WALKER

SINGLES
Jacky/The Plague – Philips 1628 (1967)
Joanna/Always Coming Back to You (UK) – Philips 1662 (1968)

Scott Walker

The Rope And The Colt/Concerto Pour Guitar (France) – Philips B.370780.F (1968)

Lights Of Cincinnati/Two Weeks Since You've Gone (UK) – Philips 1793 (1969)

Til The Band Comes In/Jean The Machine (Holland) – Philips 6006-107 (1970) Pic sleeve

I Still See You/My Way Home (UK) – Philips 6006-168 (1971)

The Me I Never Knew/This Way Mary (UK) – Philips 6006-311 (1973)

A Woman Left Lonely/Where Love Has Died – CBS 1795 (1973)

Delta Dawn/We Had It All – CBS 2521 (1974)

Track 3/Blanket Roll Blues – Virgin VS 666 (1984) Pic sleeve

Man From Reno/Indecent Sacrifice (France) – Fontana CD 682 382-2 (June 1993)

EPs

SCOTT ENGEL: I Broke My Own Heart/What Do You Say/Are These Really Mine/Crazy in Love With You (UK) – Liberty 2261, released 1966, recorded 1962

GREAT SCOTT: Jacky/When Joanna Loved Me/The Plague/Mathilde – Philips MCP-1006 (Cassette only) (1967)

LPs

LOOKING BACK WITH SCOTT WALKER: Too Young/I Don't Want To Know/Comin' Home/Bluebell/Paper Doll/Sunday/When I Kiss You Goodnight/Sing Boy Sing/Too Young To Know/Take This Love/Till You Return/When You See Her/All I Do Is Dream of You/Everybody But Me – Ember 3393, released 1967, recorded 1958/59

SANDY NELSON (with Scott on bass): LET THERE BE DRUMS (USA) – Imperial 9159/12080 (1962)

THE ROUTERS (with Scott on bass): LET'S GO WITH THE ROUTERS (USA) – Warner Bros 1490 (1963)

SCOTT ENGEL AND JOHN STEWART: I ONLY CAME TO DANCE WITH YOU: I Only Came To Dance With You/Chick's Choice/Ham Hocks/Swingin' At The Batcave/Wallflower/Without Your Love/Diskoteque/Greens/Lottin' Dottin' Da Da/Nashville – (USA) Tower 5026, recorded 1963 as The Dalton Brothers – released 1966

SCOTT: Mathilde/Montague Terrace (In Blue)/Angelica/The Lady

Came From Baltimore/When Joanna Loved Me/My Death/The
Big Hurt/Such A Small Love/Through A Long and Sleepless
Night/You're Gonna Hear From Me/Always Coming Back To
You/Amsterdam – Philips 7816 (1967)

SCOTT 2: Jacky/Best Of Both Worlds/The Amorous Humphrey
Plugg/Black Sheep Boy/Next/The Girls From The Streets/Plastic
Palace People/Wait Until Dark/The Girls And The Dogs/Win-
dows Of The World/The Bridge/Come Next Spring – Philips
7840 (1968)

SCOTT 3: It's Raining Today/Copenhagen/Rosemary/Big Louise/
We Came Through/Butterfly/Two Ragged Soldiers/30 Century
Man/Winter Night/Two Weeks Since You've Gone/Sons Of/
Funeral Tango/If You Go Away – Philips 7882 (1969)

SCOTT SINGS SONGS FROM HIS TV SERIES: I Have Dreamed/
Impossible Dream/Will You Still Be Mine/When The World Was
Young/Who (Will Take My Place)/If She Walked Into My Life/
The Song Is You/The Look Of Love/Country Girl/Someone To
Light Up My Life/Only The Young/Lost In The Stars – Philips
7900 (1969)

NOEL SCOTT ENGEL

SCOTT 4: The Seventh Seal/On Your Own Again/World's Strongest
Man/Angels Of Ashes/Boy Child/The Old Man's Back Again/
Hero Of The War/Duchess/Get Behind Me/Rhymes of Goodbye
– Philips 7913 (1969)

SCOTT WALKER

BEST OF SCOTT WALKER – Vol 1: Joanna/Montague Terrace (In
Blue)/Jacky/Copenhagen/Big Louise/Mathilde/Plastic Palace
People/If She Walked Into My Life/Lady Came From Baltimore/
The Impossible Dream – Philips 7910 (1970) (re-issues)

TIL THE BAND COMES IN: Prologue/Little Things (That Keep Us
Together)/Joe/Thanks For Chicago Mr James/Long About Now/
Time Operator/Jean The Machine/Cowbells Shakin'/Til The
Band Comes In/The War Is Over/Stormy/The Hills of Yesterday/
Reuben James/What Are You Doing The Rest Of Your Life/It's
Over – Philips 6308 035 (1970)

THIS IS SCOTT WALKER – Vol 1: Lady Came From Baltimore/

When Joanna Loved Me/Amsterdam/Always Coming Back To You/Mathilde/Montague Terrace (In Blue)/Angelica/Jacky/Best Of Both Worlds/Plastic Palace People/Black Sheep Boy/Copenhagen – Philips 6382 007 (1971) (re-issues)

THIS IS SCOTT WALKER – Vol 2: Impossible Dream/Windows Of The World/Come Next Spring/Will You Still Be Mine/Look Of Love/Lost In The Stars/If You Go Away/Sons Of/Two Ragged Soldiers/It's Raining Today/What Are You Doing The Rest of Your Life/Til The Band Comes In – Philips 6382 052 (1972) (re-issues)

THE MOVIEGOER: This Way Mary/Speak Softly Love/Glory Road/That Night/Summer Of '42/Easy Come Easy Go/Ballad of Sacco and Vanzetti/Face In The Crowd/Joe Hill/Loss of Love/All His Children/Come Saturday Morning – Philips 6308 120 (1972)

THE BEST OF SCOTT WALKER: Joanna/Speak Softly Love/Summer of '42/Copenhagen/Angelica/Jacky/Lights Of Cincinnati/Glory Road/Best Of Both Worlds/Lady Came From Baltimore/When Joanna Loved Me/Mathilde – Contour 6870 (1972) (re-issues)

ANY DAY NOW: Any Day Now/All My Love's Laughter/Do I Love You/Maria Bethania/Cowboy/When You Get Right Down To It/Ain't No Sunshine/The Me I Never Knew/If Ships Were Made To Sail/We Could Be Flying – Philips 6308 148 (1973)

ATTENTION: SCOTT WALKER: Jacky/Do I Love You/We Could Be Flying/Who (Will Take My Place)/Black Sheep Boy/If You Go Away/Joanna/Come Next Spring/Lights Of Cincinnati/Stormy/Windows Of The World/Get Behind Me – Fontana 6438 083 (1973) (re-issues)

STRETCH: Sunshine/Just One Smile/A Woman Left Lonely/No Easy Way Down/That's How I Got To Memphis/Use Me/Frisco Depot/Someone Who Cared/Where Does Brown Begin/Where Love Has Died/I'll Be Home – CBS 65725 (1973)

THE ROMANTIC SCOTT WALKER: Will You Still Be Mine/I Have Dreamed/When The World Was Young/Who (Will Take My Place)/If She Walked Into My Life/Impossible Dream/Mathilde/Montague Terrace (In Blue)/Angelica/My Death/Lady Came From Baltimore/When Joanna Loved Me – Philips 6850 013 (1973) (re-issues)

WE HAD IT ALL: Low Down Freedom/We Had It All/Black Rose/Ride Me Down Easy/You're Young And You'll Forget/The House

Song/Whatever Happened to Saturday Night/Sundown/Old Five And Dimers Like Me/Delta Dawn – CBS 80254 (1974)

SPOTLIGHT ON SCOTT WALKER: Do I Love You/Joanna/Country Girl/Speak Softly Love/I Will Wait For You/Summer Of '42/We Could Be Flying/Who (Will Take My Place)/If/Lost In The Stars/Lights Of Cincinnati/What Are You Doing The Rest Of Your Life/I Still See You/When Joanna Loved Me/Stormy/Little Things (That Keep Us Together)/Big Louise/Copenhagen/Joe/My Way Home/Butterfly/Get Behind Me/Jacky/Sons Of/Next/If You Go Away/Mathilde/Amsterdam/The Girls And The Dogs/Funeral Tango – Philips 6625 017 (1976) Double album (re-issues)

FIRE ESCAPE IN THE SKY: THE GOD-LIKE GENIUS OF SCOTT WALKER: Such A Small Love/Big Louise/Little Things (That Keep Us Together)/Plastic Palace People/The Girls From The Street/It's Raining Today/The Seventh Seal/The Amorous Humphrey Plugg/Angels Of Ashes/Boy Child/Montague Terrace (In Blue)/Always Coming Back To You – Zoo 2 (1981) (re-issues)

SCOTT WALKER SINGS JACQUES BREL: Jacky/Next/The Girls And The Dogs/If You Go Away/Funeral Tango/Mathilde/Amsterdam/Sons Of/My Death/Little Things (That Keep Us Together) – Phonogram 6359 090 (1981) (re-issues)

THE BEST OF SCOTT WALKER: Joanna/Lights Of Cincinnati/Will You Still Be Mine/I Will Wait For You/Montague Terrace (In Blue)/When Joanna Loved Me/Jacky/The Lady Came From Baltimore/If She Walked Into My Life/The Me I Never Knew/If You Go Away/The Impossible Dream – Phonogram 6381 073 (1982) (re-issues)

SCOTT ENGEL: SCOTT: Jacky/Black Sheep Boy/Windows Of The World/The Big Hurt/The Amorous Humphrey Plugg/Rhymes Of Goodbye/Best of Both Worlds/If You Go Away/Mathilde/Angelica/The Lady Came From Baltimore/Always Coming Back To You/When Joanna Loved Me/The Old Man's Back Again/Plastic Palace People/Wait Until Dark/Copenhagen/It's Raining Today/Funeral Tango/Montague Terrace (In Blue)/I Have Dreamed/Country Girl/Who (Will Take My Place)/The Impossible Dream – Philips 7564 002 (Cassette only) (re-issues)

CLIMATE OF HUNTER: Rawhide/Dealer/Track 3/Sleepwalker's Woman/Track 5/Track 6/Track 7/Blanket Roll Blues – Virgin V2303 (1984)

BOY CHILD – THE BEST OF 1967–70: The Plague/Montague Terrace (In Blue)/Such A Small Love/The Amorous Humphrey Plugg/Plastic Palace People/The Bridge/Big Louise/We Came Through/The Seventh Seal/Boy Child/The Old Man's Back Again/Prologue/Little Things (That Keep Us Together)/Time Operator – Fontana 8428323-1 (1990) (re-issues)

COMPACT DISCS

CLIMATE OF HUNTER – Virgin CD V2303 (1989)

BOY CHILD – THE BEST OF 1967–70 – Fontana 842832-2 (1990) (re-issues)

SCOTT WALKER SINGS JACQUES BREL – Fontana 838212-2 (1991) (re-issues)

SCOTT – Fontana 510 879-2 (1992) (re-issue) (Cassette 510 879-4)

SCOTT 2 – Fontana 510 880-2 (1992) (re-issue) (Cassette 510 880-4)

SCOTT 3 – Fontana 510 881-2 (1992) (re-issue) (Cassette 510 881-4)

SCOTT 4 – Fontana 510 882-2 (1992) (re-issue) (Cassette 510 882-4)

MAN FROM RENO/INDECENT SACRIFICE (France) – Fontana CD single 862 382-2. Cassette single – Fontana 862 382-4 (1993)

Sources

INTRODUCTION

New Musical Express (21/10/66)
NME Annual 1968

CHAPTER 1 – BOY CHILD

New Musical Express (1/1/77)
'Those Rebellious Years' (source unknown)
Betty Engel, letter to Bob Farmer (2/8/66)
Disc & Music Echo (30/7/66)
Music Maker (January 1967)
NME Annual 1966

CHAPTER 2 – PEOPLE GET READY

CBC press release 1973
Disc & Music Echo (26/12/70)
NME Annual 1966
Disc & Music Echo (6/8/66)
Melody Maker (5/4/69)
Interview with Gary Leeds (4/4/93)
Phone interview with Jack Nitzsche (7/7/93)

CHAPTER 3 – MY SHIP IS COMING IN

Disc Weekly (11/12/65)
Disc Weekly (15/5/65)
CBS press release 1973
Betty Engel, letter to Bob Farmer (2/8/66)

Scott Walker

Interview with Chris Welch (6/4/93)
Melody Maker (12/3/66)
Disc Weekly (28/8/65)
Interview with Gary Leeds (4/4/93)
New Musical Express (21/5/65)
Melody Maker (5/4/69)
Interview with Keith Altham (23/3/93)
Phone interview with Mary Arnold (2/8/93)
Interview with Bobby Hamilton (22/4/93)
Phone interview with Allan McDougall (21/8/93)
Interview with Brian Sommerville (28/7/93)
Disc Weekly (16/10/65)
Disc Weekly (17/7/65)
Melody Maker (7/8/65)

CHAPTER 4 – MAKE IT EASY ON YOURSELF

Source unknown
TV Mirror & Disc News (February 1958)
Interview with Peter Olliff (23/4/93)
Phone interview with Freddie Winrose (27/7/93)
Music Maker (January 1967)
Interview with Reg Guest (26/3/93)
CBS press release 1973

CHAPTER 5 – GET BEHIND ME

NME Annual 1968
Interview with Barrie Martin (22/4/93)
Disc & Music Echo (26/12/70)
Interview with Jonathan King (24/6/93)
Melody Maker (5/1/74)
New Musical Express (no date)
Melody Maker (30/7/66)
Melody Maker (7/8/65)
Rave (November 1966)
Interview with Irene Dunford (18/3/93)
Betty Engel, letter to Bob Farmer (2/8/66)
Disc & Music Echo (13/8/66)
Interview with Chris Welch (6/4/93)

Interview with Brian Sommerville (28/7/93)
Melody Maker (12/3/66)

CHAPTER 6 – WE CAME THROUGH

CBS press release 1973
Interview with Bobby Hamilton (22/4/93)
Interview with Irene Dunford (18/3/93)
Disc Weekly (25/9/65)
Disc Weekly (27/11/65)
New Musical Express (26/11/65)
Disc Weekly (4/12/65)
Disc Weekly (11/12/65)
Reg and Ron Kray with Fred Dineage, *Our Story* (Sidgwick & Jackson 1988)
Interview with Keith Altham (23/3/93)
Melody Maker (1/1/66)
Melody Maker (12/2/66)
Phone interview with Allan McDougall (21/8/93)

CHAPTER 7 – THROUGH A LONG AND SLEEPLESS NIGHT

Melody Maker (26/3/66)
Interview with Gary Leeds (23/5/93)
Melody Maker (12/3/66)
Melody Maker (26/3/66)
Disc & Music Echo (26/12/70)
New Musical Express (21/1/67)
Interview with Bobby Hamilton (22/4/93)
Phone interview with Graham Alexander (29/4/93)
Interview with Reg Guest (26/3/93)
Melody Maker (3/9/66)

CHAPTER 8 – IN MY ROOM

NME Annual 1968
Melody Maker (30/7/66)
Melody Maker (June 1966)
Disc & Music Echo (20/8/66)
Interview with Bobby Hamilton (22/4/93)
Melody Maker (3/9/66)

Scott Walker

Interview with Irene Dunford (18/3/93)
Disc & Music Echo (26/12/70)
Fab 208 (15/10/66)
Phone interview with Mary Arnold (3/8/93)
Interview with Jonathan King (24/6/93)
Phone interview with Gary Leeds (15/7/93)
Interview with Brian Sommerville (28/7/93)
Fab 208 (21/7/67)
NME Annual 1968
Melody Maker (August 1966)
Interview with Barrie Martin (22/4/93)
Melody Maker (1/10/66)
Interview with Keith Altham (23/3/93)
Disc & Music Echo (17/9/66)
New Musical Express (8/10/66)

CHAPTER 9 – I DON'T WANT TO HEAR IT ANYMORE

New Musical Express (13/5/67)
New Musical Express (21/10/66)
Melody Maker (5/11/67)
Interview with Brian Sommerville (28/7/93)
Interview with Barrie Martin (22/4/93)
Melody Maker (19/11/66)
Interview with Gary Leeds (23/5/93)
NME Annual 1968
Melody Maker (18/3/67)
Interview with Keith Altham (23/3/67)
Disc & Music Echo (4/3/67)
Melody Maker (13/5/67)
CBS press release 1973
Sunday People (16/2/92)

CHAPTER 10 – STAND BY ME

Rave (June 1967)
Rave (August 1968)
Interview with Barrie Martin (22/4/93)
Interview with Brian Sommerville (28/7/93)
Interview with Jonathan King (24/6/93)

Edmund White, *Genet* (Chatto & Windus 1993)
Rave (June 1967)
Rave (September 1967)
New Musical Express (1/1/77)
Rave (February 1968)
Music Maker (January 1967)
Melody Maker (29/7/67)
NME Annual 1968
Melody Maker (26/8/68)
Interview with Bobby Hamilton (22/4/93)
Melody Maker (16/9/67)
Melody Maker (9/12/67)
New Musical Express (16/12/67)
New Musical Express (17/3/84)
Interview with Keith Altham (23/3/93)
Disc & Music Echo (9/12/67)
Melody Maker (13/5/67)
New Musical Express (13/1/68)
New Musical Express (20/1/68)

CHAPTER 11 – BLACK SHEEP BOY

Sunday Mirror (9/6/68)
Disc & Music Echo (17/2/68)
Hot Press (9/8/90)
Disc & Music Echo (4/5/68)
Phone interview with Mary Arnold (12/8/93)
New Musical Express (25/5/68)
Disc & Music Echo (2/8/68)
New Musical Express (22/6/68)
New Musical Express (29/6/68)
New Musical Express (6/7/68)
Guardian (5/6/93)
Disc & Music Echo (6/4/68)
Rave (August 1968)
Record Mirror & Disc (7/2/76)
Disc & Music Echo (18/5/68)
Interview with Gary Leeds (23/5/68)
Disc & Music Echo (5/10/68)
Disc & Music Echo (26/10/68)

Scott Walker

NME Annual 1969
Melody Maker (30/11/68)
Disc & Music Echo (15/2/69)
Disc & Music Echo (12/4/69)
Melody Maker (12/4/69)
Melody Maker (8/3/69)
Interview with Keith Altham (23/3/93)
Disc & Music Echo (28/6/69)

CHAPTER 12 – THE BIG HURT

New Musical Express (November 1976)
Disc & Music Echo (22/6/69)
Disc & Music Echo (26/4/69)
Melody Maker (8/3/69)
Melody Maker (5/7/69)
Disc & Music Echo (26/4/69)
Disc & Music Echo (5/7/69)
Melody Maker (28/6/69)
Interview with Jonathan King (24/6/69)
Melody Maker (5/7/69)
Disc & Music Echo (7/6/69)
Phone interview with Mary Arnold (12/8/93)
Phone interview with Bobby Hamilton (13/8/93)
Daily Telegraph (28/7/69)
Phone interview with Terry Smith (6/7/93)
Interview with Keith Altham (23/3/93)
New Musical Express (11/7/81)
Interview with Chris Welch (6/4/93)
Disc & Music Echo (6/12/69)
New Musical Express (1/1/77)
Melody Maker (19/4/69)

CHAPTER 13 – IF YOU GO AWAY

Melody Maker (7/3/70)
Phone interview with Dorte Teglbjaerg (20/8/93)
Music Now (5/12/70)
Interview with Keith Altham (1/4/93)
Melody Maker (7/8/65)

Interview with Barrie Martin (7/7/93)
Interview with Dick Leahy (19/8/93)
'Til The Band Comes In sleeve notes (12/70)
Sunday Mirror (29/11/70)
NME Gordon Coxhill (date unknown)
Interview with Paddy Fleming (3/5/93)
Phone interview with Hal Shaper (2/7/93)
NME (29/11/75)

CHAPTER 14 – SOMEONE WHO CARED

Rave (7/68)
Phone interview with Dorte Teglbjaerg (20/8/93)
Interview with Gary Leeds (7/4/93)
Music Now (5/12/70)
NME (1/1/77)
Phone interview with Robin Edwards (2/8/93)
Vox (5/92)
Any Day Now sleeve notes (5/73)
Interview with Peter Olliff (12/5/93)
Interview with B. J. Cole (15/3/92)
Interview with Del Newman (23/5/93)
CBS press release accompanying Stretch (11/73)
Melody Maker (8/12/73)
Melody Maker (5/1/74)
Phone interview with Maurice Oberstein (8/7/93)

CHAPTER 15 – ALWAYS COMING BACK TO YOU

Melody Maker (19/4/69)
Phone interview with Paul Kinder (25/6/93)
Melody Maker (?/76)
Phone interview with Mike Peyton (24/6/93)
Interview with B. J. Cole (15/3/92)
Phone interview with Freddie Winrose (9/7/93)

CHAPTER 16 – THE ELECTRICIAN

Melody Maker (?/76)
Interview with Dick Leahy (19/8/93)

Scott Walker

Interview with Gary Leeds (7/4/93)
Phone interview with David Apps (20/8/93)
Phone interview with Paul Kinder (25/6/93)
NME (1/1/77)
Gary Leeds (*The Walkers* 1992 fanzine interview)
Scott Walker BFBS German radio interview (1/4/84)
Phone interview with Robin Edwards (2/8/93)
NME (17/3/84)
Phone interview with Simon Draper (12/7/93)

CHAPTER 17 – ON YOUR OWN AGAIN

Phone interview with Simon Draper (13/9/93)
Phone interview with Al Clark (24/9/93)
Phone interview with Martin Callingford (21/9/93)
Phone interview with Mick Houghton (15/9/93)
New Musical Express (17/3/84)
Fred Dellar, *Where Did You Go To My Lovely?* (W. H. Allen & C
   1983)
New Musical Express (11/7/81)
Interview with Chris Welch (6/4/93)
Phone interview with Ed Bicknell
Phone interview with Jeremy Lascelles (6/9/93)
Phone interview with Brian Gascoigne (28/9/93)
Juke (August 1981)
Alan Bangs, *Night Flights*
The Tube (23/3/84)
Phone interview with Muriel Gray (5/8/93)
Interview with Charles Negus-Fancey (9/7/93)

CHAPTER 18 – 30 CENTURY MAN

Phone interview with Ed Bicknell
Phone interview with Simon Draper (13/9/93)
Phone interview with Brian Gascoigne (28/9/93)
Phone interview with Jeremy Lascelles (6/9/93)
Phone interview with Tim Rice (29/9/93)
Phone interview with Phil Smee (29/7/93)
New Musical Express (17/3/84)
Disc & Music Echo (17/2/68)

Weekend Telegraph (26/6/90)
Daily Express (1/5/92)
Sunday People (16/2/92)
Interview with Keith Altham (23/3/93)
Phone interview with Dave Dee (30/7/93)
Phone interview with Geoff Travis (19/7/93)
Interview with Charles Negus-Fancey (9/7/93)
Interview with B. J. Cole
Phone interview with Martin Callingford (21/7/93)
Interview with Mike Peyton (9/7/93)
Phone interview with Maurice Oberstein

CHAPTER 19 – NO REGRETS

Source unknown
Interview with Charles Negus-Fancey (9/7/93)
Melody Maker (18/1/92)
Radio Cologne interview (March 1984)
Sunday Telegraph (23/6/90)
Disc Weekly (5/3/66)
New Musical Express (25/1/92)

EPILOGUE

Sunday People (16/2/92)
Interview with Gary Leeds (23/5/93)
Interview with Brandy Maus

Index